AMERICAN WOMEN

images and realities

AMERICAN WOMEN
Images and Realities

Advisory Editors
ANNETTE K. BAXTER
LEON STEIN

A Note About This Volume

At 14, Thomas Branagan (1774-1843) terminated a miserable childhood by running off to sea. Ten years later, having seen much of the world, some of it as an African slaver, he settled in Philadelphia. In his 20 volumes of prose and poetry are found a gift for romantic rhetoric, deep compassion for the poor and oppressed, an appealing personality and prose style. Deep feeling vibrates in his anti-slavery publication *A Preliminary Essay on the Oppression of the Exiled Sons of Africa* (Arno Press, 1969) and a preacher's anger at male corruption rings in this defense of the hard-pressed virtues of women—a tract in advance of its time.

THE

EXCELLENCY

OF

The Female Character

VINDICATED

BY THOMAS BRANAGAN

ARNO PRESS

A New York Times Company
New York • 1972

Reprint Edition 1972 by Arno Press Inc.

Reprinted from a copy in The Princeton
University Library

American Women: Images and Realities
ISBN for complete set: 0-405-04445-3
See last pages of this volume for titles.

Manufactured in the United States of America

Publisher's Note: This volume was reprinted
from the best available copy

- - - - - - - - - - - - -

Library of Congress Cataloging in Publication Data

Branagan, Thomas, b. 1774.
   The excellency of the female character vindicated.

   (American women: images and realities)
   Reprint of the 2d ed., published in 1808.
   1. Woman--Social and moral questions. I. Title.
II. Series.
HQ1423.B8 1972   301.41'2   72-2592
ISBN 0-405-04449-6

THE

EXCELLENCY

OF

The Female Character

VINDICATED

Scott sc

FRONTISPIECE.

THE

EXCELLENCY

OF

Ꮯꜧe Ϝemale Ꮯꜧaracter

VINDICATED;

BEING

AN INVESTIGATION

RELATIVE TO THE CAUSE AND EFFECTS

OF

THE ENCROACHMENTS OF MEN

UPON

THE RIGHTS OF WOMEN,

AND

THE TOO FREQUENT DEGRADATION AND
CONSEQUENT MISFORTUNES

OF

THE FAIR SEX.

SECOND EDITION.

BY THOMAS BRANAGAN,
Author of the " Beauties of Philanthropy," &c. &c.

PHILADELPHIA:
PRINTED BY J. RAKESTRAW.
1808.

EPISTLE DEDICATORY.

ALL that need be said in favour of the subsequent work, (and which should be a sufficient recommendation to entitle it to the patronage of every friend to female virtue, and especially such parents as intend their children to be their comfort in life and an honour to them after their decease), is, that it is intended as a counterpoise to those vile and vulgar publications which are continually teeming from our presses, and which secretly instil the most destructive moral poison into the minds of the rising generation, and eventually prove the destruction of thousands of the giddy, the volatile, and the gay. There is no doubt but that this performance (if parents would, judiciously, put it into their children's hands) would not only prove an antidote to obviate the influence of such pernicious publications, but also incline the juvenile mind to pursue, admire, and gain the intrinsic virtue, *that pearl of great price*, which alone can adorn the sex, and which is infinitely superior to beauty, riches and fame, or even honours, sceptres, and crowns, for " beauty unchaste is beauty in disgrace " In order to prove the authenticity of the above assertion, I would ask, what is a female crowned with beauty, honour, and riches, without virtue ? I answer, like the painted sepulchre, all beautiful without, but rottenness and putrefaction within : what is she without information? I answer, no better than the wild Indian who traverses the banks of the Ohio. But, to reverse the question, what is a real virtuous and pious female, adorned with personal beauty and intellectual acquirements? She is no less than the glory of man, the ornament of nature, the favourite of Heaven, and the daughter of Jehovah himself. Another cogent circumstance I would suggest, which should irresistibly stimulate parents to put such performances as this in their daughter's hands, and that is—a thousand snares on every side (in addition to injurious books) are laid to entice them from the flowery paths of virtue, even while their parents live, and more especially after their death. In order to demonstrate the fatality of parents neglecting this precaution, witness the thousands of incontinent females who crowd our cities, of all ranks and of all ages, many of whom are the degenerate children of the most respectable parents, and who, through paternal neglect, are the pests of society, instead of being the virtuous mothers of respectable and honourable families. Finally, the present performance is enriched with the most elegant selected (and some original) poetry, in order to make it an entertaining as well as valuable acquisition to the fair sex, for whose benefit it was composed, and to whom it is dedicated with the most profound respect and veneration by their real friend, and humble servant,

THE AUTHOR.

ADVERTISEMENT.

THERE is no doubt but many inaccuracies will be discovered by the microscope of criticism, in the subsequent desultory performance. Even the most superficial observer may descry inadvertent tautology; the author has seen this himself when perusing his manuscript, but he found it difficult to correct it. He was unwilling to obliterate the sentiments alluded to, which were, of course, reassumed, with considerable variations ; and, at any rate, were of such importance, as to induce him almost to conclude, they could not be too often repeated, in order to inform the minds, and reform the hearts, of the persons he was solicitous to benefit. He conceived it not only excusable, but, in some respects, ne-

cessary to repeat sentiments intrinsically momentous and intimately connected with their
present and future welfare. The author's
phraseology and animadversions will prove,
to a demonstration, that, so far from courting
the literary fame, which authors in general
are so enamoured with, he turns his back,
not only on this intellectual vapour, but even
on the road that leads to popularity. His primary object, nay, the happiness, the only
heaven he desires to anticipate here, or enjoy
hereafter, is in pleasing his munificent Creator, gaining his approbation, promoting his
glory, and the real happiness of mankind.
With respect to literary acquirements, he pro-
fesses (contrary to the general mode of his
cotemporaries) to be a novice, as it respects
the radical rules of composition; and, as
such, acknowledges his work to be beneath
the notice of intelligent and candid critics,
who he hopes will consider the subject matter
of this performance, and not the arrangement
of words, and to whose superior discernment
he submits it with the most humble and distinguished deference. But, at the same time, the

*snarling critic and literary debauchee, who
may be inclined to retail their customary aspersions, and, with the satanic grin of envy,
endeavour to invalidate a work that lays the
axe to the root of their villainies, though the
author would look upon such with a glance
of pity, as persons who facilitate their own
ruin, and enhance their own infelicity (for
there is no vice so capable of rendering a human being so completely wretched as envy;)
yet their illiberal animadversions and malevolent aspersions, he treats with the smile
of contemptuous disregard; and he thinks it
is consistent with his moral duty, to treat,
with a total and deserved neglect, the scur-
rility of such ingenious calumniators. The
author humbly acknowledges that he has been
indifferent to the systematical arrangement
of this publication; because he is well assured that those who oppose the popular vices of
the age, will be reprobated with their works,
however elegant or correct they may be, by
the votaries of fashion; and plain honest
people will be as well pleased with unadorned
and unaffected admonitions, as if they were*

illustrated with the flowers of rhetoric, the embellishments of fancy, and the refinement of composition. Yet he has been exceedingly solicitous to introduce no matter in this performance, but what is (to say the least of it) calculated to promote the best interests of the human family. He therefore earnestly hopes, that his female readers will attend, seriously attend to his admonitions, which are eventually connected with their present honour and future glory!! Finally, he would recommend to their solemn consideration, the subsequent beautiful and appropriate lines of Robert Burns :

> " The sacred flame of well plac'd love,
> Luxuriantly indulge it,
> But never tempt th' illicit rove,
> Tho' nothing should divulge it ;
> I wave the quantum of the sin,
> The hazard of concealing,
> But Oh ! it hardens all within,
> And petrifies the feeling."

New-York, Sept. 15, 1807

PREFACE.

I THINK I am correct, when I affirm, that no subject, at the present crisis, can be exhibited for public inspection, more deserving serious attention than the present : and at no period of the world has the subject before us called more loudly for consideration than it now does. Will any man have the effrontery to deny this assertion, or to suggest a contrary sentiment; when it is considered, that on the female part of society, at first, devolves the important care of the rising generation ; those who must be the defenders of our natural rights, the supporters of our valuable privileges. It is they who form the mind to think, who first " teach the young idea how to shoot," when it is most susceptible of impression. It is they who possess charms to captivate the wisest and enamour the best of men; to lead monarchs in golden chains, and even decide the fate of nations. It is they who may be considered the most superlatively amiable, and transcendently charming part of the architecture of the Eternal. It is they, to use the emphatic language of a scriptural writer,

"*Who have borne the king and all the people that bare rule by sea and land. Even of them came they; and they nourished them up that planted the vine-yards from whence the wine cometh. These also make garments for men, these bring glory unto men; and without women cannot men be. Yea, and if men have gathered together gold and silver, or any other goodly thing, Do they not love a woman which is comely in favour and beauty? And letting all those things go, Do they not gape, and even with open mouth fix their eyes fast on her; and have not all men more desire unto her than unto silver or gold, or any goodly thing whatsoever? A man leaveth his own father that brought him up, and his own country, and cleaveth unto his wife. He sticketh not to spend his life with his wife, and remembereth neither father nor*

mother nor country. By this also ye must
know, that women have dominion over you :
do ye not labour and toil, and give and bring
all to the woman ? Yea, a man taketh his
sword, and goeth his way to rob, and to steal,
to sail upon the sea and upon the rivers ; and
looketh upon a lion, and goeth in the darkness ;
and when he hath stolen, spoiled, and robbed,
he bringeth it to his love. Wherefore a man
loveth his wife better than father or mother.
Yea, many there be, that have run out of their
wits for women, and become servants for
their sakes. Many also have perished, have
erred and sinned, for women. And now,
Do ye not believe me ? Is not the king great
in his power ? Do not all regions fear to
touch him ? Yet did I see him and Apome, the
king's concubine, the daughter of the admirable Barticus, sitting at the right hand
of the king, and taking the crown from the
king's head, and setting it upon her own
head : she also struck the king with her left
hand. And yet for all this, the king gaped
and gazed upon her with open mouth : if she
laughed upon him, he laughed also : but if she

took any displeasure at him, the king was fain to flatter, that she might be reconciled to him again. O, ye men, How can it be but women should be strong, seeing they do thus ?"

Finally, it is with them that the profoundest politicians, wisest statesmen, most invincible champions, greatest generals, ingenious artists, and even pulpit orators, spend, on an average, two-thirds of their most happy and pleasurable moments. Then, is it of no importance to inform the mind and establish the virtue of women ; to erect ramparts, in order to stop seduction in its mad, and too successful career ; shut the floodgates of temptation which modern fashions have opened; shelter female innocence from the innovations of libertinism ; and, finally, nurture the smallest bud of their juvenile virtue to its full blossom, and thereby promote individual tranquillity, domestic felicity, national prosperity, and the honour and happiness of posterity.

Esdras, iv. 15—32.

EXCELLENCY

OF

THE FEMALE CHARACTER

VINDICATED.

———◆———

CHAPTER I.

Preliminary Observations on Modern Fashions, and
their Effects on Society.

———◆———

WHEN so many spurious, futile, and
pernicious publications are teeming from our
presses, which tend to destroy social intercourse, legitimate association, female innocence, and moral obligation ; and which are
read with avidity, disseminated with alacrity, and rewarded with popularity : when
it can be proved, to a mathematical certainty,
that as soon as depravity of morals in a nation becomes general, popular, and fashionable, the seed of destruction is engendered,
the preliminary to degradation is advancing,
and that nation begins to nod to its fall : I
say, when this is the case, may I not ven-

ture to take up my pen to endeavour at least
to counterpoise the deleterious effects which
the numerous, popular, though injudicious,
publications of this degenerate age, unquestionably have to destroy female virtue
and domestic tranquillity. I will be bold to
say, that a debauchee the most artful, or a
libertine the most proficient in the arts of
seduction, could not wish a more efficacious
auxiliary, a more effectual stimulus to facilitate his designs, and to accomplish his
wishes, than the female fashions, and many of the popular publications which are, *a-
la-mode*, the order of the day.

My primary object, in the subsequent
strictures, is to demonstrate, by arguments
as plain as A B C, and clear as a ray of light,
that the radical causes of the miseries and
premature degradation of a large majority
of the human race, are the effects of paternal indulgence and fraternal neglect.

Though my talents for composition are
not to be compared to those of some, who
merely use them for the purpose of exciting
the laughter of the volatile and the gay;
and, at the same time, meet the disappro-
bation of the wise and the good, cause a
blush on the cheek of modesty, and a groan
from the breast of philanthropy; yet every
friend to the human family will, I am con-

fident, be inclined to approve of my well meant endeavours for the good of mankind, though they cannot applaud my qualifications. But it should, in justice, be remembered, that while the writers alluded to are abundantly supplied with opportunities for composition, pecuniary and scholastic resources and conveniencies, I am destitute of all these accommodations.

Stimulated by disinterested philanthropy, after the avocations of each day is past, I appropriate that season which others necessarily spend in sleep to the arrangement, and composition of this and my other works.

The following, therefore, may be very properly called, " Midnight Thoughts on the Wretchedness existing in civilized Society ;" which, in many respects, may be considered an abyss of human degeneracy, strewed with briars and thorns, instead of a terrestrial paradise, carpetted with roses, which would undoubtedly be the case, were the votaries of civilization as tenacious of maintaining the characters of virtuous and benevolent persons, as they are those of honourable and right honourable, reverend and right reverend, excellency, &c. &c. The most superficial view of civilized and savage nations, where literature flourishes, or where ignorance prevails, will furnish the philanthropist with woeful exhibitions, that are enough to make female delicacy shudder, sensibility sigh, and humanity to melt into tears ; and what enhances the painful sensation is, the melancholy reflection, that the miseries alluded to, are not diminishing, through the influence and examples of the virtuous, but are, alas! accumulating through the baneful allurements of the vicious.

When I survey actual scenes, which seem almost too tragical to be authentic, too romantic to be real, too horrible to meet the ear or eye of the humane ; and when I reflect that it is utterly impossible for me to remedy those scenes of human woe, an involuntary desire rushes into my mind to be lodged in some solitary wilderness, where I might weep for the wretchedness and degradation of my fellow-creatures, children of the same original parents, created for high beatitude in heaven, and to be lords of the creation on earth, a little lower than the angels, but, on account of moral evil, reduced one step below the brute, and but one above infernal spirits.

I profess to be a philanthropist. I seek no better name. And none but such can anticipate thé painful feelings which I endure while surveying, in sympathetic thought, the sufferings of the human family from Adam to his youngest son. And though the retrospect is gloomy and produces sad regret, the mind, unbidden, still recurs to the same melancholy exhibitions, still anticipates the same tragical catastrophes.

How little think the rich and the great, while basking in the sun-shine of prosperity, swimming in wealth, and enveloped in luxuries, while spending their golden moments in useless mirth, if not sensual gratifications ; how little do they think, that while they are crowned with abundance, many are bereaved of the necessaries of life ! while they are solaced by their friends, many are cruelly tortured by their enemies, without an eye to pity, or a hand to help ! How many are innocently bound in galling chains and shut up in dungeons, while they strut in their splendid mansions ; who eat the bread of woe and drink the cup of grief, while they are regaled with the most savory dishes and the most delicious viands ! How many are scorched by the vertical rays of the sun in the torrid zone, while others are pierced by the untimely blasts in the frigid zone ; who shrink for shelter in vain into the cheerless abode of penury ;

while they are accommodated with artificial canopies to court the gentle breezes, or with warm retreats to beguile the severity of winter's gloomy reign! How many are exposed to all the horrors of sanguinary warfare, when nation arises against nation, army against army, family against family, and individual against individual, who arm for the war, and rush with the fury of lions, and the impetuosity of demons to spill each other's blood; while they are enjoying peace and all its concomitant blessings! How many weeping children stand around the dying beds of their tender, but, alas! expiring parents. Like monumental grief, they stand to take a long and last farewell, while their parents' solicitude for their welfare continues to the last. A blessing is all their patrimonial inheritance; and with it they are thrown defenceless and forlorn on an unfriendly and unfeeling world! Here I must cease. My palpitating, tremulous heart almost weeps blood at anticipating the nameless and latent woes that await the unconscious innocents. Fain would I relinquish the painful prospective, but it recurs with redoubled force to my wounded mind. And you, my dear children, my earthly riches, and my all, who are now wrapped in the arms of peaceful slumber, unconscious of your future fate, and dead to future woe, perhaps, these scenes of toil, these incessant struggles with human depravity, degradation and poverty; these sad vicissitudes which render life one scene of suffering and woe, will be your portion, when your earthly parents are mouldering to their native dust, the sport of worms and the victims of corruption. What tongue can tell, what imagination can conceive the miseries peculiar to the defenceless orphan, especially if a female; perhaps led into the devious paths of folly by the votaries of seduction, those murderers of the human soul, those traitors to the human race, who, like the prowling wolf in the woodlands, or the voracious shark in the briny deep, go about seeking whom they may destroy and ruin. Torture of mind, agony of heart, depravity of morals, a torpid insensibility to all moral obligations, are the result of their ravages on the person of the ruined female orphan.

How much more merciful would it be for the seducers and traducers of defenceless female innocence, to assassinate the unconscious victims of their brutal lust, and send them guiltless to a world of spirits, before they lay the foundation of accumulated crimes and complicated degradation. I had almost said, that murder was no crime when com-

pared to seduction ; because the former may
free the soul from terrestrial infelicity, and
land it in eternal glory ; while the latter produces supreme wretchedness here, and unutterable torment hereafter; for, if I have
no intention to commit a crime, but am solicited and persuaded by another to perpetrate it, that person is the efficient, the virtual cause of whatever sufferings I endure
for the perpetration of that crime. How
great, how enormously great, must the guilt
of such characters be, who take a peculiar
delight to undermine the foundation of civil
society, by committing such sable crimes,
as cry to Heaven for more plagues than vengeance has in store; for there is a train of
evils too horrid to mention connected with
this crime more than any other : for instance, in the case of murder, one person
is only injured : in drunkenness, the delinquent is generally the greatest sufferer : in
envy, the culprit is always the most tormented : and the thief who robs me of my
purse, robs me of trash which may easily be
replaced with industry and economy : but
the villain who robs the innocent defense-
less virgin of her virtue, bereaves society
of a gem that might become its brightest
ornament, and its boast ; namely, the virtuous mother of a respectable family ; and

lets loose, sends forth, constitutes and quali-
fies a pest, a curse, a disgrace, to society,
who will in future live to ensnare and en-
slave others, trample upon her own character, expose her constitution, murder her
soul, and at last die the victim of a fearful
and fatal disorder, and a tortured mind,
cursing with her last breath the murderer of
her body and soul.

This is no theatrical exhibition, no speculative reasoning : the misfortune is, these observations are too true. To particularize the
real number of prostitutes who crowd our
city, (some of them not more than twelve or
fourteen years old) would make even a
hoary headed debauchee shrink appalled,
and shock the most unprincipled libertine.
And the reason these shocking sights are
viewed with indifference by the professors
of religion, as well as the profane, is, because
they are so common and numerous that the
heart of charity is not warmed by viewing
them. The social tear of benevolence forgets to flow unbidden, and the wide wish of
philanthropy to dilate for them.

As we inadvertently suggested a few spontaneous thoughts to those who call themselves
the rich and the great, we will take the liberty
to resume the subject by the following desultory remarks.

The rich, as well as the poor, are particularly interested in the subject of our investigation. Indeed, the prosperity, nay, the very existence of society, is connected with it. The children of rich parents are, by no means, out of the reach of disaster; and, however they may feed their vanity and nurture their pride, they are, in common with others, obnoxious to diversified vicissitudes, misfortunes and temptations. With sympathetic pity, I view the futile, vain, and absurd pursuits of the personages who compose what are called the higher circles, though many of them are not only the children of poor parents, but were originally poor themselves; but either by industry or economy, by fraud or force, have accumulated riches, and of course popularity; when lo! they forget their origin, and look down with sovereign contempt upon their poor brethren.

When the rich are so peculiarly favoured by Providence above millions of their fellow-creatures, how great must their ingratitude be, if they neglect to return their thankful acknowledgments to the Author of all their Mercies; and with their lives, as well as their lips, celebrate the great Creator's praise. Let us inquire for what purpose does the Deity bestow riches upon a

part of the human race. Is it to spend in
vanity and superfluity? Surely not: but to
be appropriated to the most benevolent purposes, to wit, the support of God's poor ;
for he sends the poor and needy to the rich
man's door, to try his heart ; and the same
pity which he shows to them, will God show
to him at a future day. And every rich man
should pray for power to say and feel the
force of these lines :

> " Teach me to feel another's woe,
> And hide the fault I see :
> The mercy I to others show,
> That mercy show to me."

There are three grand objects that the
rich have in view whilst accumulating this
world's goods. First, a false notion they
entertain of the power and respectability of
riches; a desire of making a magnificent appearance in the world ; and, above all, a re-
solution to leave their children independent
fortunes. These are the phantoms which
too many live and die in the pursuit of, who
spend their short probationary state, in pro-
viding with great economy and industry, for
their children, that which proves their ruin
and disgrace. Riches cannot produce a moment of real happiness, though all in the
world were at our disposal. Nay, riches
have the direct tendency to destroy all real

felicity by drawing man from the pursuit of religious duties ; and are often the source of burdensome cares and perplexing disquietudes.

How preposterous and absurd it is for people to spend their time in hoarding up riches, for the splendid accommodation of their children, when they are in their graves ; and yet, forsooth, neglect to inculcate the precepts of moral rectitude and virtue on their juvenile minds. The thought never occurs to them, that wealth can only make them appear externally happy and respectable, but that virtue alone can make them appear externally and feel internally happy, amidst all the vicissitudes incident to our mortal state. They will not learn wisdom from experience. We see the extravagant children of parsimonious parents, spend in vanity and dissipation the immense fortunes accumulated by their progenitors : and when that is gone, having been brought up in idleness, and unaccustomed to industry, the spendthrift makes use of unlawful means to replenish his purse ; and he is consequently brought to a premature and ignominious end. Thus are they, by the impolicy of their injudicious parents, incapacitated for performing their duty to society, and to their Almighty Creator. Finally, when a man accumulates riches for the purpose of offering sacrifice at the shrine of vanity and ambition, he falls into sundry temptations, and pierces himself and progeny with many sorrows. He opens the floodgates of temptation upon them temporally, and shuts the gates of Heaven against them eternally. Hence, we find it is not only the children of the poor that excite our sympathetic commiseration, but also those of the rich. It would be too tedious and painful, and perhaps indelicate to mention the most prominent snares and temptations to which they are exposed. Their education ; the examples placed before them ; the sentiments inculcated upon their minds, are all too often in open hostility with the best interests of their immortal parts, as well as their domestic tranquillity. Where there is not sufficient virtue found in parents and teachers, to administer wholesome instruction, there can be found no aliment for domestic tranquillity. It is among the rich and great that not only war, but those scandalous fashions imported from abroad originate. The middling class soon participate in these fashions however immodest. And, finally, the commonality, if they cannot literally imitate, will, at any rate, mimic their superiors in point of wealth. There is an approbious gradation in this, as in all other vices. With a superficial glance, we may recognize ladies high in estimation, and in the highest circles, slaves to the fashions in their most obscene and indecent extremes. We may even see the consorts and daughters of the guardians of the public weal strutting through the streets, with the disgraceful and obscene appearances peculiar to lewd women, with appendages and exhibitions which I am ashamed to name. We may then ask, without at present descending to particulars, is there a grade in humiliation to which we may not be reduced ? Is there a vice we may not render fashionable ? Is there a precipice of luxurious indulgence down which we may not precipitate ourselves, when it is fashionable so to do ? One of the most pernicious circumstances attending the vice under consideration is, that it is most prevalent amongst the characters that should discourage it most. Were they to discountenance and disapprove, by the most vindictive censures, and condemn the votaries thereof to the retreats of neglect and contempt, the most beneficial consequences would unquestionably result. Were we to take a countermarch into the rear of time, and view the rigid virtues of our ancestors, we might easily refuse to be slaves

to fashion ; and we need not fear to be out*
casts and a derision. But alas! a scrupu*
lous delicacy towards the articles of modern politeness, which too often adhere to
the gown and band, the clergy as well as
the laity, seems to fetter, in adamantine
chains, every circle and rank in society : yes,
even the clergy themselves have been very
diffident in giving umbrage to conscious
criminality. They have viewed, with complacency, that on which they should have
looked with detestation and horror. They
have spoken peace, peace, when God had
not intended it. Even grave divines, whose
appearance commands respect, and who
are celebrated for their profound erudition,
will view with indifference, and even without
cautioning, their auditories arrayed in all the
indelicate fashions and voluptuous appendages peculiar to the age in which we live.

When, therefore, our spiritual guides exhibit such lassitude in the discharge of the
duty they owe to their fellow-creatures and
to their God, and which they have solemnly
undertaken to fulfil ; to whom shall we look,
or where shall we turn to find wholesome
admonitions ? If the sacred temples of the
Eternal are periodically crowded with the
votaries of fashion ; and if the ambassadors
of Heaven suffer them to come in and go

out without suggesting even a mild reproof, can we expect any thing better than that the most obscene fashions that ever disfigured and disgraced the human family, should become the order of the day.

I smile to myself when I take a retrospective view of the ludicrous* fashions

---

* In confirmation of the above assertion, I will subjoin the following letter :

To the Editor of the American Magazine.

SIR,

I hope to be pardoned, if I find fault with things which are, or have been, or will be.

The long trails of the ladies gowns were a fashion in which all regard to taste was sacrificed. It appears impossible, that ladies, who are under no bias, and influenced solely by a regard to elegance, should adopt such a fashion—a fashion that, besides its inconvenience and the expense it incurs, can hardly be reconciled with neatness. It is perfectly right, in manufacturing countries, for ladies to draw fifty or a hundred thousand yards of silk upon the ground :* for the destruction of it is a public benefit. But it betrays a total *want of taste and elegance in dress;* and when the American ladies adopted the fashion, they paid fifteen or twenty thousand pounds to foreign nations, for the *trouble* of being *very inelegantly* dressed.

The enormous head-dresses, which were fashionable, a few years ago, were beyond the bounds of taste, and so troublesome as to be very short-lived.—

---

* *The children of the poor might be clothed with their trimmings.*

of former times; the diversity and peculiarity of which are too tedious to mention; but I blush with shame, and am almost pet-

---

Huge bonnets, loaded with finery are equally—But these must not be mentioned the present year.

The long-quartered shoe, for a long time, kept in countenance a very indelicate custom, of putting on shoes in the streets and in public assemblies.

A lady could hardly walk a square, or go down a country dance, without being obliged to stop and pull up the quarters of her shoes. The gentlemen were often in the same situation. Is this consistent with taste, elegance or convenience?

But when long-quartered shoes were discarded, large buckles succeeded; which are not only disproportioned to the foot, but very painful. Such is the size, that a gentleman cannot wear a buckle without a false strap; and even then it is a chance, that his straps will be flapping about his feet, as he walks the streets or is dancing. Besides, it is impossible to suit so large a buckle to the foot—it must be painful—and it is amusing enough to hear a beau damning his buckles for giving him uneasiness; that is, *damning fashion.*

The best proportioned shoe will always keep upon the foot, and the best proportioned buckle will always sit easy. *True taste* never deviates from these proportions.

Americans could hardly run into absurdities of these kinds, were they to consult their own taste or interest. It is the authority of foreign manners which keeps us in subjection, and gives a kind of sanction to follies, which are pardonable in Europe, but inexcusable in America.

TITUS BLUNT

rified with horror and solicitude for the honour of human nature, when I survey the female fashions of modern times, which are both ludicrous and lascivious to behold. On the commencement of the female fashions alluded to, through the instrumentality of which,

"Those charms alas! that virtue bids them screen,
By every wanton libertine are seen."

The fashions adopted by the males were tantamount with those of the females; particularly as it respected their wearing worsted pantaloons, which sometimes fitted them like stockings, and exhibited spectacles which were only on a par with female exhibitions; but the former got disgusted with the indecency and obscenity of their appearances, and relinquished the fashion as disgraceful to humanity; but the latter retained it as the ornament of their sex, though the very reverse is the case. The former's prudence was paramount to their love of fashion, when in open hostility with decency and common sense; but, alas! it was *vice versa* with the latter.

Formerly the only criterion whereby we could discriminate a virtuous from a lewd woman, was by their apparel; but now that criterion is almost banished to oblivion: indeed, many virtuous, and in other respects, reputable ladies, dress more indecent than even the vilest prostitutes. Their appearances are such as not only to entice, but almost to force the male of ardent passions to acts of violence,* as well as the arts of seduction. And our wonder will vanish when we remember, that " strong temptation with the best prevail." What temptation, then can be more invincible to a certain description of men, than a beautiful woman dressed with **** ; but I must cease delineating even the outlines of the fascinating sight. It would be unpardonable indelicacy in me to paint what prudence must conceal; or to depicture one half of the obscenity of female fashions : but the reader will himself save me the trouble by anticipating the sights which he sees daily exhibited : or, let him take a summer's evening walk on the battery; and he will see dis-

---

* Surely some amendment should be made to the law applicable to such crimes : or, laws should be enacted to keep female fashions within the bounds of common decency : and to fix the distinction between lewd and virtuous women.——Shall a wanton female act and dress in such a manner as to solicit the amorous male to acts of outrage? And shall he, according to law, be condemned to death, while the lascivious female, who was the primary cause of the evil, is suffered to pass on with impunity? It is unjust, partial, and ungenerous.

played in magnitude what I dare not even depict in miniature.

There is nothing in nature more capricious, contagious, and, at the same time, contaminating, than fashion : hence, appearances and personages, which are now beheld with approbation and complacency, would, twenty years ago, have been seen with shame, disgust and execration : and hence, mankind, in the different ages of the world, have practised the most unnatural and diabolical evils and vices, till they became both familiar and fashionable. To demonstrate the authenticity of our assertions, we might adduce a number of examples. The Grecians, the most refined and learned nation of antiquity, were so blinded by custom, as to constitute one thousand priestesses for one temple in the city of Corinth, dedicated to Venus, who made prostitution a part of their devotion to that unhallowed goddess. For the honour of human nature, we will not mention the multitudes of human victims sacrificed to the heathen gods ; all of which was considered laudable by the unenlightened orientals. In many parts of the world, at the present period, there are ridiculous customs established, which habit renders familiar, and which we would consider as degrading to the brutal, much more to the human creation. There are, and have been certain customs and fashions which regard things of pure indifference : and though they may appear ridiculous, they are not injurious to society : though they may excite our contempt they should not our reproach. But, on the other hand, there are fashions that are of intrinsic moment, not only as it respects their present effects, but future tendency. We will all agree, that to bring up the rising generation in the path of virtue, is an indispensable and important duty ; for, on the virtue of our children, the prosperity, nay the very existence of society depends. It will, of course, appear, that whatever precept or example is inculcated or exhibited in the present age to our youth, will have a deleterious or salutary tendency, according to its merits or demerits in the subsequent generation. We need not inquire the effects which modern fashions have on our children's minds : and indeed, it will be so till the means are stopped, and then the effects will consequently cease. We see female children mimic the fashion ; and before nature supplies them with real, they exhibit, as substitutes, in the usual form, artificial breasts.

" They first mimic fashions, only arm'd with smiles,
Then fall all ruined by seduction's wiles."

While their infatuated parents see them go, nay, sometimes lead them into the jaws of destruction, and virtually tell the libertine to tempt them, · how many innocent girls have been utterly ruined through the neglect of their parents, who are insensible of the obligations laid upon them by the God of nature, till, perhaps, it is too late to remedy the evil! Oh! how will it augment their horror in eternity, when they find that their neglect and imprudence were the radical cause of the overthrow and infelicity of their offspring in time and eternity.

Many complain of disobedient children; but who are to blame for it? Undoubtedly the parents themselves; for children may be taught almost any thing, if they are begun with in time. " They are imitative animals." They are, or will be, in miniature, what their parents or guardians are in magnitude. They will, at least, endeavour to imitate them in all they do : hence, instruction by example is more efficacious than precept ; but when both are united, the most salutary effects ensue. With my mind's eye, I view the fashionable mother at her toilet, with all the apparatus connected with it, particularly the looking-glass before her face. While she is exerting all her ingenuity to beautify her person, and to exhibit

her charms in the most advantageous manner, the daughters, both young and old, recognize all her movements, surround her
toilet, mimic her pride, and become adepts
at the business, before they arrive even at
the years of accountability. We must cease
drawing this baneful picture, and investi-
gating the secret recesses of female vanity.
Were I to draw the picture at full length,
and say all that might be said on the subject,
Satan himself could scarce refrain from blushing; Heaven would drop a tear; and hell
would groan and reverberate the fatal effects
of such injudicious, vain, and cruel conduct.
Is this the way to bring up the most amiable
part of God's creation? Is it, or can it be, the
will of the Eternal, that parents should spend
their time in teaching their children how to
decorate their persons like butterflies? (I
will not say like harlots.) Has God intrusted an immortal spirit, created for high beatitude, to your care, O parents! in order to
have it taught how to offer sacrifice at the
shrine of vanity? how to prostitute its noble
qualifications on the altar of pride and self-
consequence? how to obey the suggestions
and mandates of Satan? how to become
slaves to idleness, the fashions, and fopperies of the age? Your own common sense,
your own consciences will answer in the

negative, and will testify that the very reverse of what you now do is your duty
as rational beings : you should, both by precept and example, endeavour with indefatigable assiduity to improve the intellectual and
moral faculties of your offspring. By this
means, you will lay the foundation of a life of
happiness and utility ; but, by a contrary line
of conduct, you will facilitate their ruin ;
and, I believe, their blood will be required at
your hands by the impartial Judge and Sovereign of the skies. If we, for a moment,
reflect on the shortness of time, the certainty
of the approach of death, and the vanity of
riches, (which this messenger will, sooner
or later, force us to relinquish), as well as
on the intrinsic excellency of virtue, and the
deformity of vice, we shall immediately be
convinced of the propriety and cogency of
my arguments. Were the votaries of fashion
to let one solemn thought of their mortality
impress their minds, it would cause them to
forego their vanities.

Can any thing be more ludicrous, than
curling their hair in sable ringlets to dangle
over their eyes, obstruct their sight, and
thus incommode themselves, merely because
it is fashionable.

Were they to recollect, while decorating
their dying bodies, and neglecting the im-

provement of their immortal spirits, that very soon the bodies which they so much admire and prize, and on which they sacrifice so much precious time and talents, will be deposited in silent graves. Then their sparkling eyes, ruby lips, ruddy faces, delicate and majestic persons, will become the food of worms ; will no longer bloom, but soon return to the dust from whence they came : as a beauteous flower in the fragrant vale that blooms with native lustre, charms the eyes of every beholder, and dances in the vernal breeze ; when, lo ! at an unsuspected moment, the storms arise, the winds blow, the rains beat upon the devoted flower, which bows its charming head, withers, dies, and intermingles with the clods of the valley.

But the greatest misfortune of all is, that the children inherit the vices of their parents with their riches, and, when *they* are laid in their tombs, loose the reins to the domination of every sensual propensity ; and the riches that were accumulated by assiduity are spent with prodigality, precipitancy, and profligacy, and facilitate the premature ruin of the sprightly, volatile heir, by putting it in his power to commit many dreadful crimes which he would never have had an opportunity of perpetrating, were it not for his

D

wealth. Riches prove eventually a curse to thousands, because they do not use them as good stewards of the Almighty Judge, to whom they must give a strict account of their stewardship. The greatest assiduity and perseverance are surely necessary on the part of parents to keep their children from being infected by the vices of the age ; for, while we live in a world where public morals are corrupted, it is no easy matter to avoid contracting a habit of some fashionable vices. For the popularity of fashion, the allurements of pleasure, the seductions of vanity, the gallantry of certain favourite vices, all conspire to impair the upright in heart, and to destroy the generosity and rectitude of the finer feelings. The fascinating method, the light air, the artful sophistry and adulation, with which libertinism turns to jest the scruples of virtue, and ridicules the precepts of moral rectitude, too often destroy the importance with which the juvenile mind was wont to admire and nurture them. It is, therefore, of great importance, that the precepts of virtue should be inculcated forcibly, not superficially ; demonstratively, as well as theoretically. None but the philanthropist and sincere christian can judge of the fatality of the contagious and popular vices which at present, as well as formerly, have brought de-

struction upon nations, desolation upon families, discord amongst friends, and ruin upon both the bodies and souls of men. For
the debauchee, or fashionable libertine, being a stranger to the endearing connexions
and affections by which families are connected, never anticipates the afflictions and dismay which his lawless crimes produce, in
the bosoms of virtuous retirement. He
thinks little about the tears he will cause
to flow, and the anguish and despair he will
create. Not unlike the spider which spreads
his fallacious snare, and watches with anxious solicitude the moment the unconscious
fly approaches it, when he rushes on his innocent prey, which struggles to gain its
liberty and life, but, alas! in vain; and if it
should extricate itself, it is so debilitated
and wounded that it never recovers strength,
but lingers life in perfect misery. Thus these
pests of society lay wait to entangle and destroy innocent females, who have no friends
to defend them, and no relatives to redress
their wrongs. If a solitary gleam of pity
flushes across his iron mind, it is instantly
effaced by the more potent call of lawless
passion. If the principles of religion and
moral rectitude recur to his memory, they
are rejected as the offspring of fanaticism,
that do not belong to the character of a gen-

tleman. He thinks he may enjoy the license which custom proffers and human laws do not prohibit. As for God and his laws, such characters pay very little regard to them. Since then temptations and snares stand thick through all the ground, the syren's voice is heard on every side, to lead the rising generation to ruin, should not parents, therefore, be perseveringly solicitous to fortify the minds of their children against the evil day, when they may be exposed to all the force of temptation from Satan and wicked men, when *they* are laid in their graves, and can no longer protect and defend them? Surely they should. But, alas! how contrary do many parents act to this line of conduct! They not only suffer their female progeny to go unreproved into the very jaws of destruction, but even facilitate their ruin themselves. Little do they think, that they themselves will have to answer to God for the evils resulting to the rising generation from their negligence; for, surely, children that are formally devoted, by their infatuated parents, to be the slaves of fashion and idleness, will, of course, become, not the ornaments, but the pests of society. A folio volume would not contain what might be said, in displaying modern fashions, and their deleterious tendencies. And the misfortune is, that many parents encourage their children to become the votaries of fashion, long before they arrive at years of maturity. You may see little miss Amelia mimicking the fashions, with all the affected airs of a coquette, before she has seen her twelfth year ; and little master Tommy, at the same age, with his pantaloons up to his chin, his waistcoat about six inches long, his half boots with tassels, a watch in his fob, a club under his arm, and a segar in his mouth, strutting along with his arms a-kembo, with all the self-consequence of a nabob. Can it be possible, that such parents ever recollect for what purpose man was created. I repeat the sentiment, and it cannot be too often repeated, while parents are so thoughtless, for what end God intrusted them with the care of children, I should have said immortal spirits, capable of high beatitude. Was it that they should consider them as animal machines, and forsooth learn them to dance and sing, and spend their precious time in the pursuit of vanity and sensual gratification, and to prostitute their talents to the most unworthy purposes : in short, their lives in the service, not of their friend, but of their enemy : not of their Heavenly Father, but of Satan.

I smile to myself when I take a retrospective view of the routine of the formalities
and ceremonies, through which the children
of those called the higher class pass, while
attaining, and prior to their being metamorphosed to what are called ladies and gentlemen ; but that smile is changed to a frown
of indignation, when I recollect the dreadful consequences resulting to the unconscious
innocents, who are prematurely contaminated
with pride and vanity; and who become, as
it were mechanically, or by instinct, the devoted victims of concupiscence and sensuality, or, to what leads directly to these evils,
namely, fashion.

When I recollect these gigantic evils, for
my mind unbidden still recurs to the same
topic, disgusted with the baneful retrospect,
and alarmed for the consequences, I can only
lament the infatuation and degradation of
my unhappy fellow-travellers to the tomb,
who are one day arrayed in all the pomp and
pageantry of fashion, and the next wrapped
in their winding-sheets ; one day, blooming
with health and beauty, and bursting with
pride ; and the next inanimate clay ; one
day, with all the affectation of pedants, the coquetry of jilts, the formality of devotees, and
the agility of play-actors, skipping through
the ball-room ; the next, stretched out on

the cooling-board. Like the beauteous lily, waving on the dewy lawn, displaying its snow white face, dancing in the winds, and receiving the exhilarating sun-beams in full effusions; when lo! in a moment, the atmosphere is clouded, the sun shrouds his golden face, the storms arise, the rain descends in deluges, overloads the gay plant, till it droops and kisses the ground : when the rude winds invade and tear it up by the roots. It lies extended on the lawn, its beauty forever fled, and mingles with the dust.

Thus, one month, the proud votary of fashion thinks the ground scarcely good enough for her to walk upon ; next month, she is deposited six feet below that ground, mouldering to dust, and the food of worms. But when we extend our ideas to the indelicacy, indecency, and fatality of female fashion, and view its votaries, one day, with all the enticing wiles of Joseph's beauteous, though incontinent mistress, and with all the charms of a Helen, exhibited to the greatest advantage, to attract the eyes and provoke the lust of the degenerate, and thus cause them to sin against the Eternal; I say, how dreadful is the thought, yet how true, that, one day, the votary of fashion is thus leading the unguarded into the devious paths of folly ;

and the next, she is arraigned at the bar of God, to answer for the concomitant evils resulting from such imprudent and wicked conduct, of which nature it undoubtedly is. Indeed, I am bold to say, that some fashionable females would be less fascinating, were they to go altogether naked : for instance, a person may display in part an object, which will be truly captivating by exhibiting the most attracting part to view, and screening the rest as still more delightful ; whereby the beholder is stimulated, with tenfold solicitude, to recognize that which is screened, his fancy depicting it in imaginary colours, as possessed with intrinsic excellencies, which, were he to behold in its native colours, he would be quickly undeceived. Indeed some ladies carry fashions to such an extreme, as to be but one degree above nakedness. I have myself seen—But here let me stop. Decency*

---

* I hope the reader will excuse the indelicacy of some expressions used in this work. I am willing to apologize for the same ; but I think, in point of justice, the votaries of fashion should first make an apology to the public for giving the cause, they being, unquestionably, under more cogent obligations so to do, than I am ; for I scarcely exhibit in miniature, what they freely display in magnitude. Indeed it gives me pain to be so pointed in my animadversions; but it is indispensably necessary : for, without this,

forbids me to depict what some expose, who perhaps would be offended to be called immodest.

" Their robes so fashion'd, that degenerate men
May fancy all the wondrous charms within !
And thus each dame, all beautified by art,
Attracts the wanton eye, th' unhallow'd heart;
Those charms, alas! that virtue bids them screen,
By ev'ry lawless libertine are seen :
This makes seduction seem both fine and gay,
While weeping virtue walks disrob'd away.
Here all our guilt, and all our sorrows lie,
Hence youths and maids to certain ruin fly.
By nature man's deprav'd; this makes him worse,
Impels to guilt that proves an endless curse ;
They fix their eyes upon each swelling breast,
The vices reigning will declare the rest.
Oh ! what's th' enchanting eye, the ruddy face,
" Beauty unchaste, is beauty in disgrace ;"
And yet in them is every art and charm,
To win the wisest, and the coldest warm :
Fond love, the gentle vow, the gay desire,
The kind deceit, and still reviving fire;
Silence that speaks with eloquence of eyes,
That captivate the good, the great, the wise,
Languor that fascinates, all conq'ring charms,
That tempts the sage, and e'en the stoic warms.
Yet, Oh ! the pride, the glory of our race,
For want of prudence, is the world's disgrace ;

---

my writing on the subject will be in vain. When licentious fashions or practices become habitual, there is no possible means of exhibiting their deformity, but by painting them in the most prominent manner, and lively colours.

Guilt, which in ages past in darkness lay,
Is now the pride and order of the day.
But this degen'racy is big with woe,
T* social order a destructive foe,;
The race of mankind are by nature frail,
And strong temptations with the best prevail.
Th' enticing ladies who their charms expose,
At once ensnare, and are ensnar'd by foes;
Each am'rous fop with greedy eyes surveys
Their charms expos'd, and covets still to gaze ;
This makes the husband soon forget his spouse,
For man is false nor recollects his vows;
With wild inconstancy for all he burns,
Each shameless miss subdues his heart by turns;
He views each true or artificial charm,
These fatal sights his sleeping passions warm :
Seduction is his last resource—hence woe,
Disgrace, and shame o'erwhelm th' ensnaring foe ;
And hence, Oh ! hence, such num'rous rakes we see,
And idle women, plung'd in misery ;
Hence misses who have scarce twelve winters seen,
Become the victims of degen'rate men.
So lost from shepherd, and its mourning dam,
Through some lone desert roves a straggling lamb,
No danger fears, but as she idly strays,
Round ev'ry bush the heedless wanton plays,
Till raging wolves the beauteous toy surround,
Or tigers slay her on the crimson ground ;
Then from her guiltless heart the purple flows,
A precious morsel for the hungry foes.
By dire example ruin'd, thus wretched lies
Many a youthful dame with streaming eyes ,
No more their lips like dewy roses glow,
Their weary eyes no peaceful slumbers know ,
But left to strike their pensive breasts in vain,
And curse the authors of their lasting pain.

—◆—

CHAPTER II.

Miscellaneous and desultory strictures, intended to demonstrate the authenticity of the antecedant argu, ments, and respectfully submitted to the candid consideration of parents generally.

I HAVE, in the preceding chapter, delineated a few desultory and spontaneous thoughts on fashion. Refinement in composition, or elegance in arrangement, has been no part of my object and design, which are simply to deliver my sentiments unadorned and unadulterated, descending to particulars when necessary, and animadverting on the most popular vices, when introduced on the carpet. My primary object is to be useful, without paying the least regard to the critic's malicious sneers, the debauchee's vindictive frowns, or the fashionable dame's consequential declamations. The adulation of perishing mortals, I do not solicit, nor deprecate their censures ; for, though I love all men, I fear no man, being perfectly independent in this respect.

A large field for contemplation presents to my view a train of interesting commonplace thoughts, connected with my subject, which are so natural, and, at the same time, so reasonable, that one would suppose it altogether superfluous to suggest them ; but if we may judge people by their relative conduct, we must come to this conclusion, that if they are apprised of these thoughts, and well informed respecting the subject matter of our investigation, they have a queer way of showing their information. For instance, can we, for a moment, suppose, on the most superficial view of the manner in which many parents bring up their children, that they are convinced, when the love of unwarrantable pleasures, imprudent companions, fashionable appendages, however indecent, are allowed to attract the attention, engross the affections, and envelope the practices of children, their degradation, contamination, and, perhaps, even destruction, approaches with long and steady strides. Surely, we cannot believe that they are convinced of this truth, though it is as plain to behold as the beams of the sun in an unclouded atmosphere. We all know, that intemperance, by enervating the mind and debilitating the body, produces a state of wretchedness, while temperance has the contrary effect ; and even imprudence in dress, and a deleterious obsequi-

ousness to injudicious as well as indecent
fashions, have brought many a young woman, in the meredian of youth, to a premature death, by producing the most destructive disorders; while, on the contrary, the
prudent, judicious female, ,by not listening
to the solicitations of wayward fancy, and
by refusing to expose her constitution for
the gratification of her vanity, and in obedience to the capricious mandates of fashion,
lives to become an useful and ornamental
member of civil society, the virtuous wife
of a reputable husband, the prudent mother
of a happy, as well as numerous progeny;
and though her personal charms may not be
equal to others, yet her virtue more than
doubly compensates for it; for virtue, like
the shining gold, or glistening jewel, the
more it is used, the more resplendent it appears, and a more brilliant radiance it ac-
quires. Thus, the sun, in his western de-
clination, darts his horizontal beams less
glittering, but more captivating, than in his
meridian glory, when majestically grand he
displays at once his magnitude and beauty.
This similitude illustrates the characteristic
of an amiable woman, possessed with personal charms in mediocrity, without affectation, but blessed with sentimental charms in
superabundance without pedantry. But, to

E

what shall we liken the affected coquette, whose very physiognomy expresses to every beholder the quintessence of vanity and self-consequence. Though her beauty transcended that of the sun at noon day; yet would her affectation and haughtiness draw a vail over it, and excite contempt, instead of admiration, like the sable cloud, that big with showers, shrouds the radiant sun in solemn sadness, and causes a gloom to rest even upon the beauteous flower garden.

We would compare such a one (and many such there are) to a wolf clothed with a lamb's skin. By his mimickry and affectation, the deception is recognized, and he receives contempt and execration.

The horse is a beautiful and useful animal, and is of course admired and esteemed. The leopard is still more beautiful to behold, yet he is viewed with horror, and avoided with dismay. What a pity it is, that the proud and imperious votaries of fashion, while at their toilets, or strutting along the streets, will not ask their own hearts these solemn questions : What are we ? Atoms of creation, particles of dust. Where are we? On this terraqueous ball, spending a few revolving moments, as probationary, accountable, and sensitive beings, on whom are bestowed, by the liberal hand of the

Architect of Nature, transcendently excellent and ornamental qualifications, for the express purpose of promoting the glory, and doing the will of the Eternal Creator, to whom we must account for the expenditure of our riches, talents and time.

When we leave this earthly ball, what will become of our immortal parts? We shall undoubtedly be arraigned at the august tribunal of the Eternal; there to receive, from the impartial Judge, rewards or punishments, according to the merit or demerit of our actions. We shall then ascertain, that our probationary state, at least when compared to eternity, is like a dream, or a flash of lightning in the atmosphere, one moment seen, the next vanished forever. Is it then right or reasonable for us to spend our fleeting moments in gratifying our capricious passions, in indulging our unwarrantable pleasures, and in offering incense at the shrine of vanity? No. As we are not only probationary, but social and immortal beings, it is an insult to common sense, a perversion of our nature, and a mortal sin against the eternal Author and supporter of concord and peace, to spend our time in idleness and dissipation, not only in neglecting to do good, but in doing much evil, prostituting our persons, time, riches, and talents to the most unworthy purposes. These are serious considerations: and however the volatile and gay may flirt and sneer at them, the day is fast approaching when sickness will seize, and medicine fail them. Then they will anticipate all the solemnities of a dying hour, and feel, as well as know, that Jehovah is inexorable in justice, and irrevocable in his decrees, as they respect the proud and impenitent; and, at the same time, great in goodness to the humble and pious, upon whom he showers in copious abundance his divine blessings and benedictions. He is their source of consolation under trouble. He fortifies their minds in temptations; and, when about to take a long and last farewell of all things here below, a convoy of celestial heralds are sent to bear the happy soul exulting and triumphant on their golden wings up to the palace of God and his angels.

> Swift, and more swift the radiant heralds go,
> As swift as lightning, and as white as snow.

Parents should always remember, that for every child the Almighty has intrusted to their charge, he has assigned a portion of work in his vineyard; for, surely, we must believe, that he has not, will not, and cannot create an immortal spirit without hav ing some glorious end in view. For my own part, I am confident in the opinion, that there is not an individual of the human family (idiots and lunatics excepted), who has not one or more talents imparted, and a portion of salutary labour appropriated for the exercise of that talent or talents, by the improvement of which he may, in a greater or less degree, promote the glory of God, the cause of virtue, and the good of mankind. And on parents the important task falls, to cultivate the intellectual faculties of their children at an early age, that they may answer the salutary end of their creation, when arrived at the years of accountability. If they neglect this part of their duty to God and their children, they are guilty of the crimes they commit, and of the good they neglect: and let them flatter themselves as they may, they will have to answer for the same to the God of Nature. The natural consequences that result from children's being allowed by their parents or guardians to remain in ignorance and disobedience, are the contamination of the source of virtue, the perversion of their natural endowments, and the surrendering of them to the influence and domination of the most discordant passions and jarring dispositions: and when these are allowed to extend their baneful influence, the whole moral character is poisoned, the motives to laudable actions are annihilated, and disgrace, guilt, and misery are accumulated ; by which means, the unconscious children of injudicious parents are too often precipitated into a labyrinth of premature misery, and, perhaps, final ruin. Swallowed in the vortex of immorality before the principles of moral rectitude were inculcated on their juvenile minds, before the super-excellence of virtue had been exhibited to their indiscriminate view, or before its transcendent beauties had been even anticipated. Their ungovernable passions produce a train of evils. First, intemperance leads the van: complicated disease follows : sloth, pride, poverty, and dispair bring up the rear, and precipitate the unhappy beings loaded with sins of the deepest die, and enveloped with sorrows of tenfold magnitude, into eternity, cursing forever the authors of their lasting wretchedness. But, alas ! it is not only the children of such cruel parents that are prematurely contaminated by sentimental or practical seduction, but even those of prudent and virtuous people when first setting out in life, while yet strangers to the syren's voice, the charming hypocrite's solicitations; when every unhallowed pleasure entices, and every new object exhibits an air of novelty ; the seducing spirit gains the ascendency ; virtue retires disrobed and in tears ; tranquillity is forever banished ; irregular and even criminal desires are gratified, being first metamorphosed to venial weakness ; habit grows invincible ; guilt grows gigantic ; and debauchery is accounted laudable, till death stops the juvenile wantons in their mad career, and levels them with the clods of the valley ; while their disconsolate parents remain unimpeached, having done their duty to them while in their minority. How often has it happened, that young persons have begun the world with blooming prospects and virtuous dispositions ; but, alas ! by associating with wicked companions, and by indulging in unwarrantable propensities, their blooming prospects are blasted in the bud, like the opening flower scorched by the sun, or blasted by the impetuous whirlwind ; and though they bid fair to be the support, yet they eventually prove to be the pests of civil society. Thus, the sun rises majestically grand, tips the blue mountains with a golden ray, exhilarates the plain, gilds the atmosphere with orient light, and promises a charming day ; when, lo ! the sable curtains of the sky are let down, the sun is vanished, the showers descend, and conclude the weeping day with solemn sadness.

Those who call themselves the rich, the great, and the lords of the creation, are often envied by the lower class ; but, alas! their embarrassing and fleeting situations in life should command our pity, instead of exciting our envy. Many an aching head reclines upon a downy pillow. Many a sorrowful heart is conveyed from place to place in a gilded chariot. Many a volatile outside appearance conceals unutterable wretchedness within. Riches nurture pride ; and pride disorders the heart ; and the fountain of happiness being poisoned, the streams are consequently affected. Though every other painful sensation were prohibited from disturbing the rich man's mind, yet the solemn thought of the approach of death, with all his ghastly terrors, to force him to relinquish his splendid possessions in favour of others, to exchange his pompous palace for a loathsome grave, are enough to blast all his pleasures, to imbitter all his sweets, and to annihilate his hopes of future joy : especially when he takes a retrospective view of his rare virtues and multiplied crimes ; of the good he has omitted to do, and of the evils he has done, he laments that he has let his golden moments pass without improvement. The concomitants that attend his departure from the paths of innocence and virtue, appear to his wounded

mind, as the spectre of a murdered person
appears in the midnight hour to the assassin
while slumbering on his bed, calling in vain
for the comforts of peaceful repose. He
curses the unhappy moment he first cast his
eyes on the gardens of unhallowed pleasure. He remembers with what timidity
and trembling he first ventured to participate
the lawless revelling of his jovial companions,
still casting a longing lingering glance on the
forsaken path of virtue, with a purpose to return at a future period ; but, alas ! one enticing snare is followed by another still more
so, and the same with licentious acts, till
the remembrance of his former virtue is
obliterated from his mind, and even a relish
for the happiness of innocence and integrity.
He then becomes an easy victim of dissipation, is entangled in business, immersed in
luxury, filled with vanity, degraded by iniquity, and is easily whirled down the vortex
of sensuality into the ocean of complete misery, while the most superficial glance of his
former happy days, fills him with horror and
regret. Thus, the man who in his pleasure
boat sails down the river Thames views with
delight the beautiful country seats and their
romantic scenery, the blushing parterres, the
scented meads, the diversified flower-gardens,

the lofty trees peeping over trees, and waving
their verdant foliage ; but, lo ! while he is
delighting himself with the enchanting sight,
a sudden squall of wind, descending upon
his little boat, breaks the mast, and bears
the sail away. The rising gale still blows
the boat down the river, the man not being
able to manage her, the sail being lost, she
is at length ushered into the foaming ocean,
where the mountain waves threaten to make
the man's pleasure-boat his coffin. He laments his folly for coming so far from home
without making any preparation for inci-
dental dangers. He blames his own neglect
for the dilemma in which he finds himself ;
and each wave he views augments his horror, while he sees, or thinks he sees, grim
death sit frowning on each wave. He casts
many a long look on the forsaken shore,
hoping to gain it ; but he hopes in vain.

Indeed, it often happens, that the accumulation of wealth completely metamorphoses many persons from what they were
in a state of mediocrity. From being the
votaries of virtue, they become the votaries
of vanity. From offering the grateful tribute of thanksgiving at the altar of God, they
offer the sacrifice of adulation at the shrine
of avarice. The case of Hazael presents itself to illustrate my arguments. When the

prophet Elisha told him of the barbarous cruelties he would commit, he was petrified with horror, abhorred the very idea of such barbarity, and exclaimed in the language of detestation : " *But what, is thy servant a dog that he should do, this great thing ?*" But, alas ! following years demonstrated the truth 'of the prophet's words. When he became king of Syria; ambition and cruelty took possession of his rational faculties ; he was so far changed, as to take a dire delight in perpetrating what he before shuddered to anticipate. He became a monster in the shape of a man : whose delight was violence and murder ; for it appears, he smote the children of Israel in all their coasts, and oppressed them during all the days of king Jehoahaz. I might also mention Alexander the great, whose history tends to demonstrate the authenticity of my arguments. In his youth, he was truly a person of an amiable mind ; and even on the commencement of his victorious career as a general, he was remarkable for his moderation and virtue ; an instance of which, I would beg leave to relate, which does him great honour, and deserves to be had in perpetual remembrance.

" The evening after an engagement with the Persians, Alexander invited his chief

officers to a feast, at which he himself presided, notwithstanding he had been wounded that day in battle. The festivity, however, had scarce begun, when they were in-
terrupted by sad lamentations from a neighbouring tent, which at first they considered
as a fresh alarm, but they were soon taught
that it came from the tent in which the
wife and mother of Darius was kept, who
were expressing their sorrow for the supposed death of Darius. An eunuch, who
had seen his cloak in the hands of a soldier,
imagining he was killed, brought them these
dreadful tidings. Alexander, however, sent
one of his officers to undeceive them, and to
inform them that the emperor was still alive.
The women, little used to the appearance of
strangers, upon the arrival of the Macedo-
nian soldier, imagining he was sent to put
them to death, threw themselves at his feet,
and entreated him to spare them a little
while. They were ready, they said, to die :
and only desired to bury Darius, before
they should suffer. The soldier assured
them, that the monarch whom they deplor-
ed, was still living, and he gave Sysigambis
his hand to raise her from the ground.

"The next day Alexander, after visiting
the wounded, caused the last honours to be
paid to the dead in the presence of the whole

army, drawn up in the most splendid order
of battle. He treated the Persians of distinction in the same manner, and permitted
Darius' mother to bury whatever person she
pleased according to the customs and ceremonies practised in her country. After this,
he sent a message to the queens to inform
them, that he was coming to pay them a
visit ; and accordingly, commanding all his
train to withdraw, he entered the tent, ac-
companied only by Hephæstion, who made
so cautious and discreet a use of the liberty
granted him, that he seemed to take it not
so much out of inclination, as from a desire
to obey the king, who would have it so.
They were of the same age, but Hephæstion
was taller, so that the queens took him first
for the king, and paid him their respects as
such. But some captive eunuchs shewing
them Alexander, Sysigambis fell prostrate
before him, and entreated pardon for her
mistake, but the king raising her from the
ground, assured her that this his friend was
also another Alexander; and after comfort-
ing her and her attendants, took the son of
Darius that was yet but a child in his arms.
The infant, without discovering the least terror, stretched out his arms to the conqueror,
who being affected by its confidence, said
to Hephæstion, ' Oh! that Darius had some

I

share, some portion of this infant's generosity.'—This interview has done more honour to Alexander's character, than all the rest of his conquests: the gentleness of his manners to the suppliant captives, his chastity and continence, when he had the power to enforce obedience, were setting an example to heroes, which it has been the pride of many since to imitate."

Yet, alas! notwithstanding this favourable commencement, his end was truly wretched: before which he degenerated from his antecedent qualifications through the influence and medium of unexampled success; so that he was considered by the surrounding nations as the scourge of God and destroyer of the human race. And while he enslaved the world, he was himself a slave to intemperance, by which he was brought to an untimely grave. I might adduce a large number of examples to show that riches prove a curse to thousands by feeding their imperious vanity and pride; and, at the same time, annihilating their social virtue and humility. One would think it impossible for people to be haughty and proud, when the thoughts of death and the grave rush into their minds; but, alas! they suffer not the interesting thoughts to rest upon their vitiated hearts till the die is cast, and they feel as well as know, that the Almighty is just as well as good, wise as well as merciful.

Some suppose that the rich, who bask in the sunshine of prosperity, are happy, without being miserable ; are joyful, without participating any degree of sorrow ; but, let them know, that the rich, in common with the poor, have their portion of human woe to bear ; and often the disappointments of vice are greater than those of virtue. What self-denial that religion imposes, is more agonizing than the predominent influence of envy, revenge, parsimony, avarice, and a train of evils too horrid to mention ? The Eternal prohibits his children from nothing but what would be injurious to them. Those who obey his requirings, enjoy a paradise on earth, in reflecting that they, with a sincere heart, endeavour to do his will. Thus, in the midst of misfortune and disappointment, the virtuous are crowned with joy and peace, while the vicious are tormented with the thoughts of their present guilt, and the prospect of their future misery. And let the wicked man think what he may, he can never get to heaven without repentance, nor escape the notice of the all-seeing eye. Though he should vault into the sky, precipitate down to the lower regions, or fly to the uttermost parts of the earth, there

an omnipotent God would be present to punish him.

But the most potent argument we can advance to prove the validity of our hypothesis, and the cogency of the duty of parents
to their children respecting their intellectual improvement, is the solemn reflection of
the immateriality of the soul. And when
this reflection presents itself to my mind, I
can scarcely avoid being irritated at the
murderous folly of those parents, who act
towards their children, as if they were animal machines, not immortal spirits; and
thus lay the foundation of their present and
future misery. Hence, the many digres-
sions that are observable in this performance. However, I am not writing to please
the ear, but to profit the heart. Truth is,
I conceive, most resplendent when most simplified; and to attempt to garnish it with the
appendages of metaphysical erudition, in order to enforce and beautify it, is like painting a diamond with a view to make it more
brilliant. Sophistry, not truth, needs these
appendages.

I conceive it to be the duty of an author,
who writes for the good, not for the praise
of man, to make his readers reflect, not
laugh; to study utility more than elegance;
brevity more than redundance; to forego

prolixity and exhibit variety. A well-poised sentiment, a simplified argument, supported by reasou and common sense, an instantaneous exhibition of a common fact, will have a better tendency to convince the understanding, inform the mind, and reform the heart, than volumes of elegant, refined but futile composition. A literary work possessed of energy, vivacity and utility can only be useful to a certain description of persons.

Is it not virtually committing intellectual massacre, when parents not only neglect to impress on the juvenile minds of their progeny the mild precepe of our holy religion, but suffer them to run through the slippery paths of youth with unrestrained passions. Thus, the injudicious farmer suffers his colt to remain in the woodlands (instead of raising and nurturing it under his immediate inspection) till it has gained its native strength, with accumulated fierceness. The owner, being pressed by his wants, now pursues, endeavouring to recover his horse, but in vain. The horse is rendered useless to him, and dangerous to the public through his neglect. Thus thousands of children are not only useless to their parents, but bring their grey hairs with sorrow to the grave, through their wildness and disobedience. And they not only endanger the peace of others by their blind impetuosity, but hurry themselves headlong into excesses which terminate in their ruin.

The child of a savage, and that of a sage, are the same by nature. By letting them both remain uncultivated, they will be equally wild, though it may be their quickness of cultivation may not be the same on their intellectual improvement. There is, therefore, no part of parental duty more important than bridling the passions of children at an early age : and that parent, whether rich or poor, noble or ignoble, who succeeds in breaking his child's temper, while in a state of minority, has purchased the most invaluable blessing for him, and has gained the highest attainment peculiar to our rational nature.

Wherever we turn our eyes, we see objects to demonstrate this speculative reasoning. In one direction, we see the virtuous happy man who is master of his passions, sit calm in tumults, and amidst contending parties and busy multitudes; while, in the opposite direction, we discover the vicious wretched man mastered by his passions, led from one extreme to another, blasting the enjoyments of his neighbours, strewing the path of life with thorns, and rendering the sacred recesses of domestic tranquillity a vale of tears.

Let us for a moment cast our eyes on the theatre of war in Europe, and ask our hearts the cause of all this havoc, slaughter, discord, devastation, and anarchy which we behold. —While individuals, families, and nations arm for war, and, on the most trifling occasions, rush against each other with the fury of roaring lions, and with the impetuosity of maniacs, malevolent and furious to spill each other's blood, the answer is ready, the reason is obvious, to wit, PASSION! unrestrained, unhallowed PASSION. And it is not the present age only that has been famous, or rather infamous, for the depredations of sanguinary warfare, but also former generations have tinged the verdant green with crimson red; have cast libations of human blood into the briny deep; have raised whole hecatombs of human bodies, as trophies in honour of the goddess of victory. And when we descend from national to individual suicide, we behold, with an equal degree of horror, the tragical catastrophes resulting from domestic and individual discord: here we see revenge, envy, covetousness, jealousy, rage, with unbridled license: here the outlawed villain sends the glittering death through the guiltless body of the inoffensive traveller; robs him of his money, while his blood is yet warm on the reeking blade. There the legal villain, on account of some trifling misunderstanding, calls his brother into the field, and sends the leaden ball through his body with impunity, while he screens himself from all imputation under the august canopy of public patronage or popular custom ; but we must forbear delineating even the outlines of the dreadful picture.

However, we will attempt a little farther to show* the dissimilarity between the man that is a slave to his passions, and him that has conquered them. By painting the latter character more plainly, we may recognize the infinite advantages of a virtuous life. The consolatory effect of virtue on the human mind, will not admit of a shadow of doubt, much less of dispute. A thousand volumes would not contain even a specimen of the happiness which those persons enjoy who are the possessors of social virtue. There is one sensation of celestial origin which he inherits, if he is in affluent circumstances ; and that is, the opportunity given him to spread benefactions, and con-

---

* The most effectual method to demonstrate the deformity of vice, and beauty of virtue, is, by contrasting them, and by particularizing the dissimilarty in favour of virtue.

sequent comforts amongst his indigent fellow-men ; and thus to increase his own, by establishing their comforts. He rejoices in the good which they enjoy, and they in the good which he bestows ; but the approving voice of his conscience, with the exhilarating smiles of Heaven which he anticipates, exceeds description. Those heavenly sensations may be felt, but they can never be expressed. What are the pleasures of the voluptuous, of the epicure, or of the votaries of fashion, when compared to his ? They are beastly indulgence, and sensual gratification. It is like comparing a drop of water to the ocean, a grain of sand to this terraqueous ball, a candle to the sun, or hell to heaven.

All nature smiles upon him, and he upon the face of nature. The most superficial view of the bounties and beauties of this expansive creation, dilates his heart, enraptures all his intellectual faculties. He calls upon the universe, and the universe calls upon him, to praise the Divine Benefactor, the Parent of Good. He sees

> " In native white and red,
>   The rose and lily stand,
> And free from pride their beauties spread,
>   To shew his skilful hand.

The lark mounts to the sky,
    With unambitious song,
And bears her Maker's praise on high,
    Upon he artless tongue."

When he sees autumn approaching majestically grand, loaded with bounties, to reward the farmer's toil, he lifts an affectionate thought, an humble acknowledgment,
in pure praises to the Eternal Benefactor
from whom all blessings flow. His enjoyments are refined ; they penetrate the heart;
they ennoble the mind, they produce the
most lively gratitude. And nothing con-
tributes, in so high a degree, to enliven
prosperity, as gratitude ; and nothing is
more pleasing to the Deity himself, than a
thankful heart ; which is the chief return he
requires for his accumulated benedictions.
For

    " God is paid when man receives ,
    To enjoy is to obey."

While the wicked man can, or rather will,
only trace the source of his prosperity and
riches to supernumerary success and local
advantages ; the good man sees them all
coming from the hand of that God, who
hath conducted, protected, and preserved
him from his cradle, and through each intervening period of his life. While the

wicked only enjoy prosperity the short period of the present state ; the righteous reap more solid peace from the anticipation of future glory, and felicity in a world of spirits than from all their earthly possessions. One only participates the pleasure peculiar to midnight robbers, who, in their revellings are haunted with the fear of detection, and consequent punishment : the other enjoys pure sentimental delight, ineffable comfort, without fear or intimidation ; as the virtuous son of a gracious king, confiding in his father's munificence, participates his liberality with full assurance of his paternal protection and approbation. The case of David, king of Israel, presents itself to prove the assertion. See, with what an amiable simplicity and divine assurance he expresses his confidence in, and grateful acknowledgments to, his Father and Sovereign, *the King of kings and Lord of lords.*

" *The Lord is my shepherd; I shall not want. He maketh me to lie down in green pastures; he leadeth me beside the still waters. He restoreth my soul; he leadeth me in the paths of righteousness for his name's sake. Yea, though I walk through the valley of the shadow of death, I will fear no evil: for thou art with me; thy rod and thy staff*

*they comfort me. Thou preparest a table
before me in the presence of mine enemies:
thou anointest my head with oil; my cup
runneth over. Surely goodness and mercy
shall follow me all the days of my life: and
I will dwell in the house of the Lord for
ever.*"

Is it not of the very first importance, that
parents should inculcate the principles of virtuous sensibility and moral obligation upon
the juvenile minds of their children, since
it is evident, that the good things of this
world, cannot be enjoyed without the con-
curring influence of religion and virtue, much
less those of the world to come. True they
may flourish in the eyes of the world, swim
in wealth, be intoxicated in vanity, and
engrossed with the formalities of life; but
all this will not produce an hour's real peace.
Sensual gratification they may enjoy, but
never true peace; for if the wretched child
of fortune was to appropriate to himself a
moment of serious reflection, the fear of
death would soon chastise the latent joy,
and bid it hence depart. Thus he is miserable within, but splendid without; rebuked
by his conscience; applauded by his sycophants, who hope to gain, by their adulation, pecuniary emoluments: but, when his

riches take wings and fly away, his flatterers will fly away with them. Or, when death snatches him away from them, he will be soon forgotten, and on his monumental stone may, with propriety, be written the following epitaph:

" How, lov'd, how valu'd, once, avails thee not,
To whom related, or by whom begot;
A heap of dust alone remains of thee,
'Tis all thou art, and all the proud shall be."

No doubt many will be ready to conclude, that I degrade, instead of exalting and vindicating, the excellency of the female character, and will be ready to reprobate the freedom I use in my animadversions; but the vices and follies of the age call for them. The female character is excellent indeed, when their deportment is consistent with the end and design of their creation, to wit: the glory of God, their own peace, and to be man's help-meet. With respect to the purity and benevolence of my intentions, I can appeal to the Searcher of all hearts to witness my sincerity, and for the truth* of my as-

---

* Though I have been very careless in the composition of this work, I have, on the the other hand, been very careful to suggest no sentiments nor give any advice, but what will promote the best interests of the human family. This is not the case with many ingenious works on education, their authors take much pains to embellish their composition, but pay little regard to the accuracy.

sertions, I appeal to the conscience of the most hardened libertine, or the most imprudent votary of female fashion, to decide, whether they are not consistent with truth and propriety. I do, indeed, exalt the female character higher than the male, in those qualifications which ennoble human nature, and make it almost angelic; and those are benevolence, sympathy, commis-

---

of the sentiments they develope. The "Rights of Woman" in particular, I acknowledge is an elegant written work as it respects its composition, but the sentiments too often tend, in my humble opinion, to consolidate the errings instead of vindicating the rights of Women. She no doubt took very great pains in composing that work, and very little, to appearance, in correcting the sentiments therein.

However, as she was masculine herself, she perhaps thought all women like her in this respect. One of her sentiments, relative to boys and girls being instructed and kept in each others company as much as possible, I think is calculated to be very injurious. Indeed I am entirely of a different opinion. Boys and girls, I think, should be kept apart as much as possible, especially when advanced in years. By neglecting this precaution, many parents and teachers have given the children under their care an opportunity to lay the foundation of a life of dissipation and debauchery. I could mention young apprentice boys and girls, as well as juvenile schoolmates, nay, even brothers and sisters, who have been ruined by the neglect of their masters, teachers and parents. Yes, I could point to the children of the same parents who produced the indeliable fruits of incestious love, when they were both very young; and can it be wondered at when the stupid parents made them sleep in the same bed. Indeed, what I have seen acted between children when I was a little boy, as well as since, confirms me in the opinion that parents, teachers and masters, should keep their male and female children as much apart as possible. I will go farther and affirm, that boys and girls should not be sent to the same school together, and parents should be very cautious how they send their daughters even to boarding-schools, could they see the infinite injury children have met with from these quarters, they would weep and tremble by turns for the safety of their offspring, as well as for the unutterable evils to be seen in society, which eventually had their primary origin in the neglect of parents and teachers.

eration; and, as it respects every other acquirement which men have, or ever will
attain, I contend that the natural genius of
women can, if improved, make, on an equal
par, the same attainments. My object is to
show women themselves what noble, exalted, glorious, (and I had almost said)
heavenly beings they are, while they act con-
formable to their high vocation ; and, to
reverse the idea, what poor, helpless, and
despicable beings they are, when, instead
of answering the noble end for which they
were created, namely, to act a reasonable,
judicious, and charitable part in this world ;
to be a benefit to mankind, and the glory
of their Creator, and to enjoy his beatific
presence and glory in eternity ; they prostitute their talents in the service of Satan,
and their persons mentally, and, alas ! too
often corporeally, to the promiscuous lust
of the votaries of sensuality and libertinism. For, certainly, the fashionable female, who exposes publicly what prudence
should conceal, not only entices the male of
ardent passions to perpetrate, but also com-
mits the crime of sentimental fornication
herself ; for, surely, if he who looks upon
such a woman to lust after her, is guilty of
adultery in his heart, according to our dear
Redeemer's observation ; the woman who

entices him is equally guilty. These are se
rious considerations, which the day of judgment will abundantly develope. In order to
prove, that I am not alone in reprobating the
vices of men, I will close this chapter with
a quotation from the writings of Thomas
Ellwood, a pious and holy man, who was
imprisoned, in Great-Britain, for bearing an
honest and unaffected testimony to the truth,
as it is in Jesus, our dear and precious Redeemer. The following lines were written
while he was in prison.

"Why should my modest muse forbidden be,
To speak of that which but too many see?
Why should she, by conniving, seem t' uphold
Men's wickedness, and thereby make them bold
Still to persist in't? Why should she be shy
To call them *beasts*, who want *humanity*?
Why should she any longer silence keep,
And lie secure as one that's fast asleep?
Or, how indeed can it expected be,
That she should hold her tongue, and daily see
Those *wicked* and *enormous crimes* committed,
Which she in modesty has pretermitted?
Which but to name, would with their filth defile
Chaste ears, and cast a blemish on her style:
Yet, of so many, she cannot forbear
To mention some, which here detected are.
"Loud were the cries, which long had pierc'd mine ear,
Foul the reports, which I did daily hear.
Unheard of, *new-invented crimes* were brought,
By *fame* unto my *knowledge*, which I thought
Too foul and loathsome to have found a place
In any heart, though ne'er so *void* of grace.

This made me take a more observant view,
Whether report spake what of men is true.
" But as the celebrated southern QUEEN,
When she the court of *Solomon* had seen,
And had, with more than usual diligence,
Observ'd his splendor and magnificence,
Consider'd well his pomp, his port, his state,
The great retinue that on him did wait;
As one with admiration fill'd (no doubt
Not able longer to contain) burst out
Into such words as these; *Thrice happy king!*
Whose fame throughout the universe doth ring,
Though of thine acts I thought report too bold,
Yet now I see one half hath not been told.
Just so did I, though in another kind,
After I had intently fix'd my mind
Upon men's actions, and had duly weigh'd,
Not only what they *did*, but what they *said.*
" Was *Sodom* ever guilty of a sin,
Which *England* is not now involved in?
By *custom*, *drunkenness* so common's grown,
That most men count it a *small sin*, or *none:*
Ranting and *roaring* they affirm to be,
The true characters of *gentility.*
Swearing and *cursing* is so much in fashion,
That 'tis esteem'd a badge of *reputation.*
What *dreadful oaths!* what *direful execrations*
On others; on themselves what *imprecations*
They tumble out, like roaring claps of thunder
As if they meant to rend the clouds asunder!
Mockers do so abound in every place,
That rare it is to meet a sober face.
Ambition, *boasting*, *vanity*, and *pride*,
With numbers numberless of sins beside,
Are grown, through use, so common, that men call
Them *peccadilloes;* small, or none at all.
" But, oh! the *luxury* and *great excess*
Which by this wanton age is us'd in *dress!*

What pains do men and women take, alas !
To make themselves for arrant *bedlam's* pass!
And he that in a modest garb is drest,
Is made the laughing-stock of all the rest.
All things to *lust* and *wantonness* are fitted,
Nothing that tends to vanity omitted.
To give a touch on every *antic fashion*,
Which hath been worn of late within this nation,
Might fill a volume, which would tire, no doubt,
The READER's patience, if not wear it out.
   " Come now, ye *ranting gallants* of the times,
Who nothing have to boast of but your *crimes*.
Blasphemous wretches ! whose *impieties*,
With rude assaults have storm'd the very skies,
And dar'd the *God of heaven ;* a dreadful stroke
Shall ye receive, by which ye shall be broke,
And in the fiery lake those torments find,
Which for such *desperadoes* are assign'd.
   "And ye, who take so great delight to curse,
As that you think yourselves a deal the worse,
Unless unto the highest strain ye swell,
And wish the *devil* make your bed in hell ;
This know, the long provoked God is come,
From whom ye must receive that dreadful doom,
Depart ye cursed, and for ever dwell,
Where beds of torment are prepared in hell."

———

   " Since what precedes was written, I have found
An accusation form'd, but without ground,
Against me, that *with uncontrolled pen,*
I too severely lash the faults of men ;
And take upon me in satiric rhymes,
To pass a rigid censure on the times.
This drew me on to add another line,
To shew them that the fault's their own, not mine.

No crime can justly to my charge be laid,
Unless it be a crime, *that truth be said.*
Nor can, without injustice, any blame
My muse for echoing the common fame.
  " If any should object, *that wise men hold,*
That truth at all times ought not to be told.
Nor that *whatever comes into one's head,*
Should straight, because 'tis true, be published.
I readily assent, because I know
Pearls before swine we are forbid to throw.
Some truths, I grant, may better be conceal'd,
Than if they out of season were reveal'd ;
Yet would I not that any, through mistake,
Should of my words a misconstruction make,
Than that should happen, I had rather be
Tax'd by the reader for prolixity.
  " Thus then, in brief, would I be understood.
If what I know, concerns my brother's good,
For him to know ; ought I not then unfold
It to him, rather than from him withhold
A benefit ? So, on the other side,
It is, I think, too plain to be deny'd,
That if I see what certainly doth tend
To the hurt of my neighbour or my friend,
I am oblig'd, by *christian charity,*
To give them warning of the danger nigh ;
To shew them, that they stand upon the brink
Of certain ruin ; and if then they sink,
By wilful running on, I shall be free
From guilt, their blood on their own heads will be
'Tis plain I think ; yet if ye can't believe it
Without a scripture-proof, lo, here* I give it.
This is the very case ; which if well weigh'd,
Will fully justify what I have said.
  " I saw men running to a precipice,
At foot of which was such a vast abyss,

---

* *Levit.* ix. 17.   *Ezek.* xxxiii.

As could have swallow'd nations so immmense,
That 'twas impossible to climb out thence.
For if a man we see, but chance to pitch,
O'er head and ears into some miry ditch;
How quickly is he smothered, unless
Some friendly hand assist in that distress !
And if, with struggling, out at length he get,
Yet how besmear'd is he with dirt. and wet !
But into this deep pit who falls, in vain
Expects a hand to help him out again.
No, 'tis of grace that men forewarned are,
And, ere their feet are taken, *shewed the snare.*
  " And warned they must be.   For so was I,
While roving in their paths of vanity ;
Toil'd and bewilder'd in a dismal night
Of thick *Egyptian* darkness, from the light :
From whence the Lord hath, by his love me drawn,
And in my heart hath caus'd his day to dawn,
His glorious day, his never-setting sun
To rise, and darkness to expel begun.
This love, as it arises, warms my heart,
And fills it with desires to impart
To others of its goodness, that none may,
For want of good direction, miss their way.

CHAPTER III.

The primary Cause of the Encroachments of Men upon the Rights of Women considered.

In most parts of the world, females are considered by the male part of society, merely as objects. of sensual convenience and domestic accommodation ; possessed with animal, but destitute of immortal spirits ; and even in christendom, many degrade and represent them as inferior, in point of intellectual faculties to the male. My object here is to investigate the radical cause of this degradation ; and, in the first place, I must impute this strange infatuation, this unnatural conclusion, to error in education, a wrong association of ideas in youth, which is handed down from one generation to another, as it were, by hereditary succession ; till that hypothesis, which is, in fact, an insult to common sense, daily experience, and the nature of things, is, by custom, reduced to a natural supposition, a received opinion.

I am very confident in the opinion, that this neglect is the cause of infinite evil in civil society, and is the parent of accumu‧ lated and unnatural crimes.

I would ask, is not a judicious education the best fortune a child, whether male or female, can receive? Why then, has a large majority of the sons of men adopted the most spurious, the most unjust, and ungenerous sentiments respecting the female character, and the most farcical and ludicrous notions respecting female education? I ask again, why, in the name of wonder, is the cultivation of the female mind, even by the refined sons of Europe, considered merely as a matter of secondary consideration, except it is amongst the rich and affluent; and even then one would suppose, by the education that many parents give their daughters, that they intend them to be play-actors or dancing-girls, instead of being the prudent and judicious mothers of respectable families; and this, I will be bold to say, is the radical cause that multitudes of these characters, called ladies, are the most useless beings, the most vain, capricious, versatile, gaudy, and affected mortals in the creation. Like the useless butterfly that appears fluttering in the sun on a summer's day, flying from flower to flower in the scented gardens, its beauteous wings are tipt with gold ; the enraptured child views it with delight and ad-

miration, all glittering to behold, and endeavours to catch the spangled prize, when
a shower descends and wraps the lovely toy
in a premature watery grave ; the disappointed child views it, languid on the plain,
its beauty for ever fled. This similitude
will hold good with respect to too many female characters, who spend their time and
talents in as useless a manner, and with the
same superficial appearance as the painted butterfly, particularly in cities ; indeed
there is a great contrast between the manners
and customs of the females of the country
and city, as well as in their mode of life :
the native grandeur, the unaffected simplicity, the rural felicity peculiar to a country
life, are, in my opinion, as much superior to
the vicissitudes, fopperies, and fashions of
a city life, as the radiance of the native rose
is superior to the artificial one. I can find
no language to prove my opinion to be
correct, more cogently than the following
appropriate lines on

PHILOSOPHIC SOLITUDE, &c.

"Let ardent heroes seek renown in arms,
Pant after fame, and rush to wars alarms.;
To shining palaces let fools·resort,
And dunces cringe to be esteem'd at court;
M ine be the pleasure of a *rural* life,
From noise remote, and ignorant of strife ;

Far from the painted belle, and white glov'd beau,
The lawless masquerade, and midnight show ;
From ladies, lap-dogs, courtiers, garters, stars,
Fops, fiddlers, tyrants, emperors, and czars.
" Full in the centre of some shady grove,
By nature form'd for solitude and love ;
On banks array'd with ever-blooming flowers,
Near beauteous landscapes, or by roseate bowers,
My neat, but simple mansion I would raise,
Unlike the sumptuous domes of modern days;
Devoid of pomp, with rural plainness form'd,
With savage game, and glossy shells adorn'd.
" No costly furniture should grace my hall;
But curling vines ascend against the wall,
Whose pliant branches should luxuriant twine,
While purple clusters, swelled with future wine
To slake my thirst, a liquid lapse distil,
From craggy rocks, and spread a limpid rill.
Along my mansion spiry firs should grow,
And gloomy yews extend the shady row,
The cedars flourish, and the poplars rise
Sublimely tall, and shoot into the skies ;
Among the leaves refreshing zephyrs play
And crowding trees exclude the noon-tide ray ;
Whereon the birds their downy nests should form,
Securely shelter'd from the batt'ring storm,
And to melodious notes their choir apply,
Soon as Aurora blush'd along the sky ;
While all around the enchanting music rings,
And every vocal grove responsive sings.
" Me to sequester'd scenes, ye muses guide,
Where nature wantons in her virgin pride,
To mossy banks, edg'd round with op'ning flowers,
Elysian fields and amaranthian bowers ;
To ambrosial founts, and sleep-inspiring rills,
To herbag'd vales, gay lawns and sunny hills.
" Welcome ye shades ! all hail, ye vernal blooms
Ye bowery thickets, and prophetic glooms !

Ye forests, hail! ye solitary woods !
Love whispering groves, and silver streaming floods !
Ye meads, that aromatic sweets exhale !
Ye birds, and all ye sylvan beauties, hail !
Oh! how I long with you to spend my days,
Invoke the muse, and try the rural lays !
    " No trumpets there with martial clangour sound,
No prostate heroes strew the crimson'd ground;
No groves of lances glitter in the air,
Nor thund'ring drums provoke the sanguine war:
But white-robed peace, and universal love
Smile in the field and brighten every grove
There all the beauties of the circling year,
In native ornamental pride appear;
Gay rosy-bosomed SPRING and *April* showers,
Wake from the tomb of earth the rising flowers :
In deeper verdure SUMMER clothes the plain,
And AUTUMN bends beneath the golden grain;
The trees weep amber, and the whispering gales
Breeze o'er the lawn, or murmur through the vales;
The flowery tribes in gay confusion bloom,
Profuse of sweets, and fragrant with perfume;
On blossoms blossoms, fruits on fruits arise,
And varied prospects glad the wand'ring eyes.
In these fair seats I'd pass the joyous day,
Where meadows flourish and where fields look gay,
From bliss to bliss with endless pleasure rove,
Seek crystal streams, or haunt the vernal grove,
Woods, fountains, lakes, the fertile fields, or shades,
Aerial mountains or subjacent glades.
    " There from the polished fetters of the great,
Triumphal piles, and gilded rooms of state;
Prime ministers and sycophantic knaves,
Illustrious villains, and illustrious slaves ;
From all the vain formality of fools,
An odious task of arbitrary rules ;
The ruffling cares which the vex'd soul annoy,
The wealth the rich possess, but not enjoy.

H

The visionary bliss the world can lend,
The insidious foe, and false designing friend,
The seven-fold fury of *Xantippe's* soul,
And *S———'s* rage that burns without controul
I'd live retir'd, contented, and serene,
Forgot, unknown, unenvied, and unseen.

  " Yet not a real hermitage I'd choose,
Nor wish to live from all the world recluse ;
But with a friend sometimes unbend the soul,
In social converse, o'er the sprightly bowl.
With cheerful *W———*, serene and wisely gay,
I'd often pass the dancing hours away :
He skill'd alike to profit and to please,
Politely talks with unaffected ease ;
Sage in debate, and faithful to his trust,
Mature in science, and severely just ;
Of soul diffusive, vast and unconfin'd,
Breathing benevolence to all mankind ;
Cautious to censure, ready to commend,
A firm, unshaken, uncorrupted friend :
In early youth fair wisdom's paths he trod,
In early youth a minister of God :
Each pupil lov'd him when at *Yale* he shone,
And every bleeding bosom weeps him gone.
Dear *A———*, too, should grace my rural seat
For ever welcome to the green retreat :
Heaven for the cause of righteousness design'd
His florid genius, and capacious mind :
Oft have I heard, amidst the adoring throng,
Celestial truths devolving from his tongue ;
High o'er the list'ning audience seen him stand,
Divinely speak, and graceful stretch his hand,
With such becoming grace and pompous sound,
With long-rob'd senators encircled round,
Before the Roman bar, while *Rome* was free,
Nor bow'd to *Cæsar's* throne the servile knee ;
Immortal *Tully* plead the patriot cause,
While every tongue resounded his applause.

Next round my board should candid *S* ——— appear,
Of manners gentle, and a friend sincere,
Averse to discord, party-rage and strife,
He sails serenely down the stream of life.
With these *three friends*, beneath a spreading shade,
Where silver fountains murmur through the glade ;
Or in cool grots, perfum'd with native flowers,
In harmless mirth I'd spend the circling hours ;
Or gravely talk, or innocently sing,
Or, in harmonious concert, strike the trembling string.
  " Amid sequester'd bowers near gliding streams,
Druids and *Bards* enjoy'd serenest dreams.
Such was the seat where courtly *Horace* sung :
And his bold harp immortal *Maro* strung :
Where tuneful *Orpheus'* unresisted lay,
Made rapid tigers bear their rage away ;
While groves attentive to the ecstatic sound
Burst from their roots, and raptur'd, danc'd around.
Such seats the venerable *Seers* of old
(When blissful years in golden circles roll'd)
Chose and admir'd : e'en goddesses and gods
(As poets feign) were fond of such abodes :
The imperial consort of fictitious *Jove*,
For fount-full *Ida* forsook the realms above.
Oft to *Idalia* on a golden cloud,
Veil'd in a mist of fragrance, *Venus* rode ;
There num'rous altars to the queen were rear'd,
And love-sick youths their am'rous vows preferr'd,
While fair-hair'd damsels (a lascivious train)
With wanton rites ador'd her gentle reign.
The silver-shafted *Huntress* of the woods,
Sought pendant shades, and bathed in cooling floods
In palmy *Delos*, by *Scammander's* side,
Or where *Cajister* roll'd his silver tide,
Melodious *Phœbus* sang ; the *Muses* round
Alternate warbling to the heavenly sound.
E'en the feign'd MONARCH of heaven's bright abode,
High thron'd in gold, of gods the sovereign god,

Oft time prefer'd the shade of *Ida's* grove
To all the ambrosial feasts, and nectar'd cups **above**.
" Behold the rosy-finger'd morning dawn,
In saffron rob'd, and blushing o'er the lawn!
Reflected from the clouds, a radiant stream,
Tips with ethereal dew the mountains brim.
The unfolding roses, and the opening flowers
Imbibe the dew, and strew the varied bowers,
Diffuse nectarious sweets around, and glow
With all the colours of the showery bow.
The industrious bees their balmy toil renew,
Buzz o'er the field and sip the rosy dew.
But yonder comes the illustrious god of day,
Invests the east, and gilds the ethereal way;
The groves rejoice, the feathered nations sing,
Echo the mountains and the vallies ring.

" Hail, orb! array'd with majesty and **fire**,
That bids each sable shade of night retire!
Fountain of light! with burning glory **crown'd**,
Darting a deluge of effulgence round!
Wak'd by thy genial and prolific ray,
Nature resumes her verdure and looks gay:
Fresh blooms the rose, the drooping plants **revive**,
The groves reflourish, and the forests live.
Deep in the teeming earth, the rip'ning ore
Confesses thy consolidating power:
Hence labour draws her tools, and artists mould
The fusile silver and the ductile gold:
Hence war is furnished, and the regal shield
Like lightning flashes o'er th' illumin'd field.
If thou so fair with delegated light,
That all heaven's splendours vanish at thy sight;
With what effulgence must the ocean glow!
From which thy borrow'd beams incessant flow
Th' exhaustless source, whose single smile supplies,
Th' unnumbered orbs that gild the spangled skies!

" Oft would I view, in admiration lost,
Heaven's sumptuous canopy, and starry host,

With levelled tube and astronomic eye,
Pursue the planets whirling through the sky ·
Immensurable vault ! where thunders roll,
And forked lightnings flash from pole to pole.
Say, railing infidel ! canst thou survey
Yon globe of fire, that gives the golden day,
The harmonious structure of this vast machine,
And not confess its Architect divine ?
Then go, vain wretch : though deathless be thy soul,
Go, swell the riot, and exhaust the bowl ;
Plunge into vice, humanity resign,
Go, fill the sty, and bristle into swine !

   " None but a power omnipotent and wise
Could frame this earth, or spread the boundless skies :
He made the whole ; at his omnific call,
From formless chaos rose this spacious ball,
And one ALMIGHTY GOD is seen in all.
By him our cup is crown'd, our table spread
With luscious wine, and life-sustaining bread.
What countless wonders doth the earth contain !
What countless wonders the unfathom'd main !
Bedrop'd with gold, their scaly nations shine,
Haunt coral groves, or lash the foaming brine.
JEHOVAH's glories blaze all nature round,
In heaven, on earth, and in the deeps profound ;
Ambitious of his name, the warblers sing,
And praise their Maker while they hail the spring :
The zephyrs breathe it, and the thunders roar,
While surge to surge, and shore resounds to shore.
But MAN, endued with an immortal mind,
His Maker's image, and for heaven design'd !
To loftier notes his raptured voice should raise,
And chaunt sublimer hymns to his Creator's praise.

   " When rising *Phœbus* ushers in the morn,
And golden beams the impurpled skies adorn :
Waked by the gentle murmur of the floods,
Or the soft music of the waving woods ;
Rising from sleep with the melodious choir,
To solemn sounds I'd tune the hallow'd lyre.

Thy name, O GOD! should tremble on my tongue,
Till every grove prov'd vocal to my song:
(Delightful task, with dawning light to sing,
Triumphant hymns to heaven's eternal King.)
Some courteous angel should my breast inspire,
Attune my lips, and guide the warbled wire,
While sportive echoes catch the sacred sound,
Swell every note, and bear the music round;
While mazy streams meandering to the main
Hang in suspense to hear the heavenly strain;
And hush'd in silence, all the feathered throng,
Attentive listen to the tuneful song.
    " Father of *Light!* exhaustless source of good!
Supreme, eternal, self-existent God!
Before the beamy sun dispens'd a ray,
Flam'd in the azure vault, and gave the day;
Before the glimm'ring moon, with borrow'd light,
Shone queen, amid the silver host of night,
High in the Heavens thou reign'dst superior Lord,
By suppliant angels worshipp'd and ador'd.
With the celestial choir then let me join,
In cheerful praises to the power divine.
To sing thy praise, do thou, O GOD! inspire
A mortal breast with more than mortal fire;
In dreadful majesty thou sitt'st enthron'd,
With light encircled, and with glory crown'd;
Through all infinitude extends thy reign,
For thee, nor heaven, nor heaven of heaven's contain;
But though thy throne is *fix'd* above the sky,
Thy *omnipresence* fills immensity.
Saints rob'd in white, to thee their anthems bring,
And radiant martyrs hallelujahs sing:
Heaven's universal host their voices raise,
In one *eternal chorus*, to thy praise;
And round thy awful throne, with one accord,
Sing, Holy, Holy, Holy is the Lord.
At thy creative voice, from ancient night,
Sprang smiling beauty, and yon worlds of light

Thou spak'st—the planetary chorus roll'd,
And all the expanse was star'd with beamy gold ,
Let there be light, said GOD,—Light instant shone,
And from the orient burst the golden sun ;
Heaven's gazing hierarchs, with glad surprize,
Saw the first morn invest the recent skies,
And straight the exulting troops thy throne surround,
With thousand thousand harps of heavenly sound :
Thrones, powers, dominions, (ever shining trains!)
Shouted thy praises in triumphant strains :
Great are thy works, they sing, and, all around,
Great are thy works, the echoing heavens resound.
The effulgent sun, insufferably bright,
Is but a beam of thy o'erflowing light ;
The tempest is thy breath the thunder hurl'd,
Tremendous roars thy vengeance o'er the world;
Thou bowest the heavens, the smoking mountains **nod,**
Rocks fall to dust, and nature owns her God ;
Pale tyrants shrink, the atheist stands aghast,
And impious kings in horror breathe their last.
To this great God alternately I'd pray,
The evening anthem, and the morning lay.

" For sovereign *gold*, I never would repine,
Nor wish the glittering dust of monarchs mine.
What though high columns heave into the skies,
Gay ceilings shine, and vaulted arches rise,
Though fretted gold the sculpter'd roof adorn,
The rubies redden, and the jaspers burn !
Or what, alas ! avails the gay attire,
To wretched man, who breathes but to expire !
Oft on the vilest, riches are bestow'd,
To shew their meanness in the sight of God.
High from a dunghil, see a *Dives* rise,
And *Titan*-like, insult the avenging skies :
The crowd in adulation, calls him Lord,
By thousands courted, flatter'd and ador'd.
In riot plung'd, and drunk with earthly joys,
No higher thought his grov'ling soul employs :

The poor he scourges with an iron rod,
And from his bosom banishes his God.
But oft, in height of wealth, and beauty's bloom,
Deluded man is fated to the tomb !
For, lo ! he sickens, swift his colour flies,
And rising mists obscure his swimming eyes,
Around his bed his weeping friends bemoan,
Extort the unwilling tear, and wish him gone ;
His sorrowing heir augments the tender shower,
Deplores his death—yet hails the dying hour.
Ah, bitter comfort ! Sad relief, to die !
Though sunk in down, beneath the canopy !
His eyes no more shall see the cheerful light,
Weigh'd down by death in everlasting night :
And now the great, the rich, the proud, the gay,
Lies breathless, cold, inanimated clay !
He, that just now was flatter'd by the crowd,
With high applause, and acclamations loud :
That steel'd his bosom to the orphan's cries,
And drew down torrents from the widow's eyes,
Whom like a god the rabble did adore—
Regard him now—and, lo ! he is no more.
  " My eyes no dazzling vestments should behold,
With gems instarr'd, and stiff with woven gold ;
But the tall ram his downy fleece afford,
To clothe, in modest garb, his frugal lord :
Thus the great Father of mankind was drest,
When shaggy hides compos'd his flowing vest ;
Doom'd to the cumb'rous load, for his offence,
When clothes supply'd the want of innocence :
But now his sons (forgetful whence they came)
Glitter in gems, and glory in their shame.
  " Oft would I wander through the dewy field,
Where clust'ring roses balmy fragrance yield ;
Or in lone grots, for contemplation made,
Converse with angels and the mighty dead.—
For all around unnumber'd spirits fly,
Waft on the breeze, or walk the liquid sky.

Inspire the poet with repeated dreams,
Who gives his hallow'd muse to sacred themes:
Protect the just, serene their gloomy hours,
Becalm their slumbers, and refresh their powers.
Methinks I see th' immortal beings fly,
And swiftly shoot athwart the streaming sky:
Hark! a melodious voice I seem to hear,
And heavenly sounds invade my list'ning ear!
"Be not afraid of us, innoxious band,
Thy cell surrounding by divine command;
E'er while, like thee, we led our lives below,
(Sad lives of pain, of misery and woe!)
Long by affliction's boist'rous tempest tost,
We reach'd at length the ever blissful coast:
Now in the embow'ring groves and lawns above,
We taste the raptures of immortal love,
Attune the golden harp in roseate bowers,
Or bind our temples with unfading flowers.
Oft on kind errands bent, we cut the air,
To guard the righteous, Heaven's peculiar care!
Avert impending harms, their minds compose,
Inspire gay dreams, and prompt their soft repose.
When from the tongue divine hosannas roll,
And sacred rapture swell the rising soul,
To heaven we bear thy prayers like rich perfumes,
Where, by the throne, the golden censer fumes:
And when with age thy head is silver'd o'er,
And cold in death thy bosom beats no more,
Thy soul exulting shall desert its clay,
And mount, triumphant, to eternal day."
But to improve the intellectual mind,
Reading should be to contemplation join'd.
First I'd collect from the Parnassian spring,
What muses dictate, and what poets sing.—
Virgil, as prince, should wear the laurel'd crown,
And other bards pay homage to his throne;
The blood of heroes now effus'd so long,
Will run forever purple through his song.

See ! how he mounts towards the blest abodes,
On planets rides, and talks with demi-gods !
How do our ravish'd spirits melt away,
When in his song *Sicilian* shepherds play !
But what a splendour strikes the dazzled eye,
When *Dido* shines in awful majesty !
Embroider'd purple clad the *Tyrian* queen,
Her motion graceful, and august her mien ,
A golden zone her royal limbs embrac'd,
A golden quiver rattled by her waist.
See her proud steed majestically prance,
Contemn the trumpet, and deride the lance !
In crimson trappings, glorious to behold,
Confus'dly gay with interwoven gold !
He champs the bit, and throws the foam around,
Impatient paws, and tears the solid ground.
How stern *Æneas* thunders through the field !
With towering helmet, and refulgent shield !
Coursers o'erturn'd, and mighty warriors slain,
Deform'd with gore, lie welt'ring on the plain.
Struck through with wounds, ill-fated chieftains lie,
Frown e'en in death, and threaten as they die.
Through the thick squadrons see the hero bound,
(His helmet flashes, and his arms resound !)
All grim with rage, he frowns o'er *Turnus'* head,
(Re-kindled ire ! for blooming *Pallas* dead,)
Then, in his bosom plung'd the shining blade—
The soul indignant sought the Stygian shade ?

 " The far fam'd bards that grac'd *Britannia's* isle,
Should next compose the venerable pile.
Great *Milton* first, for towering thought renown'd,
Parent of song, and fam'd the world around !
His glowing breast divine *Urania* fir'd,
Or God himself th' immortal bard inspir'd.
Borne on triumphant wings he takes his flight,
Explores all heaven, and treads the realms of light :
In martial pomp he clothes th' angelic train,
While warring myriads shake the ethereal plain.

His lays the verdure of the meads prolong,
And wither'd forests blossom in his song ;
First *Michael* stalks, high towering o'er the rest,
With heavenly plumage nodding on his crest,
Impenetrable arms his limbs enfold,
Eternal adamant, and burning gold !
Sparkling in fiery mail, with dire delight,
Rebellious *Satan* animates the fight :
Armipotent they sink in rolling smoke,
All heaven resounding, to its centre shook,
To crush his foes, and quell the dire alarms,
Messiah sparkled in refulgent arms ;
In radiant panoply divinely bright,
His limbs incas'd, he flash'd devouring light.
On burning wheels, o'er heaven's crystalline road
Thunder'd the chariot of the *Filial* God ;
The burning wheels on golden axles turn'd,
With flaming gems the golden axles burn'd.
Lo ! the apostate host, with terror struck,
Roll back by millions ! the empyrean shook !
Sceptres, and orbid shields, and crowns of gold,
Cherubs and seraphs in confusion roll'd ;
Till, from his hand, the triple thunder hurl'd,
Compell'd them headlong, to the infernal world.
  " Then tuneful *Pope*, whom all the nine inspire
With *sapphic* sweetness, and *pindaric* fire.
Father of verse ! melodious and divine !
Next peerless *Milton* should distinguish'd shine.
Smooth flow his numbers when he paints the grove,
Th' enraptur'd virgins list'ning into love.
But when the night and hoarse resounding storm,
Rush on the deep, and *Neptune's* face deform,
Rough runs the verse, the son'rous numbers roar
Like the hoarse surge that thunders on the shore,
But when he sings th' exhilarated swains,
Th' embowering groves, and *Windsor's* blissful plains,
Our eyes are ravish'd with the sylvan scene,
Embroider'd fields, and groves in living green :

Thames' silver streams his flowing verse admire,
And cease to murmur while he tunes his lyre.
  " Next should appear great *Dryden's* lofty muse,
For who would *Dryden's* polish'd verse refuse ?
His lips were moisten'd in *Parnassus'* spring,
And *Phœbus* taught his *laureat* son to sing.
How long did *Virgil* untranslated moan,
His beauties fading, and his flights unknown;
Till *Dryden* rose, and, in exalted strain,
Re-sang the fortune of the godlike man !
Again the *Trojan* prince with dire delight,
Dreadful in arms, demands the ling'ring fight :
Again *Camilla* glows with martial fire,
Drives armies back, and makes all *Troy* retire.
With more than native lustre *Virgil* shines,
And gains sublimer heights in *Dryden's* lines.
  " The gentle *Watts* who strings his silver lyre
To sacred odes, and Heaven's all ruling fire ;
Who scorns th' applause of the licentious stage,
And mounts yon sparkling worlds with hallow'd rage,
Compels my thoughts to wing the heavenly road,
And wafts my soul, exulting, to my God ;
No fabled *Nine*, harmonious bard ! inspire
Thy raptur'd breast with such seraphic fire ;
But prompting *Angels* warm thy boundless rage,
Direct thy thoughts and animate thy page.
Blest man ! for spotless sanctity rever'd,
Lov'd by the good, and by the guilty fear'd ;
Blest man ! from gay delusive scenes remov'd,
Thy Maker loving, by thy Maker lov'd ;
To God thou tun'st thy consecrated lays,
Nor meanly blush to sing *Jehovah's* praise.
O ! did, like thee, each laurell'd bard delight,
To paint *Religion* in her native light,
Not then with *Plays* the lab'ring press would groan,
Nor *Vice* defy the *Pulpit* and the *Throne* ;
No impious rhymer charm a vicious age,
Nor prostrate *Virtue* groan beneath their rage :

But themes divine in lofty numbers rise,
Fill the wide earth, and echo through the skies.
  " These for *Delight* ;—for *Profit* I would read,
The labour'd volumes of the learned dead :
Sagacious *Locke*, by providence design'd
T' exalt, instruct, and rectify the mind.
Th' unconquerable *Sage*,* whom virtue fir'd,
And from the tyrant's lawless rage retir'd,
When victor *Cæsar* freed unhappy *Rome*,
From *Pompey's* chains, to substitute his own.
Longinus, *Livy*, fam'd *Thucydides*,
Quintillian, *Plato*, and *Demosthenes*,
Persuasive *Tully*, and *Corduba's Sage*,†
Who fell by *Nero's* unrelenting rage ;
Him‡ whom ungrateful *Athens* doom'd to bleed,
Despis'd while living, and deplor'd when dead,
Raleigh I'd read with ever fresh delight,
While ages past rise present to my sight.
Ah ! man unblest ! he foreign realms explor'd,
Then fell a victim to his country's sword !
Nor should great *Derham* pass neglected by,
Observent sage ! to whose deep piercing eye,
Nature's stupendous works expanded lie.
Nor he, *Brittania*, thy unmatch'd renown !
(Adjudg'd to wear the philosophic crown)
Who on the solar orb uplifted rode,
And scann'd the unfathomable works of God !
Who bound the silver planets to their spheres,
And trac'd th' ecliptic curve of blazing stars !
Immortal Newton, whose illustrious name
Will shine on records of eternal fame.
  " By love directed, I would choose a wife,
To improve my bliss and ease the load of life.
Hail *Wedlock* ! hail, inviolable tye !
Perpetual fountain of domestic joy !
Love, friendship, honour, truth, and pure delight,
Harmonious mingle in the nuptial rite.

---

  * *Cato.*   † *Seneca.*   ‡ *Socrates.*

I

In Eden first the holy state began,
When perfect innocence distinguish'd man ;
The human pair th' Almighty Pontiff led,
Gay as the morning to the bridal bed ;
A dread solemnity th' espousals grac'd,
Angels the *Witnesses* and GOD the PRIEST !
All earth exulted on the nuptial hour,
And voluntary roses deck'd the bower !
The joyous birds, on every blossom'd spray,
Sung *Hymenials* to th' important day,
While *Philomela* swell'd the sponsal song,
And Paradise with gratulations rung.

  " Relate, inspiring muse ! where shall I find
A blooming virgin with an angel mind,
Unblemish'd as the white rob'd virgin choir
That fed, O *Rome !* thy consecrated fire ;
By reason aw'd, ambitious to be good,
Averse to vice, and zealous for her God ?
Relate, in what blest region can I find
Such bright perfections in a female mind ?
What *Phænix*-woman breathes the vital air,
So greatly good, and so divinely fair ?
Sure, not the gay and fashionable train,
Licentious, proud, immoral, and prophane ;
Who spend their golden hours in antic dress,
Malicious whispers and inglorious ease.—

  " Lo ! round the board a shining train appears,
In rosy beauty, and in prime of years !
This hates a flounce, and *this* a flounce approves,
This shews the trophies of her former loves ;
Folly avers that *Sylvia* drest in green,
When last at church the gaudy nymph was seen ;
Chloe condemns her optics, and will lay
'Twas azure satin, interstreak'd with grey ;
Lucy invested with judicial power,
Awards 'twas neither————and the strife is o'er.
Then parrots, lap-dogs, monkeys, squirrels, beaus,
Fans, ribbands, tuckers, patches, furbeloes,
In quick succession, through their fancies run,
And dance incessant on the flippant tongue.

And when fatigued with every other sport,
The belles prepare to grace the sacred court,
They marshall all their forces in array,
To kill with glances and destroy in play.
Two skilful *maids*, with reverential fear,
In wanton wreaths collect their silken hair ;
Two paint their cheeks, and round their temples pour
The fragrant unguent, and the ambrosial shower ;
One pulls the shape-creating stays, and one
Encircles round her waist the golden zone :
Not with more toil to improve immortal charms,
Strove *Juno, Venus,* and the *Queen of arms,*
When *Priam's* son adjudg'd the golden prize
To the resistless beauty of the skies.
At length equip'd in love's enticing arms,
With all that glitters and with all that charms,
The ideal goddesses to church repair,
Peep through the fan and mutter o'er a prayer,
Or listen to the organ's pompous sound,
Or eye the gilded images around ;
Or, deeply studied in coquettish rules,
Aim wily glances at unthinking fools ;
Or shew the lily hand with graceful air,
Or wound the fopling with a lock of hair ;
And when the hated discipline is o'er,
And *Misses* tortured with—*Repent* no more
They mount the pictur'd coach, and to the play
The celebrated idols hie away.
   " Not so the *Lass* that should my joys improve,
With solid friendship and connubial love :
A native bloom, with intermingled white,
Should set her features in a pleasing light :
Like *Helen* flushing with unrivall'd charms,
When raptur'd *Paris* darted in her arms.
But what, alas ! avails a ruby cheek,
A downy bosom, or a snowy neck !
Charms ill supply the want of innocence,
Nor beauty forms intrinsic excellence.

But in her breast let moral beauties shine,
Supernal grace and purity divine :
Sublime her reason, and her native wit
Unstrain'd with pedantry and low conceit
Her fancy lively, and her judgment free,
From female prejudice and bigotry :
Averse to idle pomp, and outward show,
The flattering coxcomb, and fantastic beau,
The fop's impertinence she would despise,
Though *sorely wounded by her radiant eyes,*
But pay due rev'rence to the exalted mind
By learning polish'd, and by wit refin'd,
Who all her virtues, without guile, commends,
And all her faults as freely reprehends.
Soft *Hymen's* rites her passion should approve,
And in her bosom glow the flames of love :
To me her soul, by sacred friendship, turn,
And I, for her, with equal friendship burn ;
In every stage of life afford relief,
Partake my joys, and sympathize my grief ;
Unshaken, walk in virtue's peaceful road,
Nor bribe her reason to pursue the mode ;
Mild as the saint whose errors are forgiven,
Calm as a vestal, and compos'd as heaven.
This be the partner, this the lovely wife
That should embellish and prolong my life ;
A nymph ! who might a second fall inspire,
And fill a glowing *Cherub* with desire !
With her I'd spend the pleasurable day,
While fleeting minutes gaily danc'd away :
With her I'd walk, delighted, o'er the green,
Through every blooming mead, the rural scene,
Or sit in open fields damask'd with flowers,
Or where cool shades embrown the noon-tide bowers,
Imparadis'd within my eager arms,
I'd reign the happy monarch of her charms ;
Oft on her panting bosom would I lay,
And, in dissolving raptures melt away :

Then lull'd, by nightingales, to balmy rest,
My blooming fair should slumber at my breast.
   " And when decripped age (frail mortals' doom)
Should bend my wither'd body to the tomb,
No warbling *Syrens* should retard my flight,
To heavenly mansions of unclouded light ;
Though death, with his imperial honours crown'd,
Terrific grin'd, and formidably frown'd,
Offences pardon'd, and remitted sin,
Should form a calm serenity within :
Blessing my *natal* and my *mortal* hour,
(My soul committed to the eternal power)
Inexorable death should smile, for I,
Who *knew* to LIVE, would never *fear* to DIE."

The question still recurs, Why the degradation of the female character ? Why are
they, or a very great proportion of them, reduced to mere cyphers in the scale of beings ?
Is it because they are devoid of those brilliant qualifications that shine so conspicuous
in the sons of men ? By no means. Those
noble qualifications if not superior, are at
least equal, in the female character ; and
nothing but the poison of false education,
the wrong association of juvenile ideas, are
the cause why the native genius and inher-
ent endowments of females do not burst forth
and shine with renovated splendor.
   We might deduce a long deduction of examples, to prove the super-excellence of the
female character, and that they have excel-

led in many of the departments of civil and savage society, and have eventually proved an ornament not only to their own but to the male sex, I refer the reader to the many volumes of female biography to prove my arguments.

Though the limits of my plan will not allow me to enlarge much, I will merely give a specimen of the heroic character of a celebrated female, taken from my " Flowers of Literature," even in an early age of the world; I mean Semiramis, the consort of Ninus, the sovereign of the ancient and celebrated city of Nineveh. She was previously the wife of one of his officers, and distinguished herself so much by her heroic exploits, that the king not only married her, but left her his crown at his death.

" This ambitious princess being desirous, in her turn to render her name immortal, in a very few years built the city of Babylon, to such an amazing extent that it far exceeded Nineveh, its walls being of a sufficient thickness to allow six chariots to go abreast.

" The quays, the bridge over the Euphrates, the hanging gardens, the prodigies of sculpture and architecture, the temple of Belus, which had in it a golden statue forty feet high, though they were not all works of Semiramis, yet they were much improved and embellished by her.

" The brevity of my plan forbids me to give a circumstantial account of the astonishing magnificence, and strength of Babylon; particularly the walls, which were fifty feet wide, 200 high, and 50 miles in circumference; and the temple of Belus, which is allowed by historians to be the same as the tower mentioned in scripture, called Babel; however, for a more particular account of this astonishing city, antecedent and subsequent to its overthrow, I would refer the reader to my Preliminary Essay, page 143.

" The last and greatest expedition of Semiramis was against India. On this occasion she raised an innumerable army out of all the provinces of her empire, and appointed Bactra for the rendezvous.

" As the strength of the Indians consisted chiefly in their great number of elephants, this artful queen had a multitude of camels accoutred in the form of elephants, in hopes of deceiving the enemy. It is said, that Perseus, long after, used the same stratagem against the Romans. But neither of them succeeded.

" The Indian king having notice of her approach, sent ambassadors to know who she was, and with what right, having never received any injury from him, she came out of wontonness to attack his dominions; adding, that her boldness should soon meet with the punishment it deserved. "Tell your master," replied the queen, "that in a little time, I myself will let him know who I am."

"She advanced immediately towards the river Indus, from which the country takes its name; and having prepared a sufficient number of boats, she attempted to cross it with her army. Their passage was a long time disputed, but after a bloody battle, she put her enemies to flight. Above a thousand of their boats were sunk, and about a hundred thousand of their men taken prisoners.

"Encouraged by this success, she advanced directly into the country, leaving sixty thousand men behind to guard the bridge of boats, which she had built over the river. —This was just what the king desired, who fled on purpose to bring her to an engagement in the heart of his country. As soon as he thought her far enough advanced, he faced about, and a second engagement ensued, more bloody than the first. The counterfeit elephants could not long sustain the shock of the true ones. These routed her army, crushing whatever came in their way.

" Semiramis did all that could be do..e, to rally and encourage her troops; but in vain. The king perceiving her engaged in the fight, advanced towards her and wounded her. The wound however did not prove mortal. The swiftness of her hórse soon carried her beyond the reach of her enemies.

" As her men crowded to the bridge, to repass the river, numbers of them perished by the disorder and confusion unavoidable on such occasions. When those that could save themselves were safely over, she destroyed the bridge, and by that means stopped the enemy; the king likewise, in obedience to an oracle, had given orders to his troops not to pass the river, nor pursue Semiramis any farther.

" The queen, having made an exchange of prisoners, returned to her own dominions, with scarce one-third of her army, which, according to Ctesias, consisted of three hundred thousand foot, and fifty thousand horse, besides the camels and chariots armed for war, of which she had a very considerable number."

Time would fail me to mention the many female characters who have signalized themselves by their ingenious, heroic, and invincible achievements, from the reign of

this celebrated woman, to that of the em-
press Catharine of Russia; and with respect to philanthropy and munificence, they
unquestionably abound more, far more
amongst the female than the male part of
society; and with reference to the finer feelings which adorn human nature, if we candidly consider them on an average, we shall
be obliged to relinquish the palm in favour of women: were I inclined, I could, perhaps, trace a line of tender feelings, benevolent emotions, in a direct course, through
every generation, and in every clime, not
excluding the most savage, from Eve, the
mother of the human family, to the members which compose that intrinsically munificent institution, entitled the *Widow's Society*, and exclusively organized by a number of respectable ladies* of New-York, for
the support and protection of helpless and
disconsolate widows and orphan children.
These respectable personages I exhibit with
delight, as living monuments to illustrate
my reasoning, and to consolidate my arguments in favour of the native excellency
of the female character; and while I admire them, may the grateful tears of the
poor unhappy orphan and widow abun-

* I would advise the ladies of Philadelphia to imitate this
laudable example, by organizing a society on a similar plan.

dantly repay their liberality : and while
I look upon them with reverential sensations, as the friends of those whom I desire
to befriend, may that Almighty Sovereign of
the skies, who delights in each beneficence
that assimilates to himself; may he view them
with such a smile of approbation as not
only to enrapture, but snatch their hearts
from terrestrial vicissitudes to celstial delight. In giving this small tribute of respectful eulogium to a society that ennobles
human nature, and constrains even angels
to smile with approbation, I must declare
that I am actuated by no sinister or interested motives. I have never seen, and perhaps
never shall see, an individual of that respectable and truly philanthropic society, but the
governess whom I called upon one day, in
Wall-street, to recommend to her consideration a poor woman I happened by accident
to see in the street, a stranger, in a strange
place, among strange people, all destitute and
forlorn. The sympathetic concern which
she testified, and the solicitude she expressed, for the poor woman's relief and accommodation, caused me to entertain the highest degree of respect and veneration for her
character; for I almost idolize the few individuals of the human race, who are real
friends to the poor and the needy ; and, at
the same time, to reverse the idea, I feel

the same time, to reverse the idea, I feel most implacable indignation, at the conduct of those innumerable characters, who are the traitors and oppressors of mankind, and, of consequence, the enemies of God.

But it is a stubborn fact, as lamentable as it is authentic, that many of the professors of religion are criminally deficient, sordidly parsimonious, palpable delinquents, with respect to their neglecting to sympathize with, and relieve, to the utmost extent of their influence, and I may add finances, the sons of affliction and the daughters of misfortune: and those religious devotees, who can behold, with dry eyes, their fellow travellers to the grave enveloped in wretchedness, and wrapped up in complicated disease, and not even anticipate a particle of tender emotion and sympathetic commiseration. Yet these characters, who can, with impunity, forego the sacred delights peculiar to the philanthropist, and neglect to fulfil the cardinal duties peculiar to christianity, would feel condemnation if they neglected to attend a social, a ceremonial, or a sacramental meeting, intended for their personal benefit.— And these think, because they attend hypocritic rites and penal creeds, that they will, of course, meet the approbation of the Deity, though they neglect the more important duties of hospitality and benevolence to their brethren—I mean the progeny of Adam collectively.

This animadversion is by no means intended for any individual character, or denomination. No man can be more divested of party prejudice than I am, political or religious. While I love God supremely, I profess to love all men affectionately, without any reference to sects or parties; these deleterious barriers, which preclude fraternal love from flowing from the centre to the circumference of the earth; and prohibit, with the effrontery of a demon, the social intercourse of heaven-bound and of heaven-born christians. I am sorry to be under the necessity of asserting, that in Christendom in general, and this city in particular, there seems to be an evident declension in christian charity amongst many of the professed votaries of revealed religion; a selfish parsimonious disposition, utterly repugnant to the principles of moral rectitude, as well as incompatible with, and uncongenial to, evangelical religion. Can a selfish penurious man be a christian? It is impossible. How different is such a character from the pious philanthropist, whose delight is to bless, (were his power equal to his affection), and circle the human family

K

in one kind embrace. The following paraphrase on a chapter of scripture will prove
the validity of this remark.

*A Paraphrase on the Thirteenth Chapter of
the First Epistle to the Corinthians.*

" Did sweeter sounds adorn my flowing tongue,
Than ever man pronounc'd or angel sung;
Had I all knowledge, human and divine,
That thought can reach, or science can define;
And had I power to give that knowledge birth,
In all the speeches of the babbling earth ;
Did Shadrach's zeal my glowing breast inspire,
To weary tortures, and rejoice in fire ;
Or had I faith like that which Israel saw,
When Moses gave them miracles, and law :
Yet gracious charity, indulgent guest,
Were not thy power exerted in my breast,
Those speeches would send up unheeded prayer.
That scorn of life would be but wild despair ;
A cymbal's sound were better than my voice ;
My faith were form ; my eloquence were noise ;
  " Charity, decent, modest, easy, kind,
Softens the high, and rears the abject mind ;
Knows with just reins, and gentle hand, to guide
Betwixt vile shame and arbitrary pride.
Not soon provok'd, she easily forgives ;
And much she suffers, as she much believes.
Soft peace she brings wherever she arrives ;
She builds our quiet, as she forms our lives ;
Lays the rough paths of peevish nature even ;
And opens in each heart a little heaven.
  " Each other gift, which God on man bestows,
Its proper bounds and due restriction knows ;

To one fix'd purpose dedicates its power ;
And finishing its act, exists no more.
Thus, in obedience to what Heaven decrees,
Knowledge shall fail, and prophecy shall cease ;
But lasting charity's more ample sway,
Nor bound by time, nor subject to decay,
In happy triumph shall forever live,
And endless good diffuse, and endless praise receive.
  " As through the artist's intervening glass,
Our eye observes the distant planets pass ;
A little we discover ; but allow,
That more remains unseen, than art can show ;
So whilst our mind its knowledge would improve,
(Its feeble eye intent on things above),
High as we may, we lift our reason up,
By faith directed, and confirmed by hope ;
Yet we are able only to survey
Dawnings of beams, and promises of day ;
Heaven's fuller effluence mocks our dazzled sight,
Too great its swiftness, and too strong its light.
  " But soon the mediate clouds shall be dispell'd ;
The Son shall soon be face to face beheld,
In all his robes, with all his glory on,
Seated sublime on his meridian throne.
  " Then constant faith, and holy hope shall die,
One lost in certainty, and one in joy :
Whilst thou more happy power, fair charity,
Triumphant sister, greatest of the three,
Thy office and thy nature still the same,
Lasting thy lamp, and unconsum'd thy flame,
Shalt still survive ————————
Shall stand before the host of heaven confest,
For ever blessing, and forever blest.

Another argument still more convincing
strikes my mind, which will demonstrate
the futility and fallacy of that man's hopes
for heaven, who is destitute of true chris-

tian charity, which alone can afford us help to fulfil, with sacred joy, the subsequent address of the Saviour and Judge of the world; which he has positively and emphatically declared, he will apply to the righteous, convened at his august tribunal on the last day: *Come ye blessed of my Father, inherit the kingdom prepared for you from the foundation of the world: For I was an hungered, and ye gave me meat: I was thirsty, and ye gave me drink: I was a stranger, and ye took me in: Naked, and ye clothed me: I was sick and ye visited me: I was in prison, and ye came unto me.*" Can any man, professor or profane, who habitually neglects to do these good works, so far insult common sense, shut his eyes against the light of reason, and basely insult his own understanding, as to have the impudence to hope or expect, that God will tell a palpable lie in the presence of assembled worlds, in applying the antecedent address to him, when he in fact, acted diametrically opposite to the subject matter of that address? Or does such a character expect to go to heaven after death? Which is virtually expecting that God will tell a falsehood, to save a fugitive delinquent. It is impossible. This argument is of itself sufficient to prove, to a demonstration, the utility and indispensable necessity of social virtue, to capacitate us to meet the approbation of Heaven, by and not for our works of hospitality and love, for after we have done all that is commanded us, we are truly unprofitable servants.

My object is not to make this a theological work. I was led inadvertently to dwell on divinity, by suggesting the few anterior thoughts in commendation of the Widows' Society for the relief and support of friendless orphans; and I request, therefore, the reader to pardon the digression, which was not properly connected with the subject of my investigation; but to which I will return after introducing the orphan's grateful prayer, and inscribing it, with respectful consideration, to the members of the said society to whom it is addressed.

THE ORPHAN'S GRATEFUL PRAYER,

A POEM,

Inscribed to the Widows' Society of N. York.

Hail! virtuous few, by heaven and earth approved,
True immitators of your gracious Lord;
In sacred union may you long agree,
By grace cemented, and true charity.
Oh! may your lives be lengthen'd out on earth,
And every day rejoice to give new birth;
May mutual love to mutual good provoke,
A three-fold cord that never can be broke;
To raise the helpless, and to soothe distress,
To bless the sick, the afflicted to redress;

K 2

To screen the orphan from the threat'ning blow,
To ease the widow's heart of latent woe ;
To cheer the faint, and gently to reprove
The stubborn heart, by offices of love.
On acts like these our God looks smiling down,
And to each heir holds out a starry crown.
May he, the sacred Monarch of the skies,
Who heard the poor unhappy orphan's cries ;
Oh! may he hear the grateful orphan's prayer,
And give you each celestial crowns to wear.
But tears of gratitude can ne'er repay,
The debt of thanks I owe, nor half display
Your pity when you wip'd the orphan's tears away.
To tell your kindness, or your love to paint,
The muse's sweetest notes appear too faint ;
To paint the tears that crystalliz'd your eyes,
Or grief that made your bosoms heave with sighs,
When Heaven brought you to see my deep distress,
And gave the heart to feel, the power to bless ;
Not all the gems Columbia's sons convey
From the Ionian through the Atlantic sea,
E'er seem'd so precious as that pearly tear,
Or should with those dear sacred sighs compare.
Your gifts to me essential joy imparts,
And proves the gracious feelings of your hearts,
Your aid supports a drooping parent's age ;
And still the widow's poignant woes assuage ;
Your aid still sooths the way-worn orphan's grief,
And to her artless cries still yields relief ;
For you my prayers to Heaven shall still be borne,
On the first breeze that hails the golden morn ;
And, Oh! thou mighty Sire of the distress'd,
Let our protectors be forever bless'd.
Their philanthropic deeds to heaven shall rise,
Behold, Oh earth! and view, ye sacred skies ;
And when their useful happy lives shall fade,
May hosts of Angels lend their blissful aid,
And on their golden wings may they arise,
To praise the Sacred Sovereign of the skies ;

To hear the glorious invitation " come,"
And to receive the plaudit of " well done;"
To join eternally the angelic lays,
And fill the heaven of heavens with grateful praise.
With glowing love my heart within me burns,
Hope, joy, and fear possess my mind by turns;
Bless'd through your means, my heart within me says,
If not my lips, my life shall speak his praise ;
Bless'd through your means, let me again proclaim,
And still repeat my grateful thanks again.
Oh ! for a quill pluck'd from some angel's wing,
Oh ! for a mighty trumpet's voice to sing
The praises of the immortal Sire above,
Who mov'd your hearts to sympathy and love ;
From heaven's high arch he saw and smil'd to see,
Your finer feelings exercis'd towards me.
He saw the tender tears unbidden flow ;
He saw and lov'd, and angels lov'd you too,
This is religion, this indeed is love,
Pleasing to God and all the powers above ;
To bless the orphan, and the widow bless;
And for the stranger spread the couch of rest.
By Heaven the orphan and the poor are sent
To try your hearts, and cause them to relent,
Then know what you now give, to Heaven is lent.
God will repay a hundred fold and more
On earth, and on the bless'd celestial shore ;
While those who view the orphan's dire distress,
Without kind pity nor their woes redress,
Shall from their Judge, on the eternal shore
Receive such pity as they gave before;
Professors who pretend to love the Lord,
Yet to his poor no succour will afford;
Their base pretensions are impertinence,
Hostile to reason and to common sense.
In future years when reigning with the just,
And all your frames lie mouldering in the dust;
Then may your offspring Heaven's true cause defend,
And future ages bless the orphan's friend;

With me, may thousands say with joy within,
I was an orphan and ye took me in ;
And may each good which can from heaven descend,
Crown with eternal joy the orphan's friend.

But it is not only in such works of beneficence, that many females excel ; but also
in the departments of literature, the republic of letters, many females have acted
distinguished parts ; have gained the laurel
crown ; have acquired celebrity, and maintained their popularity unadulterated, though
candour* obliges me to observe, that few,
comparatively speaking, have maintained
their popularity untarnished, but those who
were not only ingenious, but also truly religious, such as Lady Guion, Mrs. Rowe, and
a number of others. There is a certain degree of vanity peculiar to such characters,
who exult in the majestic walks of science.
This, though an unaccountable paradox, is
a stubborn fact. That the grovelling minded,
the sordid, the illiterate multitude should be
conceited, proud, and vain, seems no matter of astonishment to me, as they know no
better, they never recollect what diminutive
atoms of creation they are ; haughty worms,

---

* It is a lamentable fact that a majority of females
who have talents for composition, prostitute them in the
service of the novelist and romancer.

dying mortals, probationary intelligencies. But, that the literary, the philosophical, the scientific sons and daughters of men, should be proud of their acquirement, seems matter of amazement. For my own part, the more I investigate the book of creation, the more diminutive I appear. I feel almost less than nothing, when I compare myself with the extensive, the wonderful works of God; when I view, with my mind's eye, the multiplicity of worlds, in magnitude inconceivable, and radiance inexpressible; that seem, to the naked eye, to spangle the ethereal fields, and to be scattered through the milky way; or, when I, in ardent thought, soar from this, comparatively insignificant, terraqueous ball, and tread the starry skies; when I take my stand on the star that seems farthest from us at present, and view still farther, through the unmeasurable fields of ether, other stars twinkling, other suns blazing, and other moons (or, as they are philosophically termed, satellites) reflecting their borrowed rays: when I, with that inquisitiveness peculiar to mortals, proceed in my aerial journey, from star to star, from sun to sun, from system to system, with the velocity of light (and light flies at the rate of 10,000,000 of miles in a minute), for one thousand years, and still see more magnificent systems arranged, more brilliant skies expanded, and more enormous comits, flying in their eccentric ecliptics ; when, after all this astonishing intellectual flight, I find by experience, at the end of my journey, that I am only just beginning to enter the suburbs of creation, and only recognize a specimen of the works of the great Architect of Nature. Could I, after this sentimental investigation, this intellectual tour, be haughty, imperious and proud ? Surely not. But I should rather consider myself merely as a diminutive particle of creation, and, in the language of true humility, self-debasement, grateful sensations, and reverential awe, I should cry out with the Psalmist, " *What is man that thou art mindful of him, and the son of man that thou visitest me.*"

The female claim to mental equality is questioned, and their reasoning faculties depreciated, not only by Indians and infidels, but even by christian philosophers; and many authors of the most respectable talents. The celebrated Lavater, the great physiognomist, has unequivocally asserted, " that women know not how to think ; they perceive, and can associate ideas, but can go no further." How astonishing it is, that a man of Lavater's ingenuity and ce-

lebrity could believe or assert such a spurious and fallacious sentiment. Had he listened to the captivating brilliancy of the elocution of Aspasia, and ascertained the
depth of her philosophy; the powers of
whose mind struck with amazement and
admiration even the eloquent Pericles ; had
he recognized the sublime Corinna, contending with, and winning the prize from,
the famous Pindar, of Thebes, by her verse;
had he investigated with candour the ingenious, though abstruse writings of Wolston-
croft; had he been present in the councils
in which queen Elizabeth* presided ; and in
which she displayed political ingenuity superior to a majority of her predecessors, and
all her successors, he would undoubtedly
have been of a different opinion.

Indeed, I cannot help believing, that the
contempt for the mental capacity of the sex,
expressed by many learned authors, proceeds
more from envy than ignorance ; more from
want of candid consideration, than from want
of literary penetration.

I must allow that a village clown, arriv-
ing in our city from the country, and surveying the employments, the customs, and
fashions of the sex, must be constrained to

---

* She was also a proficient in the Greek and Latin
languages.

believe, that they were almost irrational beings; but were he candidly to examine the biography of a single female, distinguished for her literary acquirements, &c. he would be inclined to allow, that the ignorance, vanity, affectation, and petulance of a large majority of the sex, are the result of neglect, not incapacity : the fatal influence of the tyranny of custom, not mental imbecility. They are, indeed, possessed with great powers and great parts ; but, alas ! they are neglected and despised, while fashions and fopperies are encouraged and countenanced. And why ? because, forsooth, it is customary. Many fair ones tremble to launch into the ocean of fashion at first ; but seeing so many thousands venturing their delicate barks into this tempestuous sea, they think the crime cannot be great, and as for the danger they never fear it till too late.

> Imprudence at a distance seems not such,
> They view the sea, yet dread to launch, or touch;
> Yet still their hearts beat high for the delight ;
> They wish, but dread to plunge where joys invite,
> To taste they venture first, and then retire ;
> The taste inflames, and not allays desire :
> Another taste, and then a drink succeeds,
> From bad to worse, thus modern fashion leads.

While so many improvements are taking place in the world, it is distressing to see the most amiable part of the creation, taking a retrograde march, not to improvement, but to greater degradation. Is it impossible to break asunder the adamantine fetters, with which custom has shackled their energetic minds? Why is not their natural equality established? Why is it that in the multiplicity of revolutions and counter-revolutions that have latterly taken place in the world, the scientific improvement of females, favourable to their intellectual emancipation, has not been effected. Even the few who have magnanimously passed the boundaries of male usurpation, have too often wasted their illustrious talents in chimerical and romantic, instead of beneficial and scientific compositions. We have seen the works of women who were blest with super-eminent qualifications and superlative talents, (but too often on subjects of little use) clothed in the most sublime language.

A hundred instances might be adduced, to show, how greviously the rights of women are infringed: though they themselves are not sensible of it: even in a religious point of view, how unjustly is the female mind shackled?

In ancient times, prophetesses as well as prophets were allowed and encouraged to preach, or as it was then called prophesy;

but in modern times, a holy and almost seraphic female, the favourite of heaven, and child of God ; if her heavenly Father should move her by his spirit, to bear a testimony for him to his guilty creatures, the clergy are up in arms and unanimously say it shall not be so. Thus we see, even the will of Heaven is counteracted by the tyranny of custom. But what makes this picture tenfold more degrading to human nature and insulting to common sense, is the peculiar contrast between the character and conduct of some ministers and some of the congregations. Here we see a youth sent to college with his two brothers, one to be instructed for an attorney at law, one for an officer in the army, and the other for a minister of religion ; the juvenile preacher learns a smattering of Latin, how to write a sermon ; and, forsooth, skips from the college to the pulpit, with his head full of elocution ; but, alas ! his heart full of corruption : this young manufactured parson assumes the gown and band for liberal wages ; and while the holy, and, perhaps, eloquent female we have just depictured is compelled to silence ; she is necessitated to see this metamorphosed clergyman mount the rostrum with a skip, adjust his ministerial appendages, cry hem ! and after reading a sermon, perhaps he took out of an old book, he skips out of the pulpit again, and with a bow, a polite whisper, or a fashionable nod to a favoured miss, the ludicrous, or I should rather have said the melancholy scene is closed. The liberality of sentiment manifested by the Society of Friends, in this respect, is truly admirable and worthy of imitation; and, also, the appearance and apparel of their young women. How amiable, how modest, and how beautiful!

When it is remembered, that modesty was made for woman, and woman was made for modesty, we must say, nothing ornaments and embellishes a female more than modest apparel and a prudent demeanour, and *vice versa*, with immodesty and imprudence. Amongst these discreet females, who ennoble human nature, we not only recognize the fair sex, but also the cherishing sex, who cherish the widow and orphan, clothe the naked, and feed the poor; the pious sex, who nurture their offspring as the candidates of Heaven, and as sojourners on earth; they teach them to draw the sincere milk of the word with that of the breast. The pacific sex, who delight not in war nor the discord of nations or societies; the sympathetic sex, whose hearts melt at human woe, and who are precipitate to alleviate the sorrows of the children of affliction ; the reverential sex, who appear in social worship, with reverence and godly fear, with becoming modesty, and solemn seriousness ; but, alas ! what a contrast between them and the votaries of fashion in the house of God.

When they in splendid robes to church repair,
To see, be seen, and say a formal prayer ;
They view the images and pews abound,
Peep through their fans, and eye the beaus around, }
Then listen to the anthem's solemn sound.
Their breasts swell'd out, their necks and elbows bare,
Their eyes half screen'd with curls of golden hair ;
Hence, while the parson utters hymns of praise,
The impious fop, with lustful eyes surveys }
Their charms expos'd, and covets still to gaze.
While they unsham'd, against all sacred rules,
Dart amorous glances at the amorous fools.

I would to Heaven this was only a poetical fiction : alas ! alas ! it is too true ; nay, only the thousandth part of the degrading tale is told. This degeneracy is owing to corrupt educations, and the wrong association of ideas. For instance, when the young female is taught to adorn and beautify her person and physiognomy, in order to gain admirers, and to select a husband from the number ; she is of course mechanically led to pollute the house of God as well as the play house, (pollution it undoubtedly is), and it is more the fault of parents and teachers than of the delinquent herself; for she, no doubt, thinks it is her prerogative to exhibit her charms at every place and opportunity to advantage according to the fashion. Hence she is the virtual cause of virtual fornication,* being committed in the church at divine service, and—but I must cease the delineation: the concomitant evils are too indelicate to be named.

---

* When we remember the words of Christ, that he *who looks upon a woman to lust after her, is guilty of adultery in his heart;* and the appearances of the votaries of fashion, calculated not only to compel the bad man to sin in this manner; but are formidable and fiery darts in the hands of Satan, to pierce with anguish, to entice, if not pollute even the good man, who is, by nature, prone to such evils. I say, considering these circumstances, I am led to fear, that sometimes there is more sin committed than good effected in the house of God. If parents who habitually dress their daughters in such apparel, as to be the instruments of Satan, to lead others into sin, would recollect, that they are the auxiliaries and emissaries of hell; and the greatest culprits in the sight of Heaven, when such sins are committed, I am persuaded they would detest the fashions and their concomitant evils; and they are not only guilty in this respect, but also the murderers of their children, when they permit them unreproved to go into the ways of folly in their youth, for evil habits grow with their growth, and strengthen with their strength.

Would it not be an excellent plan for some ladies of distinction, to organize an university, similar to those established by our sex? A superb edifice to be erected for the purpose by subscription, which would testify to posterity the philanthropy and intrepidity of its founders and patrons; the institution to be trusted to female philosophers, to the exclusion of our sex. By this means the talents of females would be brought into a right channel; works of utility and science would be produced to their own honour, interest, and the benefit of society.

CHAPTER IV.

The Cause and Consequences resulting to Society from Female Degradation and Incontinence investigated.

I HAVE in the preceding pages, suggested some truly momentous, though desultory reflections : important, though unmethodical sentiments : interesting, though spontaneous animadversions, connected with the subject of our investigation.

I come now to discuss the most interesting part of my subject, and which the heads of every family will find essentially connected with their interest, honour and prosperity. I would here observe that the antecedent and subsequent animadversions are by no means intended to apply to the sex in general. The prudent and modest are by no means implicated, none but those obscene votaries of fashions, who are too often carried beyond the bounds of common decency. Heaven forbid that I should speak disrespectfully of those individuals of Adam's family, who are the ornaments of human nature and the glory of man, especially when

I remember that my mother, sisters, and my wife, are women, and that the God of Nature intended man to be their protector and defender. No person can be a more ardent and indefatigable defender of the sex than I am, when I find them the votaries of virtue, modesty, and delicate sensibility. And no man, perhaps, beholds, with more painful sensations than myself, those persons who are the objects of my highest admiration, sacrificing at the altar of fashion their virtuous accomplishments, mental qualifications, and native innocence, which alone can render them worthy of our ardent regard and reverential esteem.

There are many of the sentimental votaries of seduction, and even itinerant libertines, who will, with the effrontery of a demon, attempt to applaud and vindicate the cause of females, who riot in the unrestrained licentiousness of their wanton desires, at the expense of modesty and virtue; who have sacrificed their honour to the gross pleasures of sense; and these libertines will make no distinction between the virtuous and the vile, the innocent and the lewd; they cannot, or rather will not, ascertain the infinite superiority and intrinsic excellency of a virtuous woman, that a man of sense and honour, would delight to take as the protector of his interest, the repository of his secrets, the cabinet of his earthly riches, the solace of his sorrows, the darling of his bosom, the admired companion of his whole life, and the mother of his sweet babes; the little cherubs whose infantile smiles and artless prattle, render, in one moment, more real and refined delight, than years sacrificed in the pursuit of sordid pleasures and voluptuous gratifications. However, with men of sense and discernment, the adulation of these hypocritical calumniators (who would, perhaps, be inclined to censure me for my candid boldness, in thus admonishing the votaries of sensuality), will be treated with the smile of contemptuous disgust, and well deserved execration.

In attempting to investigate the cause of female degradation, my mind is led imperceptibly to contemplate the miserable state of millions of poor unhappy females, who, at this very moment, are the victims of the avarice, and consequently the promiscuous lust of the traitors and tyrants of mankind; I mean the exiled daughters of the African race, from whose chains death alone is expected to relieve them.

O, death! the negro's welcome friend,
" The dearest and the best,"
How joyful is the hour you bring
  The weary slave to rest.

When from the cruel tyrant's grasp,
  By friendly death he's torn ;
To taste the blest relief of those,
  Who cease on earth to mourn.

His tyrant, though he seems thus vain,
  In fortune's lap carest ;
Yet think not while he seems thus great,
  That he is truly blest.

The thought, he'll soon be food for worms
  From all his pleasures torn ;
Blasts ev'ry op'ning bud of joy,
  And makes the tyrant mourn.

To persons who have perused my antecedent publications, it will not, perhaps, be necessary to say, that the cause of those abject victims of legal barbarity, is, and ever will be uppermost in my mind : the circumstance of my witnessing so much cruelty exercised towards them during my voyages to Africa, and several of the West-India islands, has made such an impression on my mind, as time can never erase, nor mortal eloquence depict. I need not, in this place, recapitulate the unparallelled sufferings of these wretched victims of our avarice ; this I have already done in my other performances, to the best of my poor abil-

ities. Suffice it to say : The son and sire
are daily and hourly tormented by their
cruel task masters, who force them to under-
go extremity of toil and hardship : to forego not only the comforts, but even the necessaries of life. While they endure severity of toil, they receive only penury of food ;
and, to aggravate their miserable doom,
they are forced, with weeping eyes and agonizing hearts, to see their wives and daughters, not only the victims of the avarice,
but subjected to the promiscuous lust of
their oppressors.

" Ah ! how can he whose daily lot is grief,
Whose mind is vilify'd beneath the rod ;
Suppose his Maker has for him relief?
Can he believe the tongues that speak of God ?

For when he sees the female of his heart,
And his lov'd daughters torn by lust away ;
His sons the poor inheritors of smart,
Had he religion, think ye he could pray.

E'en at this moment on the burning gale,
Floats the weak wailing of the female tongue ;
And can that sex's softness nought avail ?
Must feeble women shriek amid the throng ?

Haste, haste ye winds on swiftest pinions fly,
Ere from this world of misery they go ;
Tell them their wrongs bedew a nation's eye,
Tell them Columbia blushes for their woe.*"

---

* As an apology for introducing this matter, which
some will consider as not strictly connected with my

An individual ruffian, that is the owner of an estate of 200 slaves, appropriates all the young females for his seraglio ; there is, of course, a motly race of half white and half black children, produced by the owner, yet not considered as legitimate ; they are, of course, continued as slaves : hence these promiscuously begotten children, when arrived at the years of maturity, being ignorant of their progenitors, promiscuously and unwittingly commit incest with all its beastly concomitants ; but I must cease delineating this truly degrading picture of human depravity, as being too shocking for the ear of delicacy to hear, the eye of philanthropy to view, or the heart of humanity to recognize. But I would beg leave to make a short digression, in order to suggest a few of the effects produced by this deleterious cause : and, first, the human nature, is degraded to the brutal for the pleasure of the voluptuous epicure ; the laws of nature are inverted, though not

---

subject, I would affirm it as my solemn belief, that the cruelty of Americans to the African race, will sooner or later bring the vengeance of Heaven upon our country. Hence, I feel it my indispensable duty, to warn faithfully and affectionately, my unthinking fellow citizens, every opportunity, without regarding formality. " 'Tis conscience calls, and conscience I obey."

the laws of grace : for, while the tyrant is chaining the mangled limbs and lascerated bodies of his slaves, their souls, perhaps, are, at the self-same moment, holding sweet converse with God.

The foundation of civil liberty and social virtue, is shaken to maintain the superiority of demons in human form. I will prove the validity of this assertion, by exhibiting the premature fate of Hayti, which presents itself at once to prove to a demonstration the force of my hypothesis. The thousands of white planters, who, some few years ago, were scourging, with unrelenting cruelty, the exiled sons of Africa, in that unhappy country, have been cruelly massacred by the same exiled and exasperated Africans. Only 700, out of several thousands, were spared for a time, and afterwards butchered by order of Dessalines, except a few artificers retained for local purposes.

Can any impartial man take the most superficial view of that devoted country, and not acknowledge that it is intended by the Almighty as an example and warning to the other tyrannical nations of Christendom? But, I would ask, who takes the tragical warning? Is it the republicans of America? No; they rivet, instead of breaking asun-

der, the manacles of slavery. Instead of
obviating they consolidate its influence.—
Witness the thousands of slaves recently
imported into Charleston, and from thence
scattered through the different states. Yet,
the fate of Hayti proves, that these are mortal enemies to the public weal, and are continually gnawing the vitals of the body politic.
But I anticipate the answer which the citizens of the northern states will make to the
above assertion; namely, that the Africans
in our states are treated with such mildness
and generosity, that they would, in case of
intestine commotion or foreign invasion, be
the defenders and not the destroyers of their
benefactors. Such a supposition is the first
born of absurdities. Can the mother forget her sucking child? No more can the
sons of Africa, in what part of the world
or in whatever situation they may be, forget
the sufferings they have, in conjunction with
their ancestors, endured from the hands of
the cruel and avaricious whites. The fact
is, they would be worse than the worst of
traitors, if they did not espouse the cause
of their degraded countrymen. But facts
step forward to prove the solidity of my
arguments; and, of course, render speculative reasoning unnecessary. Great numbers of blacks and mulattoes, on the com-

mencement of intestine commotion in **Cape**
Francois, when the flames of rebellion were
kindling, who were both comfortably and
respectably situated among the whites; who,
notwithstanding, on the commencement of
hostilities, were the greatest enemies they
had to encounter. And this must be the
fate of America at a future period. Unless
we forego the cause, the effects will undoubtedly be the same.

At a former period, the citizens of America were enabled, by Divine assistance, to
conquer their enemies and consolidate their
liberties. But can we have the assurance
to ask, or the impudence to expect,' Divine
assistance, in attempting to vindicate our
national honour, by endeavouring to reorgan-
ize our federal government, on the event of
intestine commotion and foreign invasion, a
million of infuriated Africans in the bowels of
our country, and an army of veterans on our
frontiers? Surely not. The moment we are
robbing others of their liberty, can we ask
or expect God to secure our own? It is impossible. It would be blasphemy against
the rectitude of heaven to ask, and an insult to its Sovereign, to expect such a thing.
But I am anticipating a subject I intend to
discuss in a separate performance, entitled,
Political and Theological Discussions on the

Signs of the Times. I will, therefore, only observe here, that our political horizon is impregnated with impending storms at the present crisis; internal factions and external commotions, seem to predict that the scourge of the world* will find a way to bring his myrmidons to America. Then we shall feel, as well as know, what it is to be oppressed.

But to return to the subject of our investigation, which I will take the liberty to illustrate by two authentic circumstances, which took place yesterday; and which will tend to consolidate my assertions respecting children.

Conversing with my next door neighbour, respecting the cause why so many children were not only disobedient and refractory, in their minority, but even a curse to their parents when arrived at the years of maturity, she very judiciously asserted, that the radical cause was their giving their children their own way, and letting their self-will be unrestrained, while young. When they grow older, their wills become so invincibly stubborn, that they are unconquerable ; and that those parents, who were thus neglectful, generally felt the consequences of their

* Bonaparte.

credulity and impolicy. In proof of which she adverted to another neighbour, who was more than once cruelly beaten by her son, till she was black and blue; and, at the same time, contrasted the case of this undutiful son with her own children, six of whom were married, and most of them had children. Yet they were as submissive, dutiful, and affectionate as when they were in a state of minority; and that they had always continued in the same state. Indeed, I took notice several times myself of the social intercourse and affectionate regard existing between her and her children, the youngest of whom is now nineteen years of age, and none of them, though persons of respectability, will undertake, even now, any business, or enter upon any important pursuit, without first asking her advice, and gaining her consent. I asked her how she attained the happy, the heavenly art, of thus bringing up, and not only gaining, but keeping the affections of her children? She said, her primary object, with respect to her children, was, from their infancy, to break their wills. To begin at one year old, and let them know that her word was a law, and that her will should not be disputed with impunity. The infants, having these elementary principles of submission instilled into their minds, obedience became natural to them. They scarcely ever deserved or received a whipping. The cause being taken away at first, the effect ceased. Hence her children have been, and, to my certain knowledge, are a blessing to her; and she has nurtured ten, and raised seven, with more facility, with more ease and pleasure, than other parents have raised one; though a widow for sixteen years, This is a lesson better than volumes of metaphysical reasoning and philosophical disquisitions on education. The sentiments are familiar to the most illiterate, and which I have endeavoured to simplify. Ye injudicious parents, whose children are an intolerable burden, if you want to learn the sacred art of gaining happiness for yourselves and for them, view this woman as in a looking glass, and see the way to gain this happy end. By indulging your children, you make yourselves infinite trouble, and give them infinite pain, both here and hereafter; in this world and that which is to come. You are in short, raising them up to be your tormentors, their own murderers, and enemies of the state. I would illustrate this assertion by a circumstance that took place yesterday. Walking past the court house, I stept in, for a few moments, to hear the trials then under discussion; and, to my no small surprise, I saw and heard an old woman, bending with age, give testimony against her undutiful son, who had robbed her of her house and property (by getting a false deed made in his own name) the only support of her old age, and afterwards turning her out of doors, to seek refuge in the public bounty.

It is now past twelve o'clock at night : the solemnity of the time, connected with the singularity of the above adventure, causes a train of spontaneous and momentous reflec tions to strike my mind. How many pa rents, now wrapped in the close embraces of slumber, circle in their arms the children who one day will bring their grey hairs with sorrow to the grave, and yet alas! these same parents perhaps will peruse and approve of these sentiments respecting their children, but will not take one step in reforming the abuses their neglect has, and perhaps will still produce. If such persons suffer for their credulity and imbecility, their suffer-ings are the just fruit of their folly and neg-lect, but, alas! their ruined, contaminated, un-conscious offspring, also suffer loss, the floods of destruction are poured upon them by the impetuosity, the invincibility, and virulence of their unbridled passions and unrestrained desires, which, like the river Nile, whose

source is a small spring or rivulet, but which
ends in a mighty river that is supplied by
supernumerary streams and winding lakes,
which all unite to augment the magnitude,
and stimulate the impetuosity of this amazing river, till it empties itself into the boundless ocean; thus the little unconscious prattling infant's desires and passions are suffered to run unrestrained, at first indeed diminutive, but accumulating by degrees from bad
to worse, as from youth to age, augmented
by itinerant vicissitudes, local circumstances,
and relative situations in life, till we see the
sullen infant metamorphosed to a potent de-
magogue, a vindictive despot, whose mandate makes legions, armed with power and
pride, march majestically fierce, at whose
approach nations tremble, or, nod to their
fall, and to gratify whose will, thousands
of human beings must be sacrificed at the
shrine of imperial authority. This is a degrading but a true picture of the present state
of civilized as well as savage nations, for
turn our eyes which ever way we will, we
see violence and oppression prevail, produced by maternal indulgence and paternal neglect. Though I am unequivocally prejudic-
ed against elaborate and refined composition
and literary embellishment in discussing a
subject of this nature, and therefore endea-

vour to avoid all unnecessary amplification; yet, as a reference to facts is the only way to render argument by theory unnecessary, the elucidation of the subject requires some degree of systematical arrangement and con- nection ; though a profusion of imagery is apt to distract the reader's attention, and bring it into a wrong channel, yet some por- tion is necessary to maintain a chain of rea- soning, and make the mind recognize the connecting links in that chain. Alas ! how many truly valuable and intrinsically momen- tous as well as scientific performances on this useful subject, are perfectly useless to all but philosophical readers, on account of extra- neous matter connected with the " rubbish of hypothesis."

I would ask, from whence do the savages of our own continent receive that invincible composure, that unconquerable patience in the midst of the greatest agonies and bodily tortures; when their enemies burn them by a slow fire, beginning at their feet, and thus consume their whole bodies. While they exult and triumph in the midst of their pain, and deride and defy their foes, and even solicit them to augment their torments ; and thus expire without a single murmur or complaint: it is the force of example connect- ed with precept which endues them with

such stubborn magnanimity. The young
indian is taught by his parents to consider
flinching and betraying signs of terror in the
moments of danger or death, as the most detestable cowardice, the most disgraceful, and
at the same time, the most humiliating picture of a wretch unfit to live on earth, and
associate with mortals, or to be received into
the ambrosial habitation of their patriotic
ancestors after death. The children even
take a pleasure in putting lighted coals of
fire on their bodies by way of experiment,
to ascertain who has the most courage :—
in the same manner children might, if begun
with in time, be taught to abhor vice and admire virtue.

Education, if properly directed, may not
only subdue wayward appetite, conquer the
feelings of nature, subjugate hereditary depravity, but even annihilate physical sensations. In the same manner might sentiments be inculcated, and practices exhibited
to the indiscriminate inspection of young
females, that might impress their minds
with such invincible disgust at the prospects
of certain fashionable crimes, that they
would hold them in the greatest abhorrence
to the period of their dissolution ; and the
same might be said, with great propriety, of
other vices.

By pursuing the idea, we may ascertain the most eligible method to call the juvenile mind, not only to investigate and admire, but even practice and participate social virtue, particularly that of benevolence; for instance, when the child is attempting to kill a fly, or any other insect, by appearing to pity and sympathize for the sufferings of the fly, and, at the same time, showing that cruelty is wrong and displeasing to God. By inculcating such sentiments, the child may be led to feel mercy, and show clemency to all the animal creation. This assertion I have proved to be a fact, from the case of my oldest son, now between four and five years old. I would also assert from my own experience, that sentimental love to God may be begotten, by representing the Almighty as a good and gracious being; as the father of the human family; that wills the good of all, and the harm of none of his children; and, to reverse the idea, the malevolent passions may be engendered by an opposite line of conduct in parents and teachers, which unhappily is too often the case. But some persons will be ready to deny the above supposition, respecting children being early impressed with a sense of the love of God, and will bring forward the cases of many children, of exem=

plary pious parents, who are, notwithstanding, the most zealous votaries of infidelity,
and champions of dissipation, though they
received a truly religious education, and
had the most upright sentiments inculcated
upon their minds, by paternal solicitude and
assiduity. All I can say in contradiction
to this sentiment is, that too many good men
use the most injudicious means to make
their children such. First, the nurse begins
with the infant almost as soon as he can
lisp, to terrify him with the idea of a superior being, that will punish with vindictive-
ness. His heavenly Parent, by such imprudent nurses, is metamorphosed to a raw-
head and bloody bones, or to a hobgoblin,
or some other phantom of the brain, to
frighten the child to sleep : thus a foundation is laid at the most important period of
life, for the most invincible prejudices, the
most unconquerable superstitions to be
built upon. Aversion and terror are engendered, while love and tenderness are annihilated ; that love which can be implanted,
I had almost said sooner than any other passion, for daily experience proves that it is
generally the easiest thing in life, to gain
the affection of a child by acts of love and
tenderness ; while, on the other hand, by
hardness and moroseness, we as easily im-

bibe in them hatred and disgust; and perhaps, at the same time, a manner of fear and
terror.

It therefore appears evident, that the only
way to induce them to place their juvenile
affection on the Deity, is by exhibiting him as
their friend, not as their enemy; as one that
loves them supremely, and not as one that
will punish them inexorably. But it is not
only by nurses, but also by parents truly religious, and even ministers of religion, that
sentiments have been depictured in children's minds, that have a direct tendency to
connect gloom and horror with religion, restraint and infelicity with godliness: hence
these premature insinuations beget a secret
disgust and detestation, and when the reins
of paternal restraint are loosened, the juvenile prisoner precipitates into the forbidden
fields of pleasure and sensuality. Like the
young foal that rushes into the fields when
the stable door is opened, he skips about
every bush, he crops the verdant green, unconscious of his danger: when lo! a lion
precipitates across the lawn, and rends the
panting victim, while the atmosphere rever-
berates with his hollow groans. Thus they
continue to gratify their unhallowed passions, till death, in conjunction with complicated disease, destroys the volatile wander-

N

er in the interdicted fields of pleasure. Were children impressed with a sense of the native clemency of God from their youth, with diligence and perseverance, and the idea of punishment and future woes, not to be connected with religion, at least, not till they could associate the ideas of God's justice and goodness together—the effects, I am morally certain, would be salutary : divine love would be begotten in infancy, and would accumulate, from youth to age, strength and influence in the juvenile mind, which would be, no doubt, the best preservative against vicious practices.

Much might be said to show the fatality and futility of associating religion with monastic gloom, and the infinite injury parents do their children by this common practice. But I must pass on, to mention a fashion prevalent amongst the great, at least, those who call themselves the great : a fashion that I will be bold to say, is in open hostility with all the interests of benevolence and paternal munificence : and that is the fashionable mode* of rich people prematurely separating their children soon after their birth, and giving them in charge

---

* How many ladies would be seen carrying a lapdog in the street, before their own offspring.

to itinerant nurses, who cannot be supposed
to feel the same tender solicitude for their
welfare as their parents must unquestionably
feel; they are, of course, resigned to the caprice of persons, who often punish them in
the most cruel manner, while the poor little
sufferers cannot tell who injured and im-
posed upon them; and female children often, very often, receive the seeds of unchastity from their nurses; which prove in
following years, the cause of their destruction: for it is well known, that many wet-
nurses are merely capacitated for their employment through the medium of unchastity.
Parents taking such characters into their families, and suffering them to associate with
their daughters, is one principal cause that so
many common prostitutes crowd our cities:
thousands of innocent girls have been ruined
by this means. And with respect to parents
putting out their little infants from under
their paternal roofs to nurse, I consider the
practice not only cruel but unnatural: it
tends to annihilate the social affections.
Filial and paternal tenderness, by this
means are almost erased from both parents
and children. This assertion, I think, I can
authenticate, not only from hypothesis, and
the nature of things, but also from experience; for my parents had adoped, and

uniformly practised the unnatural custom, of sending their children at our birth, from under their inspection, and giving us in charge to nurses in their own houses ; and I recollect one of my sisters was almost starved before it was found out by my father, who instantly had her taken home. We were generally taken from our nurses under our paternal roof again, when about three or four years old ; if we had any affection it was for our nurses ; for my own part I loved my nurse much more than my parents before and after I left her; indeed I never to my recollection felt any affection for my father, while in a state of minority ; my mother died when I was about five years old, I consequently could not exercise much social affection towards her; but my father, with whom I lived till I was sixteen years old, I always disregarded, on acconnt of the appearance of moroseness in his physiognomy, and the distance he kept his children at, though he was by no means severe : but seemed to be as destitute of paternal tenderness, as I was of filial piety. I would, therefore, recommend parents, who wish to gain, and keep their children's affections, to attend to the old proverb, " Love begets love," and nothing else but love, whether human or divine. I admire God for his magnificence ; I venerate him for his holiness ; I reverence him for his matchless power ; I esteem him for his justice : but, I love him supremely for his goodness, which is infinite, amazing, and divine !

I may, with some little modification, apply the sentiment to my fellow-travellers to a world of spirits ; I, therefore, admire the statesman that acts a judicious part in the cabinet ; I eulogize the author who displays his ingenuity in the republic of letters for useful purposes : but that man, and that man alone I love, with the love of complacency, who directs his talents with tender solicitude to the purposes, and for the accomplishment of the happiness of his fellow-creatures ; but, alas ! how seldom these philanthrophic individuals are to be found : how often do we see vanity and ambition manufacture authors, who prostitute the most illustrious talents to the most unworthy purposes, with the brilliancy of diction, the appearance of tender emotion, the flippancy of language, and the flowers of rhetoric ; they exhibit resplendent performances, which flatter to destroy ; which, under the profession of respect for the cause of virtue, hide the most deadly poison ; who kiss, like Judas, and stab like Joab ; and yet, those who profess to be critics and reviewers, applaud, as delicious trifles, those voluptuous performances ; the authors of which, exert their ingenuity to mislead the unguarded, and, with sacrilegious profanity, undermine the foundations of social virtue, overturn the ramparts of female innocence, and ransack the repository of divine revelation : perhaps a deviation from the radical rules of composition, the critics and reviewers would recognize with the microscope of criticism, and yet, forsooth, they can let these ingenious murderers of the human soul, not only pass with impunity, but heap encomiums upon them, and crown them with popularity. As well might they applaud the beautiful leopard that devours a man, or the ingenious fascinating serpent, that charms and destroys the innocent bird. Just as reasonable would it be for them to recommend the assassin for his ingenuity, who, by a secret process, a new plan, most ingenious and profound, destroys the lives of his fellow men, at the moment he appears to be saving them, and sends them off the stage of action with a smile on their countenances ; without a sigh or a groan, and insensible of bodily or mental pain ; which, of course, must be reserved for their anticipation in a

future world, where no such libidinous de-
ceptions and sophistry can be practised.
Without any comment, for in fact it needs
none, I will illustrate the anterior remarks
by transcribing a paragraph published in a
London newspaper, respecting the most popular poet of the age.

" A meeting has taken place, at Chalk-
farm, between Francis Jeffries, Esq. of
Edinburgh, and Thomas Moore, Esq. commonly called Anacreon Moore ; but by the
timely appearance of the Bow-street officers,
mischief was prevented. This meeting
was produced by a literary quarrel : Mr.
Jeffries having written an article, which was
published in the Edinburgh Review, reflecting on the poems, of the modern Anacreon ; in which he is charged with ' im-
posing corruption upon his readers, by con-
cealing it under the mask of refinement, to
reconcile them insensibly to the most vile
and vulgar sensuality, by blending its language with that of exalted feeling, and tender emotion.' How true a description is
this of one half of the poems and novels of
the day."

I would here mention a circumstance,
which has a particular tendency to degrade
the female character, and which encourages
men to encroach upon the natural rights of

women ; and that is, the ridiculous partial-
ity of mothers in particular and parents in
general, to their male, in prefference to their
female children. One would suppose, that
such characters were virtually if not practically, the votaries of Mahometanism ; that
they did not believe in the immateriality
of the souls of females ; but that they were
created and put into the world, merely for
the sensual convenience of men and for their
domestic accommodation, and, of course,
that men are of decided and transcendent
superiority to women.

The mothers who profess to be proselytes
to the christian religion, and who, of course,
believe their female offspring to be heirs of
immortality, and rewardable or punishable
according to the merit or demerit of their
actions, and their belief or unbelief in the
Son of God and Saviour of the world ; I
think such mothers should blush, when they
reflect on the moral mischief they produce
(in the rising generation) by their mental
imbecility ; they virtually teach their sons to
despise their sisters, and pay no respect to
their feelings, they destroy that urbanity of
disposition which tends to produce domestic felicity ; they sow the seeds of unsocia-
bility, which prove a barrier to preclude
the introduction of reciprocal tenderness

and all the social and sentimental affections ; they implant in their boys imperious pride, with all its subordinate auxilaries, its subdivisions, and concomitants ; and in their girls, self-degradation, mortification, and disgust : they impregnate their juvenile minds with such unsocial and deleterious sentiments, so invincible as to defy even the power of religion to eradicate. Let stubborn facts authenticate the assertion. There are men, and good men too, not pagans, but real christians, the prejudices of whose education remain unconquered ; notwithstanding the influence of religion on their minds, has made a thorough revolution and reformation in their moral deportment : yet so powerful are first impressions, that even such men (though affectionate in other respects), consider their wives merely as domestic beings, whose element is a nursery, and whose business is exclusively confined to domestic economy, and maternal solicitude, without any reference to theological vocations, scientific improvement, or intellectual refinement : but without religion, men of this description are capable of blasting the domestic peace, and casting a mental gloom over the women, who are so unfortunate as to be united with them in the bands of holy matrimony.

A female of refined sensibility would en joy as much sentimental pleasure in the company, and from hearing the conversation of a rustic, as that of such a character; an ignorant person she would be inclined to pity ; but a philosophical pedant she would despise.

Women, who are thus unhappily united, can best tell the infelicity of such marriages, the mental langour produced thereby, the painful sensations resulting from the recollection of the permanency of the conjugal state, and the impossibility of ever anticipating a moment's refined pleasure, or intellectual gratification, in the communion and intercourse of persons so different in their opinions and associations—where one party are exalted to demigods, and the other degraded to brutes.

Finally, the consequences resulting from these inimical prejudices, have been, still are, and it is to be feared will long continue, to plant with thorns the nuptial bed, which ought to be a bed of roses; and strew the intermediate path between marriage and the grave with briars; instead of its being carpetted with flowers.

I will therefore, with boldness assert, that mothers, above all other people, should be well informed in all the branches of polite literature ; in order that they may be capacitated to inform their children. When this is not the case, the children who receive a classical education, are too apt to look down with contempt, upon their illiterate mothers, when they return from colleges, and other seminaries of learning. They should, therfore, consider prudence and propriety, not as sexual virtues ; but should inculcate sentiments of delicacy upon the minds of their male, as well as female progeny : by this means that unnatural contempt for the female character, which I have been execrating, will be done away ; and that hereditary prejudice, produced by the father's impropriety, and mother's imprudence, would be obviated ; we should no more see the laws of prudence outraged ; and common decency violated* in females ; or, for distinction sake, I will call them ladies, who appropriate to themselves the name of virtuous, and profess to be the votaries of modesty ; but I would ask such characters, what kind of modesty is it which can bow at the shrine of fashion, however obscene

---

* Were such females once convinced of the excellency of their characters, and glorious endowments by nature, they would be ashamed, and relinquish their foolish and fashionable furbelows.

and capricious. If it can be called modesty, it surely must be that peculiar to lewd women.

Another grand reason I assign for the obvious degradation of a great majority of the sex, is the indelicacy with which infants are treated by servants and underlings ; and the censurable inattention of parents to this important point ; which has been the means of bringing many a reputable man's child to premature prostitution : and, while we pity the child, we must reproach the parent, as the primary cause of the same : for, no pains were taken at an early period of life by the parents, to associate the ideas of delicacy and chastity, with honour and propriety ; and, on the other hand, immodesty and indelicacy, with shame and contempt.

I say again, in unequivocal terms, that this neglect in mothers is one of the radical causes, why so many prostitutes crowd our cities and principal sea-port towns. If the mother suffers her daughter to go into the very jaws of temptation, and, at the same time, never takes any pains to guard her against those temptations, and the fatality and remorse connected with yielding to them : is it therefore any wonder they should become the victims of seduction, or wayward appetite ? It is only by exciting dis-

gust and abhorrence at the prospect of
every thought that can corrupt a pure imagination, that we can inspire the genuine
sentiments of true chastity, and unaffected
delicacy. Again, how often does it happen, that the foolish pride, and self-distinc-
tion of people, in the middling ranks of society, prematurely poison the juvenile minds
of their children, by causing them to consider grandeur and honour, indigence and
insignificance, poverty and disgrace, as sy-
nonymous terms.

When, therefore, these children, by the
extravagance of their parents, are reduced
to the painful necessity of taking their
stand in the lowest rank of society ; what
agonizing sensations must they experience,
resulting from the wrong association of
ideas in the first instances ; and what ag-
gravates their mortification at the change of
circumstances, is the melancholy consideration, that they consider themselves in the
same light, (i. e. with contempt) in which
they formerly viewed poor people, in the
humble ranks of virtuous mediocrity ; and
they conceive the world views them in the
same point of view. These unreasonable,
supercilious, and destructive sentiments,
prove the harbingers of their downfall, from
the flowery paths of virtue, to the devious

paths of folly. Alas! how often has, and
I may add, how often do the children of respectable people (in the event of their parents
death, or reduction in a pecuniary sense,) precipitate themselves into the abyss of degradation and prostitution : hence the juvenile
companions of virtuous sensibility, become
forever separated :—as two beautiful virgins
walking hand in hand through the vernal
grove, they pluck the ambrosial fruit, they
exhale the fragrance of the scented mead,
they listen to the songs of the lark, and
view the silver stream run thrilling by them,
and crown each other with laurel garlands ;
when lo ! clouds surcharge with double
darkness, the lowering atmosphere ; the
thunder bellows, and the forked lightnings
flash from pole to pole ; while each of the
terrified maidens seek for safety in different
directions : one returns to the peaceful habitation of virtuous mediocrity, while the
other seeks for shelter under the spreading
foliage of the sovereign oak : when lo ! a
lion, ranging o'er the lawn, spies the trembling maid : he rears his main, he runs, he
flies upon the devoted victim; he tears her
to pieces ; and bears her in his grim paws to
his sequestered den, in the gloomy forest.

Thus are the companions of youth for
ever separated by vice, the influence of

evil communications, and paternal negligence and folly.

If we want a proof of the authenticity of
these remarks, we need only turn our minds
to the numerous haunts of debauchery and
dissipation ; and the lamentable proof will
appear, in the persons of the most beautiful
women, clear as the sun beam. Can any
mother, who is possessed of a particle of pat-
riotism and maternal sensibility, feel unaffected at viewing, even superficially, this
true, though degrading picture ? Let her
look upon her infant, with eyes of maternal sensibility, and then view, with sympathetic commisseration, the daughters of
respectable parents, who were wrecked on
the rocks and shoals which the object of
this work is to exhibit to view, that they
may be avoided by the rising generation.

Before I conclude this chapter, I must
observe, that young women bring themselves to ruin and disgrace, by too implicitly
believing the vague promises of men ; who
flatter to deceive. Parents are certainly ex-
tremely reprehensible, for encouraging too
much familiarity between the sex ; as well
as for not carefully explaining to their
daughters, the dangers resulting therefrom.
Thousands of virgins have been ruined

by this means : but as some freedom is jus-
tifiable, and as a prudent intercourse is com-
mendable, females should act with the most
becoming reservedness and modesty, in the
presence of their suitors; assuring themselves,
that no man of real honour, or virtuous sensibility, ever did, ever will, or ever can marry
a woman who has given him reason to believe she is destitute of modesty. If the female gives her suitor such liberty, at which
modesty would blush to behold, and virtue
would weep to witness ; he, of course, sup-
poses she would, if opportunity served, and
importunity solicited, give another man
the same liberties ; and, consequently, that
she is by no means worthy to be made the
partner of his life and fortune ; if he loved
her before ever so ardently, his antecedent
love will be changed to subsequent contempt, mixed with pity ; and if his pity
should be paramount to his honour, yet the
recollection of her past immodesty would be
the cause of periodical jealousy on the one
part, and misery on the other. Yet notwithstanding the simplicity and plainness of
these remarks, how many young women
have, and how many do, become the victims of their own credulity, and man's hy-
pocrisy.

All the reason I can assign for this prodigious folly, palpable stupidity, shameful imbecility, and flagrant unchastity in many
thousands, who were previously virtuous
young women, is the neglect of their parents,
in not impressing on their minds, from their
infancy, these intrinsically momentous reflections. Indeed there are many men, who
make it their particular business in choosing
a wife, to try and prove her virtue ; if she
resists with becoming detestation and abhorrence, the least innovations on her delicacy,
it will cause her suitor not only to love, but
also to venerate her more than he did before ;
for all men, however loose in their own morals, feel the most reverential respect and
veneration for female virtue, when untarnished and unadulterated, which their sagacity soon discriminates. But there is not only
the prefixed obvious evils attending female
imprudence, resulting from paternal negligence ; but more tragical catastrophes often
are the fruits thereof. What immense
numbers of young women have, when
their foolish and injudicious conduct, has
produced the effect I have above described ; namely, to cause the men they loved,
and who also, perhaps, loved them, to re-
nounce them forever ; I say, how often has
it happened, that these unhappy females

o 2

have put an end to their own wretched existence, or have thrown themselves as abandoned prostitutes upon the town. I will
venture to affirm that there are now thousands living, who could subscribe to the
authenticity of this assertion with weeping
eyes and agonizing hearts: I therefore do
not conceive how I can be more beneficial
to society in general, and my fair readers
in particular, than by exhibiting to their
view, in a plain and pointed manner, these
obvious rocks of seduction, on which thousands of beautiful, respectable, and previously virtuous females have been dashed
to pieces; and many too, who never thought
themselves, nor even their companions or
relatives, that they ever would have come to
so tragical an end: but beauty has produced
vanity, vanity pride, and pride has paved
the way for the successful innovations of
the votaries of seduction.

Some persons, no doubt, will think that I
am too plain and pointed in my animadversions; and that I, in some instances, even
use asperity of language in my admonitions
and reproofs; to such I will say, that admitting their thoughts were correct, yet
even the purity of my motives, and my affectionate and ardent solicitude for the present and eternal happiness of my fellow mor-

tals, should plead my excuse, and cover my indiscretion in this respect, with the mantle of love; but I positively deny the correctness of their thoughts on the subject, which I will prove to the satisfaction of every candid mind, by the following similitudes.

A certain polite gentleman descries his neighbour's house wrapt in flames at midnight, while the family are all slumbering on their beds, insensible of their danger; this polite gentleman, instead of forgetting for a moment the etiquette of politeness, and rushing into their bed-chamber, and warning them of their imminent danger, raps gently at the door and calls, but calls in vain; till the flames surround, and consume them in their beds. Suppose the same man saw a lady, who happened to fall out of a pleasure boat, drowning, she sinks, her head rises again on the surface of the water, but thinking it indelicate to catch her by the hair of her head, he neglects his opportunity, and lets her drown; would not such a man be virtually a murderer? Surely he would.

By these similitudes we may see the necessity of warning souls faithfully, who are standing on the brink of present and eternal woe. The magnitude of the evil may be as-

tertained by its dreadful concomitants : and
we may see the moral turpitude of the sin,
by its prohibition in sacred and prophane
history, and the most signal and severe punishment annexed to the commission of it.
According to the Mosaic economy, the
maid who committed whoredom in her
father's house, "was *surely to be put to death*."
And there are existing laws among many of
the heathen nations, equally, and in some instances more severe, than even that ; particularly amongst the Chinese*, whose penal
laws, in this and other instances, are ex-
tremely salutary, judicious, and equitable ;
particularly as it respects their tracing t!.

---

* As children have nothing but what they receive
by nature and education from their parents, tutors,
and companions, the infamy rests ultimately on their
parents and those who have the care of their education, (especially when they live among those of their
own profession) and not on themselves, who are ignorant of their own weakness and of the evil consequences that will attend, until it is too late to prevent
them. The Chinese laws make communities answer-
able for offences committed within their respective
authorities; parents for the misbehaviour of their
children, concluding that they must have neglected
their education ; and magistrates are severely punished
for those crimes committed within the districts of
their authority. Modern Universal History, vol. viii.
pages 153. 172. Ancient Universal History, vol. viii.
page 266.

crime to its source, and recognizing the
cause as well as the effects. The parents
are punished as we have already hinted, as
the primary cause of the evil ; and the
child as the secondary cause ; and I would
ask if the laws of man judiciously traces a
crime from its commission to its source,
will the laws of God be less judicious ?
Surely not. What a pity it is that the laws
organized by the Christian governments
should not criminate those who are the
cause, as well as those who are the perpe-
trators of crimes : surely, then, parents
would be more particular how they instructed their children, when they would be an-
swerable for their negligence in this respect ; if this was the case, our prisons would
not be so crowded with vagrants of various
descriptions : surely so many prostitutes
would not crowd and disgrace our cities ;
incomparably more so, than in the most un-
civilized and savage countries. Surely a less
number of culprits would be executed, less
suicide committed, less seduction effected, less
disobedience to parents recognized, less contempt of religion, and moral obligation
shewn, fewer obscene and scandalous fashions
prevalent; and, in short, a less number of mur-
ders, thefts, and robberies committed, in what
are called christian countries. However, if

the laws of short-sighted man will not take
cognizance of the delinquency of parents for
the disobedience of their children, God will
assuredly do it, and that with a vengeance ;
and the punishment will be superior to that
of their children, according to the nature of
their negligence, and deleterious precedence :
for instance, I would ask any man of common sense and candour, does not that parent obviously deserve more contempt and
execration, for the clandestine perpetration
of crimes committed by her child, than the
child herself ; if she never suggested to her
that those crimes were incompatible with the
principles of moral rectitude ; and especially if the mother was the only vehicle of information to which the daughter could have
access ? Without any manner of doubt. I
have myself known the daughter of respectable parents, who exhibited the indelible
fruits of illicit love ; the blame was exclusively thrown upon the actual delinquents,
while the virtual culprits, namely the parents, were considered guiltless : yet, forsooth, the wickedness was transacted under
their roof, and almost under their own eyes.
And I am now acquainted with reputable
parents, who profess religion, and who are
in other respects friendly, generous neighbours ; yet act with as much indifference to

their children, with respect to their moral improvement, as if they were merely domestic animals ; particularly their eldest daughter, a young woman, who is allowed such liberties, as well as her gallant, that if she is not ruined, it will be more by good luck than good guiding. A practitioner in the arts of seduction could not desire more opportunities for the operation of his deleterious designs, than is given in this family.

I was grieved, to behold female innocence and beauty brought to the verge of destruction : and, from a sense of duty, personally but privately expostulated with and admonished the father, and pointed out the danger of giving his daughter such liberties ; and particularly depicted the case of widows, who lived the virtuous wives of respectable husbands, yet on their death, they have through the invincible arts of seduction, been lead (even such characters who, perhaps, previously thought they would sooner suffer the most painful death, than disgrace the memory of their deceased husbands and living children), from the flowery paths of chastity ; but, notwithstanding all my expostulations and animadversions, he seemed callous and insensible to the cogent solicitude I manifested for the safety of his child. He in fact, I thought, seemed to be morally dead to the future woe of his children. Is it possible such parents can be guiltless in the sight of that wise Being, who scrutinizes the cause as well as the effect of evil? It is impossible. I will be bold to say, that this destructive negligence, this paternal insensibility is the cause of the ruin of more females, than any other cause whatever. For I would ask, how can a young woman, unconscious and unguarded, who has never been apprised of her danger, by her parents, the only persons who ought to admonish her on so delicate a subject; how can she escape pollution, when opportunity, importunity and the invincibility of seduction, are all combined against her? She parleys, she reasons with her seducer; but, alas! in vain: his sophistry is paramount to all her artless logic. The libertine hears but will not understand. She falls a martyr, I will not say, to the arts of seduction, but to paternal neglect. While the female, who has been taught in the school of maternal experience, on whose juvenile mind has been impressed the indispensable duties peculiar to the female character, to whom has been pointed out the many formidable plans laid to ensnare the sex and fascinate the unguarded, the sure and certain way, also, to shun these snares and vanquish every innovation, when the adept at seduction appears with all his wiles in the presence of such a character, she views him with scorn ; and, as she considers the smallest attempt on her chastity, or the least insinuation stamped with the signature of indelicacy, as an unpardonable insult, she replies to the same with magnanimous contempt and execration, and frowns the reptile to his native insignificance ; while she insinuates that she would sooner sacrifice a thousand lives, than forego her untarnished chastity. He will shrink from the presence of the virtuous fair one, with self-condemnation, mixed with reverential admiration, as an owl from the face of day.*

---

* Many alas! too many of those fashionable females who may, with great propriety be called affected prudes, would apparently be shocked and petrified with horror at the bare mention of some words in this work ; and yet, forsooth, these very modest fair ones, the very same moment they thus blush (and, perhaps, reprobate what they consider the indelicacy of my phraseology) are not ashamed to appear in the presence of young men, both in private and public, clothed in such a lascivious manner, and assuming such wanton attitudes, as to cause the burning blush of shame to tinge the cheek of the beholder.

——⊕——

CHAPTER V.

Advice to mothers on the importance of the intellectual improvement of their daughters.

——•⧫•——

In suggesting the anterior remarks on education, I have, no doubt, widely deviated from that systematic plan and methodical arrangement peculiar to other authors, who have written on the subject. My sentiments, in many respects, are spontaneous, and the composition precipitate, desultory, and chiefly untranscribed. Though I have not studied method in the elucidation and amplification of the subject, I have, though in an eccentric manner, studied utility according to the best of my poor natural abilities. I believe the commonality of my readers, will be far sooner benefitted by that unaffected and simplified style and arrangement, which exhibits variety and avoids prolixity, though unmethodical, than the most refined and embellished composition; when too elaborate and scientific. In addressing that venerable and truly respectable class of people, the mothers of the rising generation, I feel those diffident sensations, which a conscious sense of their importance in society, and my own inability naturally inspire; how-ever, convinced as I am of the rectitude of my intentions, and well meant endeavours to promote social intercourse and domestic tranquillity, I am emboldened to proceed with distinguished deference to the persons to whom I now address the following strictures.

Civil society is divided into three distinct classes, to wit: the higher, the middling, and the lower. The first enjoy the *good things of this life* in destructive abundance; the second, in blissful mediocrity; the third often in deleterious indigence.— The middling state is the most secure, most capacitated for enjoying the benefactions of Providence, and consequently most preferable. In high life, a thousand temptations continually intervene to draw the juvenile mind astray, and to pierce the votaries of pleasure with many sorrows. It is in vain to say, that their enjoyments are more than paramount to their disquietudes; this is not a fact; their enjoyments are merely ideal, while their infelicities are real: their abundant riches cannot afford them happiness; for,

" Abundance cloys of riches, love, or song,
We want but little, nor want that little long."

as they cannot enjoy their riches with gratitude ; nor, of course, with satisfaction, they manufacture to themselves real out of imaginary evils, and perplex themselves with vexations, which merely, and exclusively originate in their own proud imperious hearts ; indeed it seems to me, that this restless, unhappy disposition is the offspring of their own ingratitude and pride.

Such proud imperious foes their toils will know,
And every hand shall work its share of woe.

I never formed an idea of the deep debauchery (or to call it by its refined name, gallantry) and the routine of dissipation prevalent amongst this class, almost in general, till I read the memoirs of Mrs. Robinson.*

---

* The misfortunes, the writings, and adventures of this lady (who is only one of thousands which might be adduced) present themselves to consolidate my arguments, establish my hypothesis, and put it out of the power of even duplicity to doubt, effrontery to prevaricate, or profligacy to equivocate, respecting the cogency of my familiar arguments. The lady alluded to was, perhaps, the handsomest woman in England. She was emphatically called " The beautiful Mrs. Robinson." The ingeniousness and purity of her heart, when she first launched into the boisterous sea of fashion, with the profound ingenuity of her head, were only equalled by the unparalleled charms of her person. Her literary performances, particularly her poetical pieces are, in my opinion, equal, if not superior, to the productions of any of

She has portrayed the splendid wretch edness, the satanic vanity, the pompous os-

---

her sex. I will not even except the ingenious Madame Dacier, who translated Homer from the Greek into the French language; or Miss Francis, who translated from the Hebrew the songs of Solomon, with notes, critical and explanatory.

The names of these ingenious women I mention with the greatest respect; and would exhibit them as literary models for those young females, who wish to make a proficiency in erudition; and, in addition, I would enumerate the names of Mrs. Cowley, Griffiths, Barbauld, Dobson, Carter, Montague, Chapone, Smith, Inchbald, Leaper, Madan, Masters, Monk, Philips, Rowe, Countess of Winchelsea, Dutchess of New-Castle, Miss Moore, Seward, Williams, Lee, and Burney.——While I exhibit these characters for the young female to imitate, in their scientific researches, I would add that were it possible for her to possess the information of them all, with the personal beauty of an angel, and yet be destitute of virtue, her beauty and learning would only tend to make her more despicable in the eyes of the world, inexcusable in the estimation of the honourable and virtuous part of society, and a hundred-fold more guilty in the sight of Heaven; for *where much information is given the more virtue* is required by the Almighty *who will punish those who know their master's will and do it not, with many stripes.* I need not say much respecting the series of misfortunes and splendid calamities that chequered Mrs. Robinson's life, which was short indeed, but full of sorrow. I would refer the reader to her memoirs in 2d vol. written by herself. For my part I confess, that I never perused the life and misfortunes of any person that has more sensibly moved my sympathy. The resolute manner tentation, the systematical coquetry, the deep and black crimes which are not only

---

in which she, for a long time, repelled the attacks on her virtue (after she entered the fashionable world), by right hon. villains, lordly debauchees, and illustrious libertines ; and the apparent reluctance with which she surrendered her honour, though assailed by the Prince of Wales, who, after using every stratagem that an adept at seduction could devise, presented her with a bond of 20,000 pounds sterling, professing much love and vowing eternal constancy. I say the long and vigorous stand she made, though assailed by such invincible, such potent temptations, and the neglect, profligacy, and barbarity of a scornful husband, which tended to sharpen the darts of seduction, very much prepossessed me in her favour and inspired me with pity for her misfortunes. But the meanness her seducer manifested after he ruined her (for whose sake she not only sacrificed her honour, but also a lucrative establishment), beggars description. He, soon after her degradation, forsook her, and even had the baseness to get the bond of 20,000 pounds returned, and gave in its room an annuity of 500 pounds. Lord Lyttleton behaved towards her with artifice, Fitzgerald with violence, and many other right honourable and noble debauchees with dissimulation ; but none behaved with such baseness as' his royal highness. The imprudence of her parents, a premature and precipitate marriage, the early introduction into the fashionable world, laid the foundation of her subsequent calamities, and premature death, which happened in the bloom of her youth. Her constitution participated in the ruin of her honour. She languished till reduced almost to a skeleton ; and died, I believe, a true penitent.

frequent, but also fashionable amongst the right honourable and right reverend votaries of seduction. However, I will forbear to particularize them, but substitute more interesting matter. Pursuing therefore, my strictures, the dishonour resulting particularly to the female character, recurs in defiance of every effort to suppress it. Hence, it seems impossible almost to avoid tautology. The alarmist, I know, sees evils which never will be realized; but on the other hand, the slavish dupe of seductive fashion never sees them till they have taken effect. In which case the magnitude of the evils, is according to the degeneracy of the fashion. It is certain, that a host of infelicities with their conscripts, recruits, and auxilaries, crowd upon the votaries of fashion and dissipation, line after line, and rank after rank, in swift succession.

When a distinguished female personage, elevated to the first dignity in community, and, of course, popular and powerful, introduces fashions, however ludicrous and obscene, those fantastical females placed near her, or even her most distant associates, will necessarily more and more assimulate, though at first shocked with the obscenity of such fashions. These debasing fashions, progressing like a gangrene, will extend from one female to another, through every grade.

We need not look far to prove the authenticity of these remarks : is it not a stubborn fact, that the conduct of these first rate fashionables, paralyze and infatuate every grade of society ? I would ask these fashionable matrons, where is the prudence that animated your ancestors? Dispelled before the baneful notions of false refinement. Where is the prudence that characterized your progenitors, who taught you (though in vain) lessons of discretion? Where is the energy and invincibility that triumphed over female imbecility and vanity ? In short, where is the domestic economy and virtue which signalized your mothers? Lulled, gently lulled to fatal slumber in the lap of venality, and voluptuous fashionable theory.

What virtuous mother does not hang her head in solemn sadness at the thought ! what cheek does not wear the crimson blush, at the degeneracy of the sex! In the bosoms that beat with the vital force of female virtue, a noble disdain should arise, at the rememberance of their domestic betrayers and seducers. Mothers, this is not a time to sit inactive, and see the last struggles of every thing dear to you— the expiring honours of your female progeny

You should endeavour, with more than maternal solicitude to snatch from ruin, or preserve entire their sacred virtue. As the mariner, with anxious solicitude throws out any floating pieces of the wreck to save his drowning shipmate ; who, swept away by a foaming billow, while the decks are white with foam, and the rude winds howl about the masts, and sing through every shroud : he struggles with the angry waves, and whistling winds, till he is at last saved through the assiduity and perseverance of his faithful companion. Thus, let mothers use every effort to save the honour and virtue of their daughters, who are almost enveloped in the vortex of popular degradation and infamy. I am not speaking of those females who have plunged into the dreadful abyss of personal prostitution ; but rather of those who pursue the direct path that leads thereto : which is, to become the slavish dupes of the obscene, the depraved fashions of the day. Let therefore such virtuous mothers, who have a spark of ancient prudence untarnished and unextinguished, shed resplendent light on the benighted paths of the juvenile females of the rising generation. Sometimes, when I view parading the streets, ladies of the first respectability, dressed in such an obscene manner, as almost enough to make an harlot blush, I ask myself, can these ladies be really prudent, who can thus sacrifice every virtuous and modest feeling at the shrine of fashion, and excite a blush on the cheek even of lewdness?—surely not. *" The tree is known by its fruit."*—Actions speak louder than professions—a woman may profess to be exemplary and virtuous; but surely when we see that woman appear in the most immodest attire, and display her charms indiscriminately, in the most obvious manner, to the eager and amorous inspection of thousands of gazing and criticising libertines; we cannot believe, though we hear vociferated daily, that this woman is a virtuous and respectable character; and though she displayed elegance in her figure, and enchanting beauty in her countenance, to surpass the beauteous Helen; every reasonable man would admire the smallest share of personal symmetry in a prudent female, more than all her exposed charms.

" Not for such ladies we would sigh,
Loving only fashion's dye,
And their charms to every eye
                  Revealing.
But we love the prudent maid
In sweet modesty array'd,
All her beauty 'neath her shade
                  Concealing.

Lady, when with graceful care
You would deck your bosom fair,
Or your golden curling hair
     With roses.

Ah ! you throw the flower away
When it glares in open day ;
The modest bud more sweets, we say
     Discloses.

The lily trampled in the street,
The rose beneath the rav'ler's feet
Or beauty sold too cheap, ne'er meet
     Our praises.

Thus charms expos'd are in disgrace,
The spark'ling eye, and ruddy face,
If void of prudence, all your race
     Disgraces.

Such nymphs may charm th' unhallow'd heart,
But confidence can ne'er impart,
Nor captivate with beauty's dart,
     A husband.

And should he be ensnar'd by show,
The spark of love he'll soon forego,
And blame his partner for his woe,
     And her brand.

For beauty soon familiar grows,
And fades as hourly fades the rose ;
But virtue still more sweets disclose
     Till doomsday.

And then the virtuous shall enjoy
Celestial peace without alloy,
And with bright saints their hours employ
     In their lay."

These are only a few of the most obvious
evils resulting from the sacrifice too many
females make at the shrine of fashion. A.

train of evils still more tragical succeeds,
and it must be an understanding benumbed
by repeated deviations from the paths of female rectitude, that would fail to discern
them, a heart that has banished conscious
propriety, that would refuse to feel them,
and a conscience opposed to the rules of
modesty, as well as the laws of God, that
would neglect to regard them. I am well
convinced, that by declaiming against the
vices of the age, particularly our darling
fashions, I erect an impregnable barrier to
preclude praise and profit, and in their room
accumulate formidable enemies. Let others
flatter to deceive and gain praise and profit
thereby, I will faithfully point out according to my ability the devious paths of folly;
and though I am well apprised, that many
parents will put books into the hands of their
children, that will tend to entice them from
the paths of female rectitude, in preference
to mine, yet this consideration, or indeed any other, shall not hinder me from
giving the unthoughtful and unconscious female a faithful warning, hoping that this
performance may be presented to some,
even of the gay votaries of fashion, by
those who are more seriously inclined, and
being perused, though perhaps only superficially, may stop them in their mad career.

Where my propositions are not supported
by the most reasonable arguments, and my
hypothesis proved from experience, I do
not wish any to believe them; but, where
this is the case, I flatter myself, I shall be
heard by the unprejudiced, though my
strictures are unadorned with the flowers of
rhetoric. Indeed, truth is most beautiful,
when most simple. Fiction and poetic poison, not truth, require the embellishment
of fancy. And, alas! how many females
have been ruined by this means, namely,
the splendid exhibition of sterling talents
and moral poison, connected by the ingenious murderers of the human soul, by
" Poetic panders, rhyming debauchees."

" Here! let us glance at Little's songs of love,
And famous Moore, the poet of the grove;
And thank the honest Scot, who drew the veil
Which hid the moral poison of his tale.
May specious vice thus ever meet its fate,
And bear the public scorn, the public hate.
Beware, Columbia's fair, and never move
A heart to cherish interdicted love.
Oh! may you never have the fate to please
Poetic panders, rhyming debauchees;
But still let modesty her banners rear,
And give the signal when such foes appear."
Ingenious murderers, sland'rers of the wise,
While grasping fame they break all social ties,
" And own no rites, but such as vice supplies "
To gain that phantom, intellectual fame,
They prostitute their souls and their good name;

Q

Nay, hand it down to ages yet unborn,
The object of their hate. disgust, and scorn,
Who, if contaminated by the tale,
Or moral poison which their works conceal ;
They'll curse their ashes mould'ring in the tomb,
And blame them for their woes and latent doom;
And at Jehovah's bar, they'll them impeach
As the first cause of vice their writings teach ;
Whose poison makes their fame* a doubtful meed,
" Whose censure is our best applause indeed."

Ye mothers, who are indifferent and regardless of the intellectual improvement of
your daughters, it is you who are most cul-
pable, when your daughters imbibe the moral
poison of such authors : it is you that have
most opportunities to put books of a contrary description into their hands ; and, it
is you, in particular, who will have to answer at the august tribunal of Jehovah, for
the pernicious consequences of your neglect
and imprudence ; do not, I conjure you,
treat these observations with a fatal and
fool-hardy indifference ; the observance of
them will promote your social happiness
through life, enable you to leave a virtuous
offspring behind you at your death, without

---

* But admitting that they were rendered the most famous and popular after their decease, what a poor satisfaction it would be to know, that degenerate mortals
eulogized their writings, while they had to answer at
the bar of God for their pernicious tendencies.

any forebodings of mind respecting their
future conduct, and will capacitate you, on
the day of resurrection, to be enabled to say,
" Here, Lord, are the children thou intrusted to my care, and I have not lost
one through my neglect or imprudence ;"
and the consequence will be, *vice versa*, in
the event of pursuing a contrary line of conduct. If your daughters were mere creatures of solitude, in whose vice or virtue,
happiness or misery, life or death, no human being was interested, if their moral
contamination did not tend to contaminate
others ; were they even, as the Mahometans
suppose, material beings, divested of immortal parts ; if no bosom glowed at their
prosperity, or bled at their misery ; if no
mourner wept in the event of their departing from the paths of female virtue ; or, if
they did not prove a most formidable snare
to others when they thus departed : if all, or
any of these suppositions were facts ; yet
then, even then they are creatures susceptible
of feelings ; and, by being put in a wrong
channel in youth, may spend their following
years in misery : and, *vice versa*, if they are
directed in the right path : for, even leaving
futurity out of view, virtue is happiness
and vice is misery in this our mortal state.

It is my firm belief, (and that belief is supported by scripture, reason, and common sense,) that it is the duty of every one, who expects to meet the approbation of our merciful God, to be merciful, not only to their own, but the children of the helpless widow. Our commiseration we cannot withdraw from them without sin, and the forfeiture of future happiness; for, surely, we cannot be so void of common sense as to suppose, that a God of unsullied veracity will tell a palpable falsehood, in the presence of assembled worlds, to save a cruel, guilty, impenitent culprit. See page 112.

How often is it the case, that mothers, either virtually or literally, by their neglect or imprudence, lay stumbling blocks before their children; and, when they turn aside from the paths of female rectitude, they exclaim against them alone, and impute all their sorrows to their disobedient children: their hearts are pierced with agony; their grey hairs are brought with sorrow to the grave; they have lost from the paths of virtue their only daughter; and with her the support and delight of their declining years. Instead of giving the rich reward (for all their parental toil and tender solicitude) of a discreet and dutiful life, she gives her body to prostitution, her char-

acter to infamy, and her soul to endless torment. She has destroyed the domestic
happiness of her parents, and caused their
rising hopes to set in sorrow ; but, perhaps,
it is almost, if not altogether, the parents
fault, for the premature ruin of their only
daughter ; did they not let her have her own
will gratified in infancy ? and, at the dawn
of reason, did they not suffer her to peruse
the most vile and voluptuous poems and
novels ? did they not harbour the adept at
seduction under their roof, and suffer him
to take such liberty with their daughter, in
private and public, as he chose, till she was

" Lur'd by the villain from her native home !"

Did they not suffer ; nay, perhaps, encourage her to follow the most obscene and vulgar fashions ? or, perhaps (which is sometimes the case) forced her, though only 17,
to marry a rich old man, 70 years of age,
contrary to her inclination and affections,
which were previously bestowed upon a
more worthy object !

If all or any of this imprudent and injudicious conduct was applicable to the wretched parents I have been depicting, they are
themselves the primary cause of their
daughter's disgrace ; and, no doubt, will
have to answer for the same at the bar of

God. It were not to be wondered at, if the shrieking spectre of their ruined child raised up before the anguished eyes of her parents, the enormous complication of nameless crimes, which eventually became the offspring of their neglect. And when deleterious disease hurries her from present degradation to future condemnation ; it were not to be wondered at, if she escaped her troubled grave, to impeach them with her blood ; to haunt their bed through declining life ; to chill their waking moments, and alarm them in their midnight slumbers.

Ye cruel and injudicious mothers, who act in this manner to your daughters, how can you reconcile such conduct to common prudence, common sense, or rationality ? I will not say religion. If you bring them up the slaves of indolence, how can you expect that they will mechanically become industrious, when suddenly their riches take wings and fly away ? But, admitting their riches were to remain stationary, which no man can boast of, yet even then industry is the main prop of life, braces the nerves, and invigorates the whole system ; while idleness relaxes and debilitates it. Do you not know, that the parents who do not provide for the safety of their children, are worse than infidels ? Can you,

without feeling the yearnings of your bowels towards your offspring, lead them to the
slippery precipice of fashion, down which
if they fall, they are plunged into an abyss
of irrecoverable despair, perpetual infamy,
with the signature of their degradation
stamped upon their foreheads, prostitution,
desolation, and woe! Concupiscence is the
preliminary, if not the foundation, of the vile
and vulgar fashions of the day, which are
an insult to common sense, and an outrage
to common decency; for what else can induce a woman of an enlightened understanding, to expose those parts that virtue
bids her screen. I will not say, that it is
this propensity which stimulates the young,
thoughtless, volatile, and gay, as they merely imitate their progenitors. Their appearance is the appearance of wantonness; their
disposition we must believe to be the disposition of wantonness; and, though their motives are laboriously varnished over, and
imputed to a love of elegance and grandeur,
they cannot conceal the gross materials thereof, or deceive the most superficial observer.
For nothing can be more plain; than, that
the female who uses such attitudes, appearances, and appendages as will tend to excite
lust in, and awake the sleeping passions of
amorous men, must, in some measure, par-

ticipate these destructive feelings; and,
were it not for the popularity of the fashions I deprecate and invalidate, the woman that would thus expose herself, would,
unquestionably, be ranked as a lewd character, if not the most common prostitute. Remove, therefore, only the popularity of the
fashion, and you make its votaries lewd
women, even in the eyes of the world.
Thus, the popularity of African slavery
renders the man innocent that enslaves
man; and thus the popularity of female
fashion, renders the female who appears in
the garb, and with the attitudes of lasciv-
iousness, unimpeachably virtuous and modest. But I would ask, does, or can vice
(because popular among the wicked), be
metamorphosed to virtue; or lewdness to
modesty? It is impossible. If, therefore,
my reasoning is correct, and I cannot see
how it can be incorrect, women who become votaries of lascivious fashion, are, in
the estimation of every reasonable and discerning man, as reprehensible as if the
fashion was not countenanced by public degeneracy of manners. But the evil tendency of this depravity is most sensibly felt by
the rising generation, who practise the evil
unconscious of the effects thereof. They
swallow the fatal bait, but see not the hook

with which they are caught by libertinism, till it is too late. Oh, ye cruel mothers! you must shut your eyes against the truth, and basely insult your own understandings and common sense, not to see the cogency of this remark. We turn with disgust and abhorrence at the appearence of the infamous character of a hoary headed woman, whose business it is to trepan and ruin the unguarded, the friendless, the fatherless young female ; but what a striking similarity is there between such a wretch and too many parents ! She ensnares literally ; they virtually. The latter accomplishes in the long, what the former does in the short run. And one is in miniature what the other is in magnitude. It is a melancholy, a stubborn fact, that the cruelty of mothers, and obscenity of female fashions, manufacture a super-abundance of prostitutes, without the aid of such detestable auxiliaries as the hoary headed dame we have just glanced at.

If all I have said has not moved the sympathy, awakened the sensibility, aroused the finer feelings of maternal solicitude, and illuminated the understandings of the characters to whom these strictures are particularly addressed ; let me then request you to accompany me, in sympathetic thought, to the scenes of debauchery and prostitution, which you perhaps have, or at least will help to create, if you persist in pursuing that line of conduct which infallibly leads to ruin. View, I conjure you, the smiling, the beauteous countenances of your female infants; and then, with your mind's eye, survey the moral mischief which indelicate fashions produce in society, and ask your own hearts this pathetic question : can I, shall I, by my neglect or imprudence, consign these innocents to such a woeful, such a shameful end ?

But, in order to illustrate my arguments, from facts, as well as speculative reasoning, go with me to yonder part of the city. It is well known for the multitudes of unfortunate females that flock thither, in which numbers of the unhappy persons I am exhibiting to view reside.

As it would only confuse our ideas, and preclude us from reasoning correctly on the subject, to examine the wretched, degraded group collectively, or even to select an individual of them, who, deformed by habitual prostitution, and debilitated by complicated disease, is now metamorphosed from a beautiful young woman (which she was in her happy days, while under the paternal and reputable roof of her affectionate parents) to an object of deformity, the glimpse of whom is enough to excite horror and consternation in the breast of a midnight assassin.

Passing by, therefore, the most gloomy and horrible part of the tragical scene, we will view the most favourable side of the picture, by selecting a young and beautiful female just launched into the gulph of dissipation, from the interdicted walks of fashion ; we will not take her portrait in the midst of her reprobate companions or nocturnal revellings, as the scenes of debauchery there displayed would shock female delicacy ; but we will behold her in a sequestered grove, near the vestibule of her prison, the repository of dissipation. See the tears of remorse stealing silently down her woe-worn cheeks. Read, for you may read, in her faded countenance, the torturing anguish of her breaking heart. Reader, canst thou survey the intellectual, nay, the real picture I am drawing, and not feel tender pity melt your glowing heart, and the tears of commiseration drench your streaming eyes ? For my part, while I write, my heart palpitates with anguish at the consideration, that thousands of such portraits are to be found in real life. But to return, for sympathy retarded me in giving the portrait of a debased ruined fellow creature.

She still weeps, with her head reclined upon her hand, and her elbow propped on her book,* her soul detests the line of life she has commenced. She abhors herself, her companions, her crimes ; but above all her vile seducer. But a few days ago, she shared all the blessings and joys of life ; and, what is the best of all, an unblemished reputation. She was surrounded by neighbours who respected, friends who loved, and parents who adored her. They found in her their every joy, and the balm of their sorrow. She hung on their hands, and received their benedictions. She inspired all their enjoyments, and animated all their hopes. But now, alas ! for ever banished from all these scenes of delight and exultation, by the artifice of a villain ; who, enticed by her fashionable appearance, thought her a suitable person to try his arts upon. He too soon succeeded in his diabolical designs ; for she was artless, nor suspected danger to be near. Being once seduced from the paths of virtue, filled with conscious guilt and shame, she flies the indignant presence of her honourable parents, and seeks that refuge in a brothel, which she relinquished in her paternal home. She mourns and pines, but pines and mourns in vain. Now left abandoned, desolate, depraved.

---

* See the Frontispiece.

> " No eye to mark her sufferings with a tear,
> No friends to pity her, nor hope to cheer ;"

she seeks, as her only alternative, to drown her sorrows in repeated dilutions of ardent spirits, as the antidote of her woes, as the solace of her anguish, as the most efficacious means of obliterating the remembrance of her former happiness, her better days. But, alas ! she mistakes the poison for the medicine ; and, while attempting to erase from her mind the remembrance and guilt of one crime, she perpetrates another.

> " Thus sin has always this attending curse,
> To back the first transgression with a worse;
> Thus rivulets grow larger by degrees,
> From creeks to rivers, rivers into seas."

Thus she becomes the premature martyr of intoxication as well as prostitution. View her, at the door of that tippling shop, extended on the ground ; not only stupid, but senseless through ebriety ; a prey to every unprincipled ruffian, and a spectacle for every unpitying passenger. But here I must cease giving this, and take another part of her portrait ; for my heart begins almost to weep tears of blood, at the true and tragical picture I am drawing. I will also forbear delineating the scandalous and beastly crimes, which attend her footsteps,

R

from the present period to that in which she is arrested, in the mad career, by that deleterious disorder peculiar to her profession. Her delicate constitution cannot support itself, under the scenes of debauchery and infamy in which she is necessarily involved. Her emaciated and languid appearance, bespeak her disorder, and is the mittimus to have her conveyed to the Poor-house. Here I will draw her picture, as it really happened in the Alms-house in Philadelphia, where myself and a bosom friend (as exemplary for his disinterested philanthropy as he was for his unaffected piety) attended every Sunday, and visited the sick and afflicted in their apartments, exhorting them to repentance and reformation, and praying with and for them. We would often, in one forenoon, address hundreds of poor unhappy children of misfortune. One part of this charitable institution we particularly attended, called "the surgical ward," on account of the wretched beings who were accommodated there, which generally consisted of worn down and emaciated prostitutes, who were taken up by the overseers of the poor, and sent to the Alms-house to die there, unknown and forgotten by every relative and friend. We have often addressed, and endeavoured to console, twenty at a time of these wretched females, on their beds, in rows round their apartment, while the silent tears of shame and regret would steal from their eyes and trickle down their cheeks. One day as I was visiting the patients in the surgical ward, I saw a young female, about seventeen years of age, who was literally reduced to a skeleton, by the fashionable disease peculiar to her profession. Part of her face, particularly her nose, was eaten away, and she was in other respects, an object that was truly shocking to behold. Her adventures and misfortunes, prior to entering the Alms-house, were nearly similar to the portrait I have already drawn. Soon after her deviation from female rectitude, she was poisoned by the fatal disease in its most virulent form. She was soon forsaken by her companions in iniquity, and was carried to the Alms-house; where she continued under the physians care for several months, still unrecovered from her fall, either mentally or corporeally. Such was her situation when I first approached her bedside; dead in sin, pierced with sorrow, and on the confines of eternity. During the time she remained in this repository of human misery, no relative, friend or acquaintance once consoled her with a pitying look, cheered her with friendly advice, or participated her anguish with a tender tear. As I approached her bed-side, she lifted up her hopeless eyes towards me ; and, in an instant, as if transfixed with conscious shame, she cast them down again, shook her head significantly, and sighed as it were mechanically. She seemed to be so worn down with grief and sorrow, as almost to be petrified with the painful recollection of her happier days, and bereaved of her intellectual faculties. I visited her, and spoke the most consoling words my commiseration could suggest, for many days, viewing her with astonishment, mixed with distress, before she seemed to attend to my admonitions. At last, awakened as from a reverie, she looked wistfully at me, while the big round tears stole from her languid eyes. She asked me, if she was not out of the reach of mercy? if she was not abandoned by heaven, earth, relatives, and friends ; as her lover proved faithless, and her parents implacable and inexorably severe? I viewed, with a palpitating heart, her hollow eyes, sunk in their sockets, and there I could almost read, that her parent's anguish wounded her more deeply than her lover's treachery : her lover, who flattered to deceive, and was so woven with serpentile deceit and villainy, that

No human foe her fatal tale could hear,
Nor Satan's self relate without a tear.

Nature would melt, and savage ferocity would relent, were the half of her sufferings and his villainy uttered. In short, she became more and more sensible of the ruinous state of her soul, as well as the emaciated state of her body, while she listened and attended to our periodical admonitions, which she did with lively gratitude and penitential sorrow ; and every time she adverted to her degraded state, the tears of regret would start from her eyes, and trickle down her cheeks. She continued in this penitent state of mind for some weeks, praying hourly to the Almighty to pardon her manifold offences, and returning us a thousand thanks for our successful admonitions ; and a few nights previous to her dissolution, she called the nurse and told her that the Almighty had blessed her with a divine sense of his acceptance and pardoning love ; that she was supremely happy, and ready and willing to be dissolved, that she might be with Christ. Before this change she was afraid to die. She got the nurse to read in the hymn book such hymns as were applicable to her condition ; and thus the penitential delinquent departed this life without a sigh or a groan, and with a placid smile that almost beautified her deformed countenance, in full hope of a glorious immortality, through the atonement and intercession of the Friend of sinners, about the 17th year of her age. Her remains were conveyed, without form or ceremony, to Potter's-field burial ground.

No friends, no parents, there in sad array,
Saw her remains in silent sadness borne ;
No tear was shed upon her grave that day,
Her name, her memory, consign'd to scorn.

Ah! hapless maid, how many like you groan,
A life of sorrow, and disgrace, and shame,
No friend to stop the melancholy moan,
Nor cheer the mind transfix'd with mighty pain.

Her nearest friend refuses to protect,
Altho' the lonely corpse is buried nigh ;
Whose solitary clay remains undeck'd,
Nor marks her grave, nor begs a passing sigh.

Yet may'st thou read this girl's pathetic lay,
And, if possess'd of pity, drop a tear ;
She was once sparkling as Sol's golden ray,
Crown'd with delight, and void of guilty fear.

But, ah! her morning sun was set at noon,
Entic'd by fashion to the devious way;
Where artful libertines, alas! too soon,
Led the mistaken maiden more astray.

Ye nymphs who boast this sacred pearl we call
The crown of virtue; woman's pride and boast:
If now you stand, oh ! tremble lest you fall,
And prove, indeed, what hapless Anna lost.

Oh ! bear in mind the melancholy day,
That robb'd her of all she accounted dear;
And read, for thou may'st read the plaintive lay,
And drop for her a sad, a silent tear.

THE EPITAPH.

Here lies the relics of a child of woe,
Born in the lap of fortune and of fame ;
Who, lur'd from home by a seductive foe,
Relinquished fortune, and an honest name.

Soon in the interdicted fatal way,
She felt the poison reach her youthful heart;
Nor friend nor comforter she found that day,
To stop its progress, or allay her smart.

To fashion first a victim she became,
The libertine then found an easy prey ;
Enamour'd by the fascinating dame,
Thus am'rous fops defenceless maidens slay.

Her fatal downfal we no more disclose,
Since God has view'd her with a pitying eye;
Whose pard'ning mercy is her sure repose,
The pardon of the Sov'reign of the sky.

She lies forgot, this all her monument,
This the spontaneous tribute of a sigh ;
Approach and read, and while your hearts relent,
Alas ! poor Anna, let each reader cry.

The reader, I hope, will excuse me for detaining her so long with the prefixed account of poor Anna. I did not intend to say more than a few words on the occasion, without the addition of any of the lines of poetry, which were composed inadvertently, as I pursued the subject. Her sufferings and penitence would not have made such a lasting impression upon my mind, had I not been a personal witness of them.

I will conclude the picture by delineating, as its counter-part, the profile of the villain who caused all this misery; hoping it may fall into the hands of some adept at the arts of seduction, or be presented to him by some friend to female innocence. For the sordid purpose of gratifying his carnal propensities, he dares, by the most vile and treacherous methods, to attack the unsuspecting virtue of a daughter, and annihilate the domestic peace and honourable name of a virtuous family; and, by abandoning a female to infamy, he makes her the instrument of enticing and vanquishing the virtuous intentions of many young men, who, in their turn, delude and ruin other innocent females, who would have remained virtuous had it not been for the fascinating snares of the female, who was previously seduced by this villain. What complicated crimes will he have to answer for at the bar of God? and what curses are heaped upon his guilty head, by the wretched parents of the girl he has ruined? Let us approach their distressed habitation; which, previous to this catastrophe, diffused respectability, tenderness, and domestic peace; enter the door and see what vexation and anguish are depictured on every countenance—the hoary father is pacing the room with hasty steps and downcast looks, and with emotions unutterable, sorrow inconceivable, and whose resentful eyes forbid the rising tears to ease his grief—the tears that would unbidden flow on any other pathetic occasion; but his honour is wounded; his pride is mortified: the pride of his declining age is sunk in the sink of infamy and prostitution; the agonizing thought will soon bring his grey hairs with sorrow to the grave. View, seated in an armed chair, with her head reclining on her hand, the mother of the unhappy girl; she was the staff of her declining years; to her she looked to baffle the evils peculiar to old age; to close her eyes in death; to enhance her joys in eternity.—But all these promised blessings have been consigned to oblivion; they have vanished with the honour of her daughter, like a tapering vapour in the atmosphere. But how must the libertine's guilt be enhanced, if, in addition to all these woes, he has produced the eternal ruin of the soul as well as the body of his victim ; and where we find one real penitent prostitute, surely we find scores that are impenitent, and die, as well as live, incorrigible sinners :—Hence the utility of a Magdalen Society, and I am glad to find that one has been recently organized in the City of Philadelphia. Is she cut off in the bloom of life in her sins, surely the reflection of such an event will not only imbitter the walks of life ; but arm with triple fury and horror the pangs of death to her merciless destroyer.

Libertine, be assured the day of retribution is at hand ; the blood of a murdered fellow-creature cries to heaven for vengeance against you, and the cry will assuredly be heard, unless prevented by a speedy repentance and reformation. The bed of death, the yawning grave, and the pit of destruction, are open, ready to receive you.

When you anticipate the solemnities of a dying hour, and feel the icy hand of death seizing you ; oh ! how dreadful will the reflection be, that you have been the destroyer, the fell murderer of those helpless persons, which laws, human and divine, enjoined you to protect and defend. Oh ! how dreadful will you feel when about launching

into a boundless eternity, loaded with guilt;
and, as it were, drenched in the blood of
your fellow-creatures: and when you have
entered the gates of death, and are approaching the mighty gulph, without bottom or
shore, what horror must seize your naked
and forsaken soul, when the first object that
faces you, with a grin of fury, in eternity, is
the screeching ghost of the girl you have
robbed of her virtue, and plundered of her
life. She is eagerly waiting to pour on
your guilty head the vengeance of Heaven,
and the wrath of eternity. But time would
fail me in giving a glimpse of the thousandth
part of the horrors of such a soul; to enhance whose misery he will see the baneful
effects of his crimes in society, ages after
his decease, the contagion will spread wide
and more wide to future generations: But
in the day of final decision, to be impeached
by his country, whose laws he trampled under his feet; by the families, whose peace
he had destroyed; the individuals, whom he
had murdered; and even the Almighty
Judge himself, whose laws he despised, and
flung his death and agonies away; inter-
cepted his glorious rays, and forbid them to
shine upon the object he murdered; and
finally, helped to people the gloomy regions
of darkness and despair; what tongue can

express, or mind conceive his guilt, and its consequent punishment.

I have been depicting the crimson crimes of the impenitent libertine, that I might have an opportunity to prove, that not only the guilt of this female delinquent, but even the guilt of the libertine himself, is in a great measure the guilt of that cruel and injudicious mother, who not only suffered her children to go into the jaws of temptation, but led them into the paths of destruction herself, both by precept and example. Surely that mother, who (by actions which speak louder than words) tempts the libertine to tempt her daughter, and gives him every opportunity to lay snares for her destruction, is the primary cause of the iniquity of both parties; therefore, all the woes I have denounced, and ten times as many, must be the portion of these parents, gentle or simple, noble or ignoble, rich or poor, who thus virtually give their unconscious and defenceless offspring, a prey to temporal and eternal destruction. Let such consider themselves the blackest and most horrible figures in the intellectual picture I have delineated.

I have already hinted, that the children of what are called the higher and lower classes of people, were in most danger of being whirled into the vortex of popular degeneracy and personal dissipation :—the first on account of their abundance, which sharpens every illicit appetite, and invigorates every versatile solicitation :—the latter, on account of their indigence and wants, which necessitates them to expose themselves and their children to a variety of vicissitudes and temptations. For instance, that poor, but virtuous family, who have more children than they can well support, are under the necessity of binding out their oldest children—if they are daughters, their virtue will be severely tried.

I know a rich merchant who is considered respectable, whose children are men and women grown, that cannot, or rather will not, let any of his female servants, young or old, pass, without using his utmost endeavours to seduce and ruin them. I would ask, how can a young girl that is bound to such a man, escape pollution?—and many, too many there are, of this same disposition, whose appearance would forbid the supposition : and not only masters, but sons, and even men servants, are always on the alert, to decoy the unguarded female, and ruin her for ever. If, therefore, the mothers of such children do not inculcate the principles of female virtue upon their juvenile minds

s

with assiduity, they may reasonably expect, that sooner or later they will fall victims, not to seduction, but maternal neglect :—whereas, if the mother (as it is her province so to do), was to point out diligently, the beauty of chastity, and the deformity of its contrary ; and that, from the first dawning of their understandings, virtue would become mechanically charming to them, and vice, particularly debauchery, would be the object of their implacable disgust and detestation ; and, thus prepared, they might pass through a host of libertines, with unsullied virtue : but how can that mother be so unaccountably stupid, as to expect that her daughter, whom she never warns of the fascinating snares by which she is surrounded, will shun these snares, the invincible snares of seduction, by which even the dame, who has counted 30 revolving years, is vanquished ; but it is not only the lower class of people whose children are thus exposed, but the middle class, who are crowned with blest mediocrity, sometimes participate the dangers, the sorrows, and sufferings of the poor. There are a thousand vicissitudes periodically intervening, which not only levels this class, but even the higher, on an equality with the lower class.

How dreadful will it be for such, who

have raised their children in idleness and vanity, to be cursed, with too unsuitable companions ; to wit, a beggar's purse, and a proud heart. Alas ! how many daughters of such families have, on such events, sacrificed their chastity sooner than their pride : but even those, who have preferred labour to prostitution, how liable are they to be led astray, by the persuasions, insinuations and seductions of designing men, if the sacred seed of virtue, has not taken deep root. Such a reduced female, who prefers virtue clothed in rags, and working in a kitchen, to vice arrayed in silks, fringed with flowers of gold, and dwelling in a palace, is transcendently amiable, and worthy to be a princess.

From these simple, familiar, and friendly remarks, all that will, may see the necessity of female virtue, to produce domestic peace, personal tranquillity, and national prosperity ; and that mother, let her be who she may, that brings up her daughters without ever attempting to improve their intellects, nurture their virtue, defend their chastity, and promote their future honour and prosperity, is, (excuse my plainness,) a pest to society, and the virtual destroyer of her family, whom she is bound, by all laws human and divine, to protect and defend.

Little do such mothers think, that their neglect and indolence will materially affect, nay, will literally eclipse, the usefulness, as well as undermine the respectability of not only their children, but their children's children, to the third and fourth generation : for instance, those daughters who are brought up, and educated merely as if they were intended to be statues to gaze upon, or to grace the seraglio of some eastern nabob, or to flutter about, in conduct and appearance, like painted butterflies, that skip from flower to flower, to display their useless variegated colours ; I say, these daughters, when they become mothers, very naturally bring their children up in the same manner they were themselves, as useless beings, cumberers of the ground ; and sometimes as public nuisances ; and thus one generation after another are contaminated through the maternal neglect of their progenitors ; and it is *vice versa* with the females of those ancestors, who brought up and educated their offspring, not as animal machines, but as reasonable and intelligent beings, created for the most exalted purposes, and with the most benevolent design. They proved by experience the ineffable delights springing from a self-approving conscience, the recollection of their fraternal and indefatigable endeavours for the glory of their God, and their families weal, diffused the most pleasurable serenity through their souls. They ascertained, by practice as well as theory, that riches, void of virtue, can never purchase an hour's real happiness, or a moment's real peace: but that virtue, without riches, can render us truly happy, not only in this world, but that which is to come: and, in short, that nothing but the practice of virtue and piety, can render a human being truly happy, and capacitate the human mind to anticipate the joys peculiar to the first-born sons of glory. While, with gratitude, we receive the blessings of nature ; while, with humility, we follow the dictates of reason; while, with affection unsullied and sincere, we return to God the grateful tribute of thanksgiving for his benedictions, we secure a paradise on earth. But, on the contrary, while we suffer our carnal appetites to subjugate our reason, captivate our hearts, and fascinate our understandings : while we suffer our turbulent passions to degrade and subdue us, either sentimentally or practically ; sorrow and sadness, shame and disgrace, infamy and horror, will intercept the smiles of heaven, and unfold its maledictions ; will darken all our prospects on earth, and prohibit us from participating her profuse bounties with gratitude ; and, of course, with pleasurable sensations. In short, while virtue strews the path to heaven with flowers, vice carpets the road to destruction with briers and thorns ; for, as virtue has its own reward, in this as well as the world of spirits ; so has vice its punishment here, as well as hereafter.

While I am advising mothers to bring up their children in the nurture and admonition of the Lord, I am well convinced of the difficulties that occur therein. I know that kings, who have governed nations ; ministers who have led their congregations heaven-ward ; generals who have vanquished armies, and subjugated nations ; could not, (or, perhaps, I more properly might say, would not) govern their children ; lead them in the flowery paths of piety, or conquer their turbulent passions.

The scholar may give a correct definition of the theory of navigation ; but would make a poor hand of navigating a ship across the pathless ocean, encountering the dangers peculiar to the mariner's life. The theoretical politician may be able to delineate the judicious plan, and suggest the most wholesome laws for governing a subjugated nation ; but little does he know what difficulties attend the practical operation of these laws, and the opposition that will be made before the boisterous passions, long-standing prejudice, and sentimental prepossessions of the people are subdued.

One thing is necessary, and all persons who are intrusted with the education of children, should attend with great punctuality to it; and that is, to study the tempers, dispositions, and constitutions of children. Without this consideration, the most indefatigable measures, the most solicitous exertions will be in vain, as there is a diversity of tempers, not only in nations and communities, but even in families. Hence, what would prove intellectual food for one child, would be poison for another. In short, it will be almost impossible to train them up so as to answer the end for which they wer created, unless instructors suit their discipline to the disposition of their pupils. As every man's face has its peculiar features, so has every juvenile mind its particular bias; even the twin children of the same parents cannot be conducted to the paths of virtue by the same method; both time and patience are requisite to ascertain the preponderating bias of children's minds: take them by this handle, and you may lead them with success and facility; but by a contrary one, your labour will be not only in vain, but you will materially injure your pupil.

When I went first to school, my teachers were inflexibly morose and severe : all was severity, and no encouragement ; the consequence of which was, instead of being constituted a scholar by attending this seminary, I was made a dunce : I was so stupified by corporeal correction, and mental intimidation, that I was rendered stupid both in and out of school. I went about nine years, and much money was expended during that time, for my tuition. Yet I firmly believe, nay, I am confident, I could learn more now in nine weeks, than I did in that nine years. I feel irritated almost when I reflect on the cruel manner in which I was used ; I not only say for trivial faults, but also for no faults at all. I well remember to have received such a severe whipping, as to be left in a gore of blood, because I could not repeat my grammar lesson verbatim, which I had done to my school fellow, with great facility, a few moments before I received my correction ; but, being terrified at the presence of my unfeeling instructor, I had forgot every word when he examined me ; I consequently was always designated by the opprobrious epi-

thet of dunce : and, in fact, I was rendered
such by the cruelty and impolicy of my instructors : for I hope I will not be considered a pedant, when I affirm that nature never
formed me such a character. Hence,
I believe a cruel and injudicious teacher is
a pest to society, and an intellectual murderer. I do not, by any means, wish to insinuate, that a teacher should not correct his
pupils ; there is a variety of ways without corporeal punishment : but, at any rate,
I must say, gentleness should always be
mingled with severity ; mildness with chas-
tisement. A teacher, in my opinion, should
never inflict corporeal punishment on his
pupils ; as it tends to debase their minds,
break their spirits, and stupify them ; to
mortify their pride, would do better than to
lacerate their backs.

> The teacher ne'er should use the harsher way,
> When love, or gentle means will bear the sway.

This advice is not so often applicable to
parents, particularly to mothers, as they too
frequently verge on the opposite extreme.
They suffer vice too often to grow luxu-
riantly in their children, before they attempt
to stop its growth ; when, alas ! it is too
late to stop its progress when arrived near
maturity. As the monarch of the moun-

tains, the sturdy oak, when it has extended its spreading foilage, and taken deep root in the ground, and its lofty top begins to nod in the air, in token of approaching maturity; in vain will the laborious farmer try to bend it, so as to answer his domestic use. I would ask, what distinguishes the human, from the brutal creation? Some will say, reason is the characteristic : but I say, reason united with religion. Some brutes exceed many men in sagacity and ingenuity; but none, no not one in devotion; to this they are all utter strangers. Should not parents, therefore, strive, judiciously strive, to cultivate that heavenly power, that divine plant which designates the superiority of the human over the brutal, to be greater than the angelic over the human creation. I feel jealous and fearful for the rising generation, perhaps I have partly anticipated* this sentiment before ; but I will, if even so, repeat it again; too often it cannot be repeated. I would ask, what is it that civilizes savage nations? I answer, the cultivation of reason and religion. And what is it that metamorphoses civilized people to bar-

---

* Sometimes I have been precluded, for many weeks by relative avocations, from proceeding with the composition of this work : and this is one principal cause of the repetition of some sentiments.

barians? I answer, the relinquishing their religion and reason, and surrendering their common sense to be the subjugated vassals of their vile and vulgar passions.

The present generation have become adepts in the practice of the most unhallowed sensuality, systematical cruelty, refined debauchery, and fashionable indelicacy, which the antecedent generation, were they to arise from the dead, would blush to witness.

> Could they behold their daughters thus adorn'd,
> By fops admired, but by good men scorn'd;
> Some sentimental jilts, and some the slaves
> Of fashions lewd, or prostitutes of knaves;
> Disgusted with the sad, the hateful sight,
> They'd fly to earth down from the realms of light;
> Reprove with frowns their vile degen'rate race,
> And then return back to their heav'nly place.

If we may judge of the next generation by the present, we must conclude that they will approximate to a state of sensuality and debauchery, that will naturally assimilate to barbarism,* that is, if our children continue to increase in degeneracy as we have. If they imitate the present vices and fashions of their parents ; and, in addition, loose the reins to the domination of their

---

* History will justify the above sentiment.

unhallowed passions, in the same quota and etiquette as we have done before them, where will social virtue find a shelter ; after we leave, perhaps, our offspring to fill up the measure of their iniquity, and force the slumbering vengeance from the skies. In the event of such a crisis, or even at the tribunal of Jehovah, how will our children accuse us in these, or words like these.— " Oh ! ye, our degenerate ancestors, you are the radical cause of our wretchedness and woe, as well as your own shame and dis‣ grace ; for, your imprudent neglect, in not instructing your children, was the means of laying up, in our profligacy and disobe- dience, the sharpest pangs of grief, regret, and shame for your own grey hairs ; by your bad example you made us bad citizens, and scattered a wicked race to corrupt the virtuous part of society, and thus remove the barrier that kept back the just vengeance of Heaven : wherefore, by your negligence you became guilty ; and, by your bad ex- ample you became doubly guilty. Now you participate our anguish, for you have to bear your own, and feel the weight of our sins : while your own consciences, and the signa‣ ture of God's displeasure, seals the authen- ticity of our accusation. You knew we were illiterate, and yet you did not instruct us; you saw that we were born in sin, and, of course, prone to evil; and yet you did not restrain us: you saw us go into the very jaws of destruction with indifference; nay, you invited us to participate in the illicit pleasures and vanities of a guilty world. That great and good Being, who is now our impartial Judge, you never held up to our view as the object of our affections, and the author of our lives: you thought no more of him and his glorious laws than the dust under your feet; and you taught us, by your example, to despise him. Finally, you saw us working out our destruction with greediness; and yet, alas! you never so much as once suggested to us the consequence of our folly; we are, therefore, consigned to eternal misery, and unutterable woes; but you are the primary cause of them all; it would have been well for us, if we never had been born of such cruel and inconsiderate parents."

Serious, solemn considerations—Oh! that parents would lay them to heart, and act towards their children, as they will wish they had done, when they come to bid them an eternal adieu here, or appear at the bar of God in company with them hereafter; if so, happy parents. The salutations and congratulations they will then receive from

T

their offspring, when launched into eternity, will be so diametrically opposite to what I have first depicted, will be so transcendently glorious, and exquisitely divine, as to beggar description, and mock all human conception.

Before I conclude, I will suggest a few spontaneous thoughts relative to matrimonial alliances, between what the world calls people of quality.

It often happens, that such persons consider riches as the nerves of the conjugal state : hence, we often find parents sacrificing their children's present peace and future prosperity at the shrine of that greedy god, Mammon. How often does it happen, that an avaricious person will marry his daughter, perhaps not more than sixteen years of age, to a man old enough to be her grandfather, merely bacause he is rich ; for the sake of filthy lucre, the girl is forced contrary to her inclinations (which, by the by in such cases as these are never consulted,) and previous engagements, to give her hand and person to one man, while another possesses her heart ; the consequence of which is, she is plunged into a labyrinth of misery, from which nothing but death can relieve her—she is almost compelled to be unfaithful to her hoary headed husband, though she may be, by nature and education, virtuous. For, how is it possible she can live happy with a man 60 years older than herself? Oh! how many beautiful young women have been ruined in this manner, by their parsimonious parents! Such parents, I will be bold to say, are more guilty in the sight of heaven, than the highway robber; for, he only takes the traveller's money; but they rob their child of peace and tranquillity here, and place such stumbling-blocks, such invincible temptations, before her, that it is almost impossible for her to retain her integrity,* and, of course, she is plundered at the shrine of avarice, of her present and eternal peace. The vengeance of eternity will surely be hurled on the heads of such cruel and avaricious parents :—far, far more guilty than the midnight assassin, whose dagger, perhaps, is the mittimus that conveys his victim to that glorious world where the wicked cease from troubling, and' the weary are for ever at rest.

It almost always happens, on such mar-

---

* I believe many young women have been thus plundered of their present and future happiness. Oh! how mortifying, to be forced, in the presence of the man she adores, to give her hand to the one she detests.

riages, that the lady, notwithstanding her virtue is unsullied, and her prudence is unimpeachable, looses her good name ; as people consider it impossible for her to be sentimentally, as well as practically virtuous, placed in such an indelicate situation ; and her old husband, well considering circumstances, naturally suspects her of coquetry ; for such men generally prove jealous husbands when possessed of young wives ; and, indeed, the young libertine will naturally lay siege to such a lady's virtue, as he suspects, that she has every reason to encourage an intrigue. Thus is she brought into the very jaws of destruction by her murderous parents, and if she miraculously escapes the many snares by which she is surrounded, without being contaminated, her good name, which is more precious than gold or silver, will undoubtedly be tarnished by calumny, and adulterated by the censorious : thus, at all events, she is robbed of her inward peace, and outward respectability, by her unrelenting parents, to whom the subsequent lines of Shakespeare are truly applicable .—

" Who steals my purse, steals trash ;
'Tis something, nothing—'twas mine, 'tis his,
And has been slave to thousands ;

But he who filches from me my good name,
Robs me of that, which not enriches him,
But makes me poor indeed."

It sometimes happens, that very young women willingly marry old men, and thus sacrifice their own persons at the shrine of Mammon ; they are, therefore, not to be pitied, as they bring wretchedness upon themselves ; they think when they get riches they will be happy ; but, alas! they find, themselves wretchedly mistaken ; they find to their sorrow, that a palace, when changed to a prison, loses all its worth.

However, it happens to them, just as it befel Elijah's servant, who took from Naaman, the Assyrian general, the talents and changes of raiment, which his master nobly refused to accept. When he returned to his master, the prophet, a curse was denounced upon him for his covetousness, and the leprosy of Naaman was that curse ; so, with his riches, he received a disease that rendered them of no utility. Thus it is with those avaricious fair ones ; they have to live with men they cannot love, as it were in a perpetual prison ; they must submit to their caprice and jealousy, and all for the love of money, which they cannot enjoy ; for what are riches when compared to peace and tranquillity of mind? The

characters of such silly avaricious fair ones
are pointedly described by Lord Lyttleton,

> " The most abandoned prostitutes are they,
> Who not to love, but avarice fall a prey :
> And naught avails a maid so wedded."

But while these cases excite our contempt,
the misfortunes of the former ones excite
our warmest commiseration ; and not only
for the females thus forced against their inclinations and prior engagements, but also
for the young men who have the cruel mortification to see their lovers forced from
their embraces, by paternal inflexibility.
Such cruel proceedings have produced many
a suicide : and brought many a loving couple
through complicated scenes of sorrow and
woe, to a premature death.

Those who are unacquainted with the
force of juvenile attachments, will laugh at
the supposition as chimerical and romantic ;
for,

> None know their grief but they who lov'd so well,
> They, only they can half their sorrows tell ;
> These, only these can pity, weep, and melt,
> Those cannot sympathize who never felt.

However superficial or imaginary it may
be in itself, I will not attempt to define.
This much I can confidently assert, as a
stubborn and melancholy fact, authenticated
by the experience of ages, that disappointed

love has slain its thousands of the human family ; and a great proportion of them, through the inflexibility and capriciousness of maternal impolicy, penurious solicitude, or family pride. How many cruel parents, with more than savage insensibility, have sacrificed their children's present and eternal happiness, before they would relinquish a particle of their sentimental pride and hereditary pretensions! Cruel parents! Surely the tyranny of a Manasseh, the haughtiness of a Nebuchadnezzar, or the voluptuousness of an Alexander, will be more tolerable in the day of judgment than the conduct of such parents.

I will take the liberty to close this chapter with a description of the ill fated love and tragical end of Palemon, abridged from Falconer's Shipwreck. The writer, no doubt, drew the incidents of his pathetic tale from real life, and it is more than probable, from his own experience, as he was a common sailor when he wrote it, and undoubtedly saw better days. The erudition, masterly style, and sterling merit displayed in his writings, demonstrate that he was a man of classical education, as well as extraordinary poetical talents, which would do honour to a Pope, or even a Milton, especially when we contrast the advantages of the one party for displaying their talents, with the disadvantages of the other.

Our author, whose name was William Falconer, Johnson, in his Lives of the Poets, informs us " was a native of Scotland, bred to the sea service, in which he spent the greatest part of his life in a very low situation. He displayed his poetical talents, at an early age, by the publication, at Edinburg, of " A Poem, sacred to the Memory of His Royal Highness, Frederick, Prince of Wales," 8vo. 1751. In the course of his sea life he appears to have really experienced the dangers so feelingly described in his poem, entitled " *The Shipwreck*," printed in 1762. The publication of this work drew him from the obscurity of his situation ; he was patronized by the Duke of York, to whom he addressed an ode, on his second departure from England as Rear Admiral, and soon after received the appointment of Purser to the Royal George. In 1769 he published a " Marine Dictionary," an acknowledged useful work, and soon afterwards embarked on board the Aurora to settle in the East Indies. In December, 1769, he arrived at the Cape of Good Hope, from whence he sailed soon after. These were the last tidings of the ship, which was never heard of afterwards.

It is generally supposed to have taken fire,
and that all the crew perished."

"Palemon's heart for beauteous Anna bled,
For her a secret flame his bosom fed.
Nor let the wretched slaves of folly scorn
This genuine passion, Nature's eldest born !
'Twas his with lasting anguish to complain,
While blooming Anna mourn'd the cause in vain.
"Graceful of form, by nature taught to please,
Of power to melt the female breast with ease ;
To her Palemon told his tender tale,
Soft as the voice of summer's evening gale.
O'erjoy'd, he saw her lovely eyes relent,
The blushing maiden smil'd with sweet consent.
Oft in the mazes of a neighb'ring grove,
Unheard, they breath'd alternate vows of love
By fond society their passion grew,
Like the young blossom fed with vernal dew.
In evil hour th' officious tongue of Fame
Betray'd the secret of their mutual flame.
With grief and anger struggling at his breast
Palemon's father heard the tale confest.
Long had he listen'd with suspicious ear,
And learnt, sagacious, this event to fear.
Too well, fair youth thy liberal heart he knew ;
A heart to nature's warm impressions true!
Full oft his wisdom strove with fruitless toil,
With avarice to pollute that generous soil
That soil, impregnated with nobler seed,
Refus'd the culture of so rank a weed.
Elate with wealth, in active commerce won,
And basking in the smile of Fortune's sun,
With scorn the parent ey'd the lowly shade,
That veil'd the beauties of this charming maid
Indignant he rebuk'd the enamour'd boy,
The flattering promise of his future joy !

He sooth'd and menac'd, anxious to reclaim
This hopeless passion or divert its aim :
Oft led the youth where circling joys delight
The ravish'd sense, or beauty charms the sight.
With all her powers enchanting music fail'd,
And pleasure's syren voice no more prevail'd.
The merchant, kindling then with proud disdain,
In look and voice assum'd a harsher strain,
In absence now his only hope remain'd ;
And such the stern decree his will ordain'd,
Deep anguish, while Palemon heard his doom,
Drew o'er his lovely face a saddening gloom.
In vain with bitter sorrow he repin'd,
No tender pity touch'd that sordid mind ;
To thee, brave Albert, was the charge consign'd.
The stately ship forsaken England's shore,
To regions far remote Palemon bore.
Incapable of change th' unhappy youth
Still lov'd fair Anna with eternal truth ;
From clime to clime an exile doom'd to roam,
His heart still panted for its secret home.
  " The moon had circled twice her wayward zone,
To him since young Arion first was known :
Who, wandering here through many a scene renown'd
In Alexandria's port the vessel found ;
Where, anxious to review his native shore,
He on the roaring wave embark'd once more
Oft by pale Cynthia's melancholy light,
With him Palemon kept the watch of night ;
In whose sad bosom many a sigh supprest,
Some painful secret of the soul confest.
Perhaps Arion soon the cause divin'd,
Tho' shunning still to probe a wounded mind,
He felt the chastity of silent woe,
Tho' glad the balm of comfort to bestow;
He, with Palemon, oft recounted o'er
The tales of hapless love in ancient lore,
Recall'd to memory by th' adjacent shore

The scene thus present, and its story known,
The lovel sigh'd for sorrows not his own.
Thus, tho' a recent date their friendship bore,
Soon the ripe metal ow'nd the quick'ning ore;
For in one tide their passions seem'd to roll,
By kindred age, and sympathy of soul.

" These o'er th' inferior naval train preside
The course determine, or the commerce guide:
O'er all the rest, an undistinguish'd crew!
Her wing of deepest shade oblivion drew.

" A sullen languor still the skies opprest
And held th' unwilling ship in strong arrest.
High in his chariot glow'd the lamp of day,
O'er da flaming with meridian ray.
Relax'd from toil the sailors range the shore,
Where famine, war, and storm are felt no more
The hour to social pleasure they resign,
And black remembrance drown in generous wine.
On deck, beneath the shading canvas spread
Rodmond a rueful tale of wonders read,
Of dragons roaring on the enchanted coast,
The hideous goblin and the yelling ghost—
But with Arion, from the sultry heat
Of noon, Palemon sought a cool retreat.
And lo! the shore with mournful prospects crown'd*
The rampart torn with many a fatal wound;
The ruin'd bulwark tottering o'er the strand;
Bewail the stroke of war's tremendous hand.
What scenes of woe this hapless isle o'erspread!
Where late thrice fifty thousand warriors bled.
Full twice twelve summers were yon towers assail'd,
Till barbarous Ottoman at last prevail'd;

---

* The intelligent reader will readily discover, that
these remarks allude to the ever memorable siege of
Candia, which was taken from the Venetians by the
Turks, in 1669; being then considered as impregnable,
and esteemed the most formidable fortress in the uni
verse.

While thundering mines the lovely plains o'erturn'd,
While heroes fell, and domes and temples burn'd.

" But now before them happier scenes arise !
Elysian vales salute their ravish'd eyes :
Olive and cedar form'd a grateful shade,
While light with gay romantic error stray'd.
The myrtles here with fond caresses twine ;
There, rich with nectar, melts the pregnant vine,
And, lo ! the stream, renown'd in classic song,
Sad Lethe, glides the silent vale along,
On mossy banks, beneath the citron grove,
The youthful wanderers found a wild alcove :
Soft o'er the fairy region langour stole,
And with sweet melancholy charm'd the soul.
Here first Palemon, while his pensive mind
For consolation on his friend reclin'd,
In pity's bleeding bosom pour'd the stream
Of love's soft anguish, and of grief supreme—
Too true thy words !—by sweet remembrance taught
My heart in secret bleeds with tender thought :
In vain it courts the solitary shade,
By every action, every look betray'd !—
The pride of generous woe disdains appeal
To hearts that unrelenting frosts congeal ;
Yet sure, if right Palemon can divine,
The sense of gentle pity dwells in thine.
Yes ! all his cares thy sympathy shall know,
And prove the kind companion of his woe.

" Albert thou know'st with skill and science grac'd,
In humble station tho' by fortune plac'd ;
Yet never seaman more serenely brave
Led Britain's conquering squadrons o'er the wave.
Where full in view Augusta's spires are seen,
With flowery lawns, and waving woods between,
A peaceful dwelling stands in modest pride,
Where Thames, slow winding, rolls his ample tide,
There live the hope and pleasure of his life,
A pious daughter, with a faithful wife.
For his return, with fond officious care,

Still every grateful object these prepare ;
Whatever can allure the smell or sight,
Or wake the drooping spirits to delight.
   "This blooming maid in virtue's path to guide,
Her anxious parents all their cares apply'd.
Her spotless soul, where soft compassion reign'd,
No vice untun'd, no sickening folly stain'd.
Not fairer grows the lily of the vale,
Whose bosom opens to the vernal gale :
Her eyes unconscious of their fatal charms,
Thrill'd every heart,with exquisite alarms :
Her face, in beauty's sweet attraction drest,
The smile of maiden innocence express'd ;
While health, that rises with the new-born day,
Breath'd o'er her cheek the softest blush of May
Still in her look complacence smil'd serene ;
She mov'd the charmer of the rural scene.
   "Twas at that season when the fields resume
Their loveliest hues, array'd in vernal bloom ;
Yon ship, rich freighted from the Italian shore,
To Thames' fair banks her costly tribute bore ;
While thus my father saw his ample hoard,
From this return, with recent treasures stor'd ;
Me, with affairs of commerce charg'd, he sent
To Albert's humble mansion ; soon I went,
Too soon, alas ! unconscious of th' event—
There, struck with sweet surprise and silent awe,
The gentle mistress of my hope I saw :
There wounded first by love's resistless arms,
My glowing bosom throbb'd with strange alarms.
My ever charming Anna ! who alone
Can all the frowns of cruel fate atone ;
Oh ! while all conscious memory holds her power,
Can I forget that sweetly painful hour,
When from those eyes, with lovely lightning fraught,
My fluttering spirits first the infection caught ;
When, as I gaz'd, my faltering tongue betray'd
The heart's quick tumults, or refus'd its aid ;

While the dim light my ravish'd eyes forsook,
And every limb unstrung with terror shook !
With all her powers dissenting reason strove
To tame at first the kindling flame of love ;
She strove in vain ! subdu'd by charms divine,
My soul a victim fell at beauty's shrine,
Oft from the din of bustling life I stray'd,
In happier scenes, to see my lovely maid.
Full oft, where Thames his wandering current leads,
We rov'd at evening hour thro' flowery meads.
There, while my heart's soft anguish I reveal'd,
To her with tender sighs my hope appeal'd.
While the sweet nymph my faithful tale believ'd,
Her snowy breast with secret tumult heav'd :
For, train'd in rural scenes from earliest youth,
Nature was hers, and innocence and truth.
She never knew the city damsel's art,
Whose frothy pertness charms the vacant heart !—
My suit prevail'd ; for love inform'd my tongue,
And on his votary's lips persuasion hung.
Her eyes with conscious sympathy withdrew,
And o'er her cheek the rosy current flew.
Thrice happy hours ! where with no dark allay,
Life's fairest sunshine gilds the vernal day !
For here the sigh that soft affection heaves,
From stings of sharper woe the soul relieves.
Elysian scenes, too happy long to last !
Too soon a storm the smiling dawn o'ercast !
Too soon some demon to my father bore
The tidings that his heart with anguish tore.—
My pride to kindle with dissuasive voice,
Awhile he labour'd to degrade my choice ;
Then, in the whirling wave of pleasure, sought
From its lov'd object to divert my thought.
With equal hope he might attempt to bind,
In chains of adamant, the lawless wind :
For love had aim'd the fatal shaft too sure ;
Hope fed the wound, and absence knew no cure.

With alienated look, each art he saw
Still baffled by superior Nature's law.
His anxious mind on various schemes revolv'd;
At last on cruel exile he resolv'd.
The rigorous doom was fix'ed! alas! how vain
To him of tender anguish to complain!
His soul, that never love's sweet influence felt,
By social sympathy could never melt;
With stern command to Albert's charge he gave,
To waft Palemon o'er the distant wave.

   " The ship was laden and prepar'd to sail,
And only waited now the leading gale.
'Twas ours, in that sad period, first to prove
The heart-felt torments of despairing love:
Th' impatient wish that never feels repose;
Desire that with perpetual current flows;
The fluctuating pangs of hope and fear;
Joy distant still, and sorrow ever near!
Thus, while the pangs of thought severer grew,
The western breezes inauspicious blew,
Hastening the moment of our last adieu.
The vessel parted on the falling tide;
Yet time one sacred hour to love supply'd.
The night was silent, and advancing fast,
The moon o'er Thames her silver mantle cast.
Impatient hope the midnight path explor'd,
And led me to the nymph my soul ador'd.
Soon her quick footsteps struck my list'ning ear;
She came confest! the lovely maid drew near!
But ah! what force of language can impart
Th' impetuous joy that glow'd in either heart!
O! ye, whose melting hearts are form'd to prove
The trembling ecstacies of genuine love!
When with delicious agony, the thought
Is to the verge of high delirium wrought;
Your secret sympathy alone can tell
What raptures then the throbbing bosom swell;
O'er all the nerves what tender tumults roll,
While love with sweet enchantment melts the soul!

"In transport lost, by trembling hope imprest,
The blushing virgin sunk upon my breast;
While her's congenial beat with fond alarms;
Dissolving softness! paradise of charms;
Flash'd from our eyes in warm transfusion flew
Our blending spirits, that each other drew!
O, bliss supreme! where virtue's self can melt
With joys that guilty pleasures never felt!
Form'd to refine the thought with chaste desire,
And kindle sweet affection's purest fire!
Ah! wherefore should my hopeless love, she cries,
While sorrow burst with interrupting sighs
For ever destin'd to lament in vain,
Such flattering fond ideas entertain?
My heart thro' scenes of fair illusion stray'd
To joys decreed for some superior maid.
'Tis mine to feel the sharpest stings of grief
Where never gentle hope affords relief.
Go then, dear youth! thy father's rage atone;
And let this tortur'd bosom beat alone!
The hovering anger yet thou may'st appease;
Go then, dear youth! nor tempt the faithless seas;
Find out some happier daughter of the town,
With fortune's fairer joys thy love to crown;
Where smiling o'er thee with indulgent ray,
Prosperity shall hail each new-born day.
Too well thou know'st good Albert's niggard fate,
Ill fitted to sustain thy father's hate:
Go then, I charge thee, by thy generous love,
That fatal to my father thus may prove!
On me alone let dark affliction fall!
Whose heart for thee will gladly suffer all.
Then haste thee hence, Palemon, ere too late,
Nor rashly hope to brave opposing fate!

"She ceas'd; while anguish in her angel face
O'er all her beauties show'd celestial grace,
Not Helen, in her bridal charms array'd,
Was half so lovely as this gentle maid.

O, soul of all my wishes! I reply'd,
Can that soft fabric stem affliction's tide!
Canst thou, fair emblem of exalted truth!
To sorrow doom the summer of thy youth;
And I, perfidious! all that sweetness see
Consign'd to lasting misery for me?
Sooner this moment may the eternal doom
Palemon in the silent earth entomb!
Attest thou moon, fair regent of the night!
Whose lustre sickens at this mournful sight;
By all the pangs divided lovers feel,
That sweet possession only knows to heal;
By all the horrors brooding o'er the deep;
Where fate and ruin sad dominion keep;
Tho' tyrant duty o'er me threat'ning stands,
And claims obedience to her stern commands;
Should fortune cruel or auspicious prove,
Her smile or frown shall never change my love!
My heart that now must every joy resign,
Incapable of change is only thine!—
O, cease to weep! this storm will yet decay,
And these sad clouds of sorrow melt away.
While through the rugged path of life we go,
All mortals taste the bitter draughts of woe,
The fam'd and great, decreed to equal pain,
Full oft in splendid wretchedness complain.
For this prosperity, with brighter ray,
In smiling contrast gilds our vital day.
Thou too, sweet maid! ere twice ten months are o'er }
Shalt hail Palemon to his native shore, }
Where never interest shall divide us more. }
   " Her struggling soul, o'erwhelm'd with tender grief
Now found an interval of short relief;
So melts the surface of the frozen stream;
Beneath the wintry sun's departing beam.
With warning haste the shades of night withdrew,
And gave the signal of a sad adieu.

As on my neck th' afflicted maiden hung,
A thousand racking doubts her spirits wrung.
She wept the terrors of the fearful wave,
Too oft, alas! the wandering lover's grave!
With soft persuasion I dispell'd her fear,
And from her check beguil'd the falling tear.
While dying fondness languish'd in her eyes,
She pour'd her soul to heaven in suppliant sighs—
Look down with pity, oh! ye pow'rs above,
Who hear the sad complaint of bleeding love!
Ye, who the secret laws of fate explore,
Alone can tell if he returns no more;
Or, if the hour of future joy remain,
Long wish'd atonement of long suffer'd pain!
Bid every guardian minister attend,
And from all ill the much lov'd youth defend!
—With grief o'erwhelm'd we parted twice in vain,
And urg'd by strong attraction met again.
At last, by cruel fortune torn apart,
While tender passion stream'd in either heart;
Our eyes transfix'd with agonizing look,
One sad farewell, one last embrace we took.
Forlorn of hope the lovely maid I left,
Pensive and pale, of every joy bereft.
She to her silent couch retir'd to weep,
While her sad swain embark'd upon the deep.

" His tale thus clos'd, from sympathy of grief,
Palemon's bosom felt a sweet relief.
The hapless bird, thus ravish'd from the skies,
Where all forlorn his lov'd companion flies,
In secret long bewails his cruel fate,
With fond remembrance of his winged mate:
Till grown familiar with a foreign train,
Composed at length, his sadly warbling strain
In sweet oblivion charms the sense of pain.

" Ye tender maids, in whose pathetic souls
Compassion's sacred stream impetuous rolls;
Whose warm affections exquisitely feel
The secret wound you tremble to reveal!

Ah! may no wanderer of the faithless main
Pour through your breast the soft delicious bane!
May never fatal tenderness approve
The fond effusions of their ardent love.
O! warn'd by friendship's counsel learn to shun
The fatal path where thousands are undone!

  "Now as the youths, returning o'er the plain
Approach'd the lonely margin of the main,
First, with attention rouz'd, Arion ey'd
The graceful lover, form'd in Nature's pride.
His frame the happiest symmetry display'd;
And locks of waving gold his neck array'd.
In every look the Paphian graces shine,
Soft-breathing o'er his cheek their bloom divine.
With lighten'd heart he smil'd serenely gay,
Like young Adonis or the son of May.
Not Cytherea from a fairer swain
Receiv'd her apple on the Trojan plain!

  " The sun's bright orb declining, all serene,
Now glanc'd obliquely o'er the woodland scene.
Creation smiles around, on every spray
The warbling birds exalt their evening lay.
Blithe skipping o'er yon' hill, the fleecy train
Join the deep chorus of the lowing plain:
The golden lime and orange there were seen,
On fragrant branches of perpetual green.
The crystal streams that velvet meadows lave,
To the green ocean roll with chiding wave.
The glassy ocean hush'd forgets to roar,
But trembling murmurs on the sandy shore:
And lo! his surface, lovely to behold,
Glows in the west, a sea of living gold!
While, all above, a thousand liveries gay
The skies with pomp ineffable array.
Arabian sweets perfume the happy plains:
Above, beneath, around inchantment reigns!
While yet the shades, on time's eternal scale,
With long vibration deepen o'er the vale;

While yet the songsters of the vocal grove
With dying numbers tune the soul to love ;
With joyful eyes th' attentive master sees
Th' auspicious omens of an eastern breeze.—
Now radiant Vesper leads the starry train,
And night slow draws her veil o'er land and main ;
Round the charg'd bowl the sailors form a ring,
By turns recount the wond'rous tale or sing ;
As love or battle, hardships of the main,
Or genial wine, awake their homely strain ;
Then some the watch of night alternate keep,
The rest lie buried in oblivious sleep.

   " Deep midnight now involves the liquid skies,
While infant breezes from the shore arise.
The waning moon, behind a watery shroud,
Pale glimmer'd o'er the long-protracted cloud.
A mighty ring around her silver throne,
With parting meteors cross'd portentous shone.
This in the troubled sky full oft prevails ;
Oft' deem'd a signal of tempestuous gales.—
While young Arion sleeps, before his sight
Tumultuous swim the visions of the night.
Now blooming Anna, with her happy swain,
Approach'd the sacred hymeneal fane :
Anon tremendous lightnings flash between,
And funeral pomp and weeping Loves are seen
Now with Palemon up a rocky steep,
Whose summit trembles o'er the roaring deep,
With painful step he climb'd : while far above
Sweet Anna charm'd them with the voice of love.
Then sudden from the slippery height they fell,
While dreadful yawn'd beneath the jaws of hell.
Amid this fearful trance, a thundering sound
He hears—and thrice the hollow decks rebound.
Upstarting from his couch, on deck he sprung ;
Thrice with shrill note the boatswain's whistle rung.
All hands unmoor! proclaims a boisterous cry :
All hands unmoor! the cavern'd rocks reply !

Rous'd from repose, aloft the sailors swarm,
And with their levers soon the windlass arm.*
The order given, up-springing with a bound,
They lodge the bars, and wheel their engine round :
At every turn the clanging pauls resound.
Uptorn reluctant from its oozy cave,
The ponderous anchor rises o'er the wave.
Along their slippery masts the yards ascend,
And high in air the canvas wings extend :
Redoubling cords the lofty canvas guide,
And thro' inextricable mazes glide.
The lunar rays with long reflection gleam,
To light the vessel o'er the silver stream :
Along the glassy plain serene she glides,
While azure radiance trembles on her sides.
From east to north the transient breezes play,
And in th' Egyptian quarter soon decay.
A calm ensues ; they dread th' adjacent shore ;
The boats with rowers arm'd are sent before :
With cordage fasten'd to the lofty prow,
Aloof to sea the stately ship they tow.†
The nervous crew their sweeping oars extend,
And pealing shouts the shore of Candia rend.
Success attends their skill ; the danger's o'er,
The port is doubled and beheld no more.

---

* The windlass is a sort of large roller, used to wind
in the cable, or heave up the anchor. It is turned
about vertically by a number of long bars or levers ; in
which operation it is prevented from recoiling, by the
pauls.

† Towing is the operation of drawing a ship forward,
by means of ropes, extended from her forepart, to one
or more of the boats rowing before her.

Now morn, her lamp pale-glimmering on the sight,
Scatter'd before her van reluctant Night.
She comes not in refulgent pomp array'd,
But sternly frowning, wrapt in sullen shade.
Above incumbent vapours, Ida's height,
Tremendous rock! emerges on the sight.
North-east the guardian isle of Standia lies,
And westward Freschin's woody capes arise.
  "The natives, while the ship departs the land,
Ashore with admiration gazing stand.
Majestically slow, before the breeze,
In silent pomp she marches on the seas.
Her milk-white bottom cast a softer gleam,
While trembling thro' the green translucent stream
High o'er the poop, the flattering winds unfurl'd
Th' imperial flag that rules the wat'ry world.
Deep-blushing armors all the tops invest,
And warlike trophies either quarter dress'd :
Then tower'd the masts; the canvass swell'd on high :
And waving streamers floated in the sky,
Thus the rich vessel moves in trim array,
Like some fair virgin on her bridal day.
Thus, like a swan she cleaves the wat'ry plain,
The pride and wonder of the Ægean main!
  " Now, while on high the freshening gale she feels,
The ship beneath her lofty pressure reels.
Th auxiliar sails that court a gentle breeze,
From their high stations sink by slow degrees.
The watchful ruler of the helm no more,
With fix'd attention, eyes the adjacent shore ;
But by the oracle of truth below,
The wond'rous magnet, guides the wayward prow
The wind, that still th'impressive canvas swell'd,
Swift and more swift the yielding bark impell'd.
Four hours the sun his high meridian throne
Had left, and o'er atlantic regions shone :
Still blacker clouds, that all the skies invade,
Draw o'er his sullied orb a dismal shade.

A squall deep low'ring blots the southern sky,
Before whose boisterous breath the waters fly.
Its weight the topsails can no more sustain.
Reef topsails, reef, the boatswain calls again !
  " Now, borne impetuous o'er the boiling deeps,
Her course to Attic shores the vessel keeps:
The pilots, as the waves behind her swell,
Still with the wheeling stern their force repel.
High o'er the poop th' audacious seas aspire,
Uproll'd in hills of fluctuating fire.
As some fell conqueror, frantic with success,
Sheds o'er the nations ruin and distress ;
So while the wat'ry wilderness he roams,
Incens'd to sevenfold rage the Tempest foams;
And ò'er the trembling pines, above, below,
Shrill thro' the cordage howls, with notes of woe.
Now thunders, wafted from the burning zone,
Growl from afar, a deaf and hollow groan !
The ship's, high battlements, to either side
For ever rocking, drink the briny tide :
It seem'd, the wrathful angel of the wind
Had all the horrors of the skies combin'd .
And here, to one ill-fated ship oppos'd,
At once the dreadful magazine disclos'd.
But lo ! at last, from tenfold darkness borne,
Forth issues o'er the wave the weeping morn,
Hail sacred vision ! who on orient wing,
The cheering dawn of light propitious bring !
All nature smiling hail'd the vivid ray,
That gave her beauties to returning day :
All but our ship that, groaning on the tide,
No kind relief, no gleam of hope descry'd.
For now, in front, her trembling inmates see
The hills of Greese, emerging on the lee.
So the lost lover views that fatal morn,
On which forever from his bosom torn,
The nymph ador'd resigns her blooming charms,
To bless with love some happier rival's arms.

So to Eliza dawn'd that cruel day,
That tore Æneas from her arms away ;
That saw him parting, never to return,
Herself in fœneral flames decreed to burn :
O yet in clouds, thou genial source of light,
Conceal thy radiant glories from our sight !
Go, with thy smile adorn the happy plain,
And gild the scenes where health and pleasure reign ;
But let not here, in scorn thy wanton beam
Insult the dreadful grandeur of my theme !

   " But now the Athenian mountains they descry,
And o'er the surge Colonna frowns on high ;
Beside the cape's projecting verge are plac'd
A range of columns, long by time defac'd ;
First planted by devotion to sustain,
In elder times, Tritonia's sacred fane.
Foams the wild beach below with mad'ning rage,
Where waves and rocks a dreadful combat wage.

   " With mournful look the seamen ey'd the strand,
Where death's inexorable jaws expand ;
Now, on the trembling shrouds, before, behind,
In mute suspense they mount into the wind.—
The genius of the deep on rapid wing,
The black eventful moment seem'd to bring.
The steersmen now received their last command
To wheel the vessel sidelong to the strand.
Twelve sailors on the foremast who depend,
High on the platform of the top ascend ;
Fatal retreat ! for while the plunging prow
Immerges headlong in the waves below,
Down prest by wat'ry weight the bowsprit bends,
And from above the stem deep-crashing rends.
Beneath her beak the floating ruins lie ;
The foremast totters, unsustain'd on high :
And now the ship, fore-lifted by the sea,
Hurls the tall fabrick backward o'er her lee ;
While in the general wreck, the faithful stay
Drags the main-topmast from its post away.

Hung from the mast the seamen strive in vain
Thro' hostile floods their vessel to regain.
The waves they buffet, till bereft of strength,
O'erpower'd they yield to cruel fate at length,
The hostile waters close around their head ;
They sink for ever, number'd with the dead !
Those who remain their fearful doom await,
Nor longer mourn their lost companions' fate.
The heart that bleeds with sorrows all its own,
Forgets the pangs of friendship to bemoan.—

" And now lash'd on by destiny severe,
With horror fraught, the dreadful scene drew near
The ship hangs hovering on the verge of death,
Hell yawns, rocks rise, and breakers roar beneath.
In vain, alas ! the sacred shades of yore
Would arm the mind with philosophic lore ;
In vain they'd teach us, at the latest breath,
To smile serene amid the pangs of death.
Ev'n Zeno's self, and Epictetus old,
This fell abyss had shudder'd to behold.
Had Socrates, for godlike virtue fam'd,
And wisest of the sons of of men proclaim'd,
Beheld this scene of frenzy and distress,
His soul had trembled to its last recess !—
O yet confirm my heart, ye powers above,
This last tremendous shock of fate to prove,
The tottering frame of reason yet sustain !
Nor let this total ruin whirl my brain !

In vain the cords and axes were prepar'd,
For now th' audacious seas insult the yard ;
High o'er the ship they throw a horrid shade,
And o'er her burst in terrible cascade.
Uplifted on the surge, to heaven she flies,
Her shatter'd top half buried in the skies ;
Then headlong plunging thunders on the ground,
Earth groans ! air trembles ! and the deeps resound.
Her giant bulk the dread concussion feels,
And quivering with the wound, in torment reels.

So reels convuls'd with agonizing throes,
The bleeding bull beneath the murd'rer's blow.
Again she plunges! hark! a second shock
Tears her strong bottom on the marble rock!
Down on the vale of death, with dismal cries,
The fated victims shuddering roll their eyes,
In wild despair; while yet another stroke,
With deep convulsion, rends the solid oak :
Till like the mine, in whose infernal cell
The lurking demons of destruction dwell,
At length asunder torn, her frame divides,
And crashing spreads in ruin o'er the tides.

 " O! where it mine with tuneful Maro's art,
To wake to sympathy the feeling heart ;
Like him the smooth and mournful verse to dress
In all the pomp of exquisite distress!
Then too severely taught by cruel fate
To share in all the perils I relate,
Then might I, with unrival'd strains deplore
Th' impervious horrors of a leeward shore.

 " As o'er the surge the stooping mainmast hung,
Still on the rigging thirty seamen clung ;
Some, struggling, on a broken crag were cast,
And there by oozy tangles grappled fast ;
Awhile they bore th' o'erwhelming billows rage,
Unequal combat with their fate to wage ;
Till all benumb'd and feeble they forego
Their slippery hold, and sink to shades below.
Some from the main-yard-arm impetuous thrown
On marble ridges, die without a groan.
Three with Palemon on their skill depend,
And from the wreck on oars and rafts descend.
Now on the mountain wave on high they ride,
Then downward plunge beneath th' involving tide ;
Till one who seems in agony to strive,
The whirling breakers heave on shore alive ;

The rest a speedier end of anguish knew,
And prest the stony beach, a lifeless crew!
  " Next, O, unhappy chief! th' eternal doom
Of Heaven decreed thee to the briny tomb!
What scenes of misery torment thy view!
What painful struggles of thy dying crew!
Thy perish'd hopes all buried in the flood,
O'erspread with corses! red with human blood!
So pierc'd with anguish hoary Priam gaz'd,
When Troy's imperial domes in ruin blaz'd;
While he, severest sorrows doom'd to feel,
Expir'd beneath the victor's murdering steel.
Thus with his helpless partners to the last.
Sad refuge! Albert hugs the floating mast;
His soul could yet sustain this mortal blow,
But droops, alas! beneath superior woe;
For now soft natures sympathetic chain
Tugs at his yearning heart with powerful strain;
His faithful wife for ever doom'd to mourn
For him, alas! who never shall return;
To black adversity's approach expos'd,
With want and hardships unforeseen enclos'd:
His lovely daughter left without a friend,
Her innocence to succour and defend:
By youth and indigence set forth a prey
To lawless guilt, that flatters to betray—
While these reflections rack his feeling mind,
Rodmond, who hung beside, his grasp resign'd;
And, as the tumbling waters o'er him roll'd,
His outstretch'd arms the master's legs enfold—
Sad Albert feels the dissolution near,
And strives in vain his fetter'd limbs to clear;
For death bids every clinching joint adhere.
All faint to heaven he throws his dying eyes,
And, " O, protect my wife and child!" he cries:
The gushing streams roll back th' unfinish'd sound
He gasps! he dies! and tumbles to the ground!
  " Five only left of all the perish'd throng,
Yet ride the pine which shoreward drives along;

With these Arion still his hold secures,
And all the assaults of hostile waves endures
O'er the dire prospect as for life he strives,
He looks if poor Palemon yet survives,
Ah ! wherefore, trusting to unequal art,
Didst thou, incautious ! from the wreck depart
Alas ! these rocks all human skill defy,
Who strikes them once beyond relief must die
And now sore wounded thou perhaps art tost
On these, or in some oozy cavern lost ;
Thus thought Arion, anxious gazing round,
In vain, his eyes no more Palemon found.
The Dæmons of destruction hover nigh,
And thick their mortal shafts commission'd fly
And now a breaking surge, with forceful sway,
Two next Arion furious tears away.
Hurl'd on the crags, behold, they grasp ! they bleed
And groaning, cling upon th' elusive weed !
Another billow bursts in boundless roar !
Arion sinks, and memory views no more !

  " Ah ! total night and horror here preside !
My stun'd ear tingles to the whizzing tide !
It is the funeral knell ! and gliding near,
Methinks the phantoms of the dead appear !

  " But, lo, emerging from the watery grave,
Again they float incumbent on the wave !
Again the dismal prospect opens round,
The wreck, the shores, the dying, and the drown'd
And see ! enfeebled by repeated shocks,
These two who scramble on th' adjacent rocks,
Their faithless hold no longer can retain,
They sink o'erwhelm'd, and never rise again !

  " Two with Arion yet the mast upbore
That now above the ridges reach'd the shore :
Still trembling to descend they downward gaze
With horror pale, and torpid with amaze :
The floods recoil ! the ground appears below !
And life's faint embers now rekindling glow ;

Awhile they wait th' exhausted waves retreat,
Then climb slow up the beach with hands and feet
O, heaven! deliver'd by whose sovereign hand.
Still on the brink of hell they shuddering stand,
Receive the languid incense they bestow,
That damp with death appears not yet to glow
To thee each soul the warm oblation pays,
With trembling ardour of unequal praise ;
In every heart dismay with wonder strives,
And hope the sicken'd spark of life revives ;
Her magic powers their exil'd health restore,
Till horror and despair are felt no more.

" A troop of Grecians who inhabit nigh,
And oft these perils of the deep descry,
Rous'd by the blust'ring tempest of the night,
Anxious had climb'd Colonna's neighbouring height
When gazing downward on th' adjacent flood,
Full to their view the scene of ruin stood.
The surf with mangled bodies strew'd around,
And those yet breathing on the sea-wash'd ground !
Tho' lost to science and the nobler arts,
Yet nature's lore inform'd their feeling hearts ;
Straight down the vale with hastening steps they hied,
Th' unhappy sufferers to assist and guide.

" Mean while, those three escap'd, beneath explore
The first advent'rous youth who reach'd the shore :
Panting, with eyes averted from the day,
Prone, helpless, on the tangly beach he lay—
It is Palemon !—Oh ! what tumults roll
With hope and terror in Arion's soul !
If yet unhurt he lives again to view
His friend and this sole remnant of our crew!
With us to travel through this foreign zone,
And share the future good or ill unknown,
Arion thus ; but, ah ! sad doom of fate,
That bleeding memory sorrows to relate ;
While yet afloat on some resisting rock,
His ribs were dash'd, and fractur'd with the shock

Heart piercing sight! those cheeks so late array'd
In beauty's bloom, are pale with mortal shade!
Distilling blood his lovely breast o'erspread;
And clogg'd the golden tresses of his head!
Nor yet the lungs by this pernicious stroke
Were wounded, or the vocal organs broke.
Down from his neck, with blazing gems array'd
Thy image, lovely Anna; hung portray'd;
Th' unconscious figure smiling all serene,
Suspended in a golden chain was seen.
Hadst thou, soft maiden! in this hour of woe,
Beheld him writhing from the deadly blow,
What force of art, what language could express
Thine agony, thine exquisite distress?
But thou, alas! art doom'd to weep in vain
For him thine eyes shall never see again!
With dumb amazement pale, Arion gaz'd,
And cautiously the wounded youth uprais'd;
Palemon then, with cruel pangs opprest,
In faltering accents thus his friend address'd:

" O! rescu'd from destruction late so nigh,
Beneath whose fatal influence doom'd I lie;
Are we then exil'd to this last retreat
Of life unhappy! thus decree'd to meet?
Ah! how unlike what yester-morn enjoy'd,
Enchanting hopes, for ever now destroy'd!
For wounded far beyond all healing power,
Palemon dies, and this his final hour;
By those fell brakers, where in vain I strove,
At once cut off from fortune life and love!
Far other scenes must soon present my sight,
That lie deep buried yet in tenfold night.
Ah! wretched father of a wretched son,
Whom thy paternal prudence has undone!
How will remembrance of this blinded care
Bend down thy head with anguish and despair!
Such dire effects from avarice arise,
That, deaf to nature's voice, and vainly wise,

With force severe endeavours to control
The noblest passions that inspire the soul.
But, O, thou sacred Power ! whose law connects
Th' eternal chain of causes and effects,
Let not thy chastening ministers of rage
Afflict with sharp remorse his feeble age !
And you, Arion ! who with these the last
Of all our crew survive the shipwreck past—
Ah, cease to mourn ! those friendly tears restrain,
Nor give my dying moments keener pain !
Since Heaven may soon thy wandering steps restore,
When parted hence, to England's distant shore ;
Shouldst thou the unwilling messenger of fate,
To him the tragic story first relate,
Oh ! friendship's generous ardour then suppress,
Nor hint the fatal cause of my distress ;
Nor let each horrid incident sustain
The lengthen'd tale to aggravate his pain.
Ah ! then remember well my last request,
For her who reigns forever in my breast ;
Yet let him prove a father and a friend,
The helpless maid to succour and defend.
Say, I this suit implor'd with parting breath,
So Heaven befriend him at his hour of death !
But, Oh ! to lovely Anna shouldst thou tell
What dire untimely end thy friend befel,
Draw o'er the dismal scene soft pity's veil,
And lightly touch the lamentable tale ;
Say, that my love, inviolably true,
No change, no diminution ever knew ;
Lo ! her bright image pendent on my neck,
Is all Palemon rescu'd from the wreck ;
Take it and say, when panting in the wave
I struggled, life and this alone to save !
   " My soul that fluttering hastens to be free,
Would yet a train of thoughts impart to thee,
But strives in vain !—the chilling ice of death
Congeals my blood, and choaks the stream of death

Resign'd she quits her comfortless abode
To course that long, unknown, eternal road.—
O, sacred Source of ever living light!
Conduct the weary wanderer in her flight!
Direct her onward to that peaceful shore,
Where peril, pain, and death are felt no more

" When thou some tale of hapless love shall hear,
That steals from pity's eye the melting tear,
Of two chaste hearts by mutual passion join'd,
To absence, sorrow, and despair consign'd,
Oh! then to swell the tides of social woe,
That heal the afflicted bosom they o'erflow.
While memory dictates, this sad shipwreck tell,
And what distress thy wretched friend befell!
Then while in streams of soft compassion crown'd,
The swains lament, and maidens weep around:
While lisping children, touch'd with infant fear,
With wonder gaze, and drop the unconscious tear:
Oh! then this moral bid their souls retain,
" All thoughts of happiness on earth are vain.*"

" The last faint accents trembled on his tongue,
That now inactive to the palate clung;
His bosom heaves a mortal groan—he dies!
And shades eternal sink upon his eyes!

" As thus defac'd in death Palemon lay,
Arion gaz'd upon the lifeless clay;
Transfix'd he stood, with awful terror fill'd,
While down his cheek the silent drops distill'd.

" Oh, ill-star'd vot'ry of unspotted truth!
Untimely perish'd in the bloom of youth,
Should e'er thy friend arrive in Albion's land,
He will obey, tho' painful thy demand:

---

* ————sed scilicet ultima semper
Expectanda dies homini; " *dicique beatus*
Ante obitum nemo supremaque funera debet."
Ovid. Metam. lib. 3.

His tongue the dreadful story shall display,
And all the horrors of this dismal day !
Disastrous day ! what ruin hast thou bred !
What anguish to the living and the dead !
How hast thou left the widow all forlorn,
And ever doom'd the orphan child to mourn;
Through life's sad journey hopeless to complain !
Can sacred justice these events ordain?
But, O, my soul ! avoid that wond'rous maze
Where reason, lost in endless error, strays !
As through this thorny vale of life we run,
Great cause of all effects, *Thy will be done !*

" Now had the Grecians on the beach arriv'd,
To aid the helpless few who yet surviv'd :
While passing they behold the waves o'erspread
With shatter'd rafts and corses of the dead ;
Three still alive, benumb'd and faint they find,
In mournful silence on a rock reclin'd :
The generous natives, mov'd with social pain,
The feeble strangers in their arms sustain ;
With pitying sighs their hapless lot deplore,
And lead them trembling from the fatal shore."

Y

CHAPTER VI.

An Address to Young Women.

IMPRESSED with tenfold solicitude for your welfare, deeply sensible of your great importance and respectability in society, and convinced that on your intellectual improvement the prosperity, nay, the very existence of society depends; seeing the hosts of dangers which will attend you in your journey through life, and being assured that unless you take prudence for your guide you will undoubtedly be enveloped in the vortex of vanity and sensuality; which will infallibly imbitter your future days, and cause you to make shipwreck at last. I say, being cogently impressed with these sentiments, as authentic as they are important, I take the liberty, with the most respectful considerations and the purest intentions, to suggest a few thoughts for your serious consideration, which, like beacons to the mariner, may point out the dangerous rocks and shoals that are profusely interspersed through the devious paths of folly. I hope you will lay aside, for a little time, the novel and the romance, and read before you judge of the merits or demerits of my arguments. You must not suppose from my animadversions, that I cherish an antipathy to the sex. No man can be a more sincere admirer of them than myself: while virtuous I admire and venerate them; but when vicious I pity them.

> " The heedless fair, who stoops to guilty joys,
> A man may pity—but he must despise."

You will, perhape, glance indifferently and superficially over the subsequent strictures, as if they were not intimately connected with your future prosperity. The volatile fair one, while under the parental roof, seldom forms an estimate, or even anticipates the losses by which her paternal fortune will be assailed; the seduction with which her honour will be environed; the pestilential vapours proceeding from the mouth of calumny and defamation, with which her sacred character will be attacked by *coup-de-main*, or the innovations of popular degeneracy, and vile and vulgar fashion, which will lay siege, not only to property, honour, and character, but also the more important interest of that immortal spark of heavenly flame, the soul; and will, no doubt, without the utmost caution and discretion, carry all by storm, without suffering the besieged party to make even an honourable capitulation. For the potency of custom, and (I had almost said) the omnipotence of fashion, precludes resistance, and guarantees success to the innovators of female delicacy.

The invincible solicitude I impressively feel or the social and celestial happiness of my fair readers, and that they may escape the moral mischief which mental incontinency, and fashionable obscenity necessarily engender, bears a striking similarity to the parental ardour which I anticipate, when, with my mind's eye, I peep into futurity, and endeavour to recognize the fate of my two darling boys, who are the sole comfort of my declining years, the solace of my sorrows, and the promoters of my earthly joy. To express the tender solicitude I feel for their future prosperity and eternal felicity, would exceed human conception ; when I, with rapture, gaze upon their smiling countenances, the agonizing thought darts spontaneously into my wounded mind, that, perhaps, these smiling, unconscious boys, when I am deposited in my solitary grave, and mouldering to my native dust, will unhappily become the destroyers of female virtue;

the murderers of the human kind, and the ministers of woe ; as perhaps, they will inherit, by hereditary succession, all the native depravity, without a particle of the sentimental philanthropy of their father.

While thus in thought I view their future woe,
And from their eyes behold their sorrows flow;
When the unthinking cherubs joyful spring,
Climb on my knees, or to my bosom cling,
Or stretch their infant arms with fond desire,
And prattling call their melancholy sire,
While round my neck their loving arms they throw, ⎫
And kiss my cheeks where tears unbidden flow, ⎬
Unconscious of my grief—their future woe. ⎭
Their dear caresses meet a sad return,
For while they smile their joyless parents mourn
While imag'd to my boding thought appears,
The many woes that wait their future years.

Gladly would I accompany them through all the intricate windings and vicissitudes peculiar to their mortal state. With what ineffable delight would I ward off the blows directed by the unwearied enemy of man, or the machinations of his mortal auxiliaries! But this is impossible. All I can give is my benedictions, flowing from a heart bursting with anxiety ; and sending up ejaculations to the Eternal, for their prosperity and preservation.

But, to return to my fair readers. The object of your pursuits, on commencing actors on the stage of life, will, no doubt, be happiness. This we as naturally pursue as we do food when hungry, drink when dry, rest when fatigued, and consolation when transfixed with sorrow. But, alas! the reason why so many millions of Adam's descendants miss the happiness they by native instinct desire; and, in its place, nurture the most formidable evils, which produce their present infelicity and eternal misery; is, first they miss the right road to happiness; secondly, they want precaution, and rush too precipitately into the busy scenes of the fashionable world. As moral agents, as intelligent, accountable beings, the Eternal enjoins, as our reasonable service, that we look to him for direction; and serve him with affection; not only in our pursuits, but even by our intentions previous to our commencing these pursuits; "*for them that honour me* (says the prophet, personating the Almighty) *I will honour, and they that despise me shall be lightly esteemed;*" and how can we despise God more than entering upon the all-important business, on the event of which our future destiny hangs, not only in this world, but that which is to come, without ever praying for his benediction, or soliciting his advice. The admonition given by David to his son, on his entering the theatre of life, is

full of meaning, and should be perused by
every young person, with the most filial solicitude, " *And thou, Solomon my son, know
thou the God of thy father, and serve him
with a perfect heart, and with a willing
mind: for the Lord searcheth all hearts, and
understandeth all the imaginations of the
thoughts: if thou seek him, he will be found
of thee; but if thou forsake him, he will cast
thee off for ever.*" To precipitate into
the busy scenes of life, unthoughtful and regardless of the event, (which is too often the
case with young people), is not only irre-
ligious, but also irrational.

The animal creation, by natural instinct,
pursues the path by which their natures
will be gratified, which I had an opportunity of
ascertaining. One day, as I was taking a solitary walk on the margin of a mighty forest, near the river Amazon, in South America, surveying the rural, wild, and romantic beauties thereof, I saw an apperture
in the sand, where a tiger had been previously digging for a nest of turtle's eggs ;
on perceiving it I turned up the sand, took
up an egg, and opened it, when a small
turtle, about the size of a Spanish dollar,
made its appearance. I placed it gently on
the sandy beach, when it instantly made towards the sea, which was some yards off,

with great alacrity, and precipitated into its native element with apparent exultation.

In this manner natural instinct teaches the irrational creation to pursue that unerring path which the wisdom of Providence has pointed out. They all answer the law of their natures; and, consequently, the will of their munificent Creator: but we, surely, must conclude, that the laws by which the human and the animal creation are governed, must be essentially different. I do not wish by any means to enter into a metaphysical disquisition, or scientific definition, of the dissimilarity between the human and brutal creation, as that would be deviating from my plan; which is, to introduce my propositions in the most obvious, familiar, and friendly manner; regardless of censure or praise. But at the same time, it will be necessary, in order to elucidate the subject, and point out the road which leads to happiness, to investigate the character of man, analyze his capability for participating celestial, as well as terrestrial happiness. His mortal and immortal powers should also be developed, in order to ascertain his capacity for enjoyment; by which the unreasonableness and irrationality of such epicures as seek, in the interdicted revels of sensuality, unsullied delight, will be made manifest. For instance, the enjoyment of the brutal creation is exclusively confined to sense : but with the human, the pleasures of sense are the most diminutive and superficial parts of their feelings : their composition consists partly of matter, and partly of spirit ; the preponderating influence and superiority is unquestionably confined to the latter. The first is corruptible ; the latter incorruptible. The combination is truly a mysterious phenomenon of animal and perishable matter, connected with intellectual and moral powers. I would also ask, was not the circumstance of the little turtle, taking a direct course down to the sea, a phenomenon, unaccountable on just philosophical principles. We should not, therefore, with materialists, doubt the unity of flesh and spirit, because we cannot ascertain the utility thereof by speculative reasoning, and philosophical hypothesis. It, therefore, plainly follows, that human happiness does not consist exclusively in the pleasure of sense.

As we are partly animal, and partly spiritual beings, we uniformly require a portion of natural and preternatural enjoyments. Thus, without nutriment, the body becomes feeble and dies ; and without spiritual food the soul becomes languid : the intellectual principle torpid ; and piety and virtue, by degrees, expire.

Is not the soul of more importance than the body? The one is the same as the shell of a nut, and the other as the kernel. Are not the enjoyments of the one, admitting they were without interruption, (which experience proves not to be a fact,) sensual, transitory, and sordid, while those of the other are superlative, transcendent, and durable? without any manner of doubt : consequently, if our premises are correct, it is unreasonable to spend all our golden moments, in pursuing, with avidity, sublunary and superficial delights, while we forego the pursuit of intellectual and celestial gratification. It is a melancholy fact, authenticated by woeful experience, that the children of men too often attend entirely to the solicitations of wayward appetite, which tends to destroy their intellectual powers.

The experience and misfortunes of mankind, as exhibited in profane as well as sacred history, proves that sensual gratifications, though enjoyed in their greatest plenitude, and, with the most profuse abundance, cannot yield a moment's uninterrupted happiness.

The epicure who strives his taste to please,
May feel the brute's delight, but not his ease.

because the brute enjoys the gratification which the epicure so much prizes without any future forebodings, or present upbraidings of conscience ; and, consequently, with the most pleasurable feelings. But this is far from being the case with the epicure. We will wave mentioning the calls of his conscience, and the forebodings of eternity, and only hint the agonizing reflection that often recurs to his mind, while eating his animal food ; to wit, that after a few more rising and setting suns, his own body, which he takes so much pains to accommodate, will, in its turn, become the prey of putrefaction and greedy worms.

I appeal not only to the epicure for the confirmation of my arguments, but to the debauchee, who eagerly dissipated his patrimonial inheritance, and conjugal felicity ; to the victim of sensuality, who sacrificed his health ; to the martyr of sordid avarice, who starved himself to death ; to the votary of fashion who perished herself to death ; to the slave of ambition and pride who sacrificed his life to gratify his vanity, and with all these characters, I might appeal to an Alexander, a Nebuchadnezzar, a Xerxes, a Nero, a Cataline, a Cleopatra, who would, methinks, were it possible, arise from their graves to consolidate my arguments ; but I

may save myself the trouble, as their histories will speak for them. Even Ovid tells
us,

"All thoughts of happiness on earth are vain."

I humbly hope the reader will excuse my
enlarging so much on this part of the subject ; my reasons are, first, I conceive that by
this means alone, I can inform my juvenile
reader's mind, and reform her heart; by reasoning the case with her, in her own florid
language, and upon her own desultory
ground, not altogether by theological, but
reasonable and perspicuous references. If
I saw a man going in a road which led directly to a precipice, down which, if he fell,
he would be dashed to pieces : if he really
thought he was pursuing the road to happiness, should it not be my first and principal
object to endeavour to convince that man
(in the style, and with the language most familiar and agreeable to him) that the road
he was in led to inevitable ruin, and not to
real happiness ?—certainly it should. If I
succeeded, by the most judicious and con-
clusive arguments, to convince him that he
was treading the interdicted road that led to
present and future misery ; and not only convinced his understanding, but also exhibited
to the indiscriminate inspection of his mind's

eye the fatal precipice, the banks of which seemed to be carpetted with flowers, interspersed with the vernal products of spring and the blushing fruits of autumn, and éven the ambrosial blossoms of paradise ; but alas ! because I was an ignoramus, not a philosopher ; a savage, not a sage ; a peasant, not a potentate ; a layman, not a reverend man ; he would not be influenced by my arguments, or led from the fatal road by my admonitions, but continued to pursue it till he was hurled down the precipice with the velocity of lightning, or like the tremendous rock that overhangs the ocean, being invaded by the impetuous torrent, is rent from its hold, and instantly whirls down, thundering, crashing, and tumbling into the foaming, swelling ocean, and sinks to the bottom.

I make this remark, as I fear some of my fellow travellers to the tomb will not attend to the force of my arguments, because they are not introduced under the patronage of some honourable or right reverend fellow worm ; though it seems almost impossible that any rational being can be so far sunk in the sink of Satanic pride and gigantic vanity, as to merit this animadversion. Yet it is certain, that too much deference is paid, and adulation offered at the shrine of pedantry; as well as unbounded plaudits, fulsome panegyric, and vociferous huzzas bestowed, not only on the political, but also the poetical murderers of the human family.

But to return to the subject of our investigation. We allow, that the great Creator, who delights to make all his intelligent and animate creatures happy, as far as their diversified natures and capacities will admit, wills, that the pleasures of sense should be a part, though a very small part indeed, of the enjoyments of his rational creatures; and, as he well knew that the too profuse participation of earthly pleasures, and the gratification of sense when carried to an extreme, had a direct tendency, not only to subvert his sacred laws of order and concord, but also was supremely prejudicial to the individuals themselves; he, therefore, in his infinite wisdom and goodness, fixed a barrier, to preclude the introduction of discord and dissipation amongst his creatures: the boundaries when fixed had their counterpart also organized or annexed, which was, that the man who passed the limits and transgressed the Eternal mandate, should in so doing, secure misery to himself, and relinquish trsnquillity and felicity. Here I would particularly observe, that no good thing that the earth does, or indeed can produce, is forbidden man to enjoy in moderation. It is the abuse, and not the use of the good things of life that are prohibited ; and why ? I answer, because God, who is particularly great in goodness and good in greatness, in this respect, knows, and every intelligent person may know the same, that abundance of any earthly substance only tends to cloy, captivate, and infelicitate the possessor, and destroy his relish for more substantial and permanent delight ; even nature herself corroborates and consolidates the inquisitions and requisitions of Heaven. She dictates in reason's ear, that disgust, langour, and infelicity, are the offspring of intemperance : that one hour spent in paternal and conjugal enjoyments, outweighs years spent in revelling and debauchery that one meal of wholesome and nutriment-al food, participated with content and a thankful heart, counterpoises all the luxurious dainties of the voluptuous and dissipated.

I feel more solicitude for the welfare of my fair readers, as I am convinced that the preponderating bias of the unexperienced mind, will be for sallying forth into the very road which I endeavour to invalidate, when they are delivered from the manacles of maternal restraint, if they have not begun to travel that deleterious road already. How

seldom do they consider the astonishing ingenuity displayed in the formation of their
mortal bodies and immortal minds : and that
they are " *fearfully and wonderfully made.*"
The delicacy and intricate windings of the
arteries and sinews, the regularity with
which every part of this astonishing system
performs its function, are truly admirable.
The wisdom manifested in the formation of
the most diminutive quadruped, or reptile,
and even the least insect that breaths the
vital air, is sufficient to excite the reverential astonishment and humble adoration of a
savage. But, alas! how few, while they
admire their own formation, reflect on the
delicacy as well as the ingenuity of it. How
easily destroyed by precipitating into the
abyss of sensuality and intemperate gratification. And, on the other hand, what superlative delight, and transcendent pleasure
it is capable of enjoying, by being obedient
to the requisitions of the Creator. I had almost said, that a faithful and grateful soul is
capable of anticipating the ecstacies of angels, and hearing the empyrean symphony.
This much I will positively assert, that even
in this world, the real good man, who main-
tains his integrity in the midst of accumulated difficulty and complicated temptations,
though mighty sorrows thicken round him,

and clouds and darkness rest upon his prospects ; every thing conspiring to discourage
him from the practice of virtue, and to encourage him in the practice of vice ; not only
his external, but his internal enemies, his
native depravity and hereditary corruptions,
all combining to entice him from the paths
of rectitude, in addition to which the iron
hand of despotism, with consequent poverty
and chilling disease, assail him ; thus, al-
though every thing, celestial and terrestrial,
seem to combine against him ; yet, notwithstanding all these discouragements, his integrity is untarnished; his faith is unadulterated, and the love he feels for his Creator
unsullied: I say, such a character brings more
glory to God than a legion of angels. But
the philosophical unbeliever may ask, what
are angels ? I answer, created intelligencers
who are in their primeval state of paradi-
siacal purity ; their faith lost in sight ; their
hope in full fruition. What are men ? they
are also created beings, placed in a state
of probation and trial, short indeed, and
transitory, prior to their introduction into
the company of superior beings. But the
question is, how are these divine enjoyments to be attained ? I answer, merely by
asking for them. " *Ask,*" says the dear
Redeemer, " *and it shall be given unto you ;*
z 2

seek and ye shall find; knock, and it shall be opened unto you." Thus, while others are sacrificing their lives, fortunes, and tranquillity in the pursuit of imaginary happiness, you may find real happiness on the most easy terms. How invincible is the passion of love, between parents and children, as well as between the sexes: and how much more invincible is the love of God for his creatures! Your earthly parents are not so near, and ought not to be so dear to you as your heavenly Parent. They are but the secondary cause of your existence; he is the first. When I see the " heaven erected face" of a beautiful woman bedaubed with paint, and depicted with affected airs, and detestable pride, I blush for the honour of human nature. Can any thing be more unreasonable, and degrading, than for such amiable, such fascinating beings thus to prostitute their intellectual powers to such unworthy purposes. Perhaps your soul recoils at the degenerate exhibition of such a vain and florid female: but remember that there is but a little space between the paths of innocent and guilty indulgence; and when that boundary is passed, the vortex of sensuality appears in view, to whirl you down the labyrinth of popular degeneracy and degradation; where you may with apparent,

but not real pleasure, pursue the same vile,
and vulgar, or at least vain routine of splendid wretchedness, and magnificent folly,
without tasting a particle of intellectual
pleasure, till death meets you in the mad
career; presents the unwelcome summons
for you to leave all your grandeur behind :
your body, which you have worshipped more
than God, will be deposited in the silent
grave, while the wretched soul, so long neglected, must account to that God for the
follies of an ill spent life. How unwillingly
the soul will leave the body on this awful
occasion, is beautifully described by Blair.

"How shocking must thy summons be, *O death!*
To him that is at ease in his possessions :
Who, counting on long years of pleasure here,
Is quite unfurnish'd for that world to come !
In that dread moment, how the frantic soul
Raves round the walls of her clay tenement,
Runs to each avenue, and shrieks for help,
But shrieks in vain !—How wishfully she looks
On all she's leaving, now no longer her's !
A little longer, yet a little longer,
Oh ! might she stay, to wash away her stains,
And fit her for her passage. Mournful sight !
Her very eyes weep blood ; and every groan
She heaves is big with horror. But the foe,
Like a staunch murd'rer, steady to his purpose,
Pursues her close through every lane of life,
Nor misses once the track, but presses on ;
Till forc'd at last to the tremendous verge,
At once she sinks to everlasting ruin.

"Sure tis a serious thing to *die !* My soul,

What a strange moment must it be, when near
Thy journey's end, thou hast the gulph in view!
That awful gulph, no mortal e'er repass'd
To tell what's doing on the other side!
Nature runs back, and shudders at the sight,
And every life-string bleeds at thoughts of parting;
For part they must: *body* and *soul* must part;
Fond couple; link'd more close than wedded pair.
This wings its way to its Almighty source,
The witness of its actions, now its judge;
That drops into the dark and noisome *grave*,
Like a disabled pitcher of no use.

   " If *death* was nothing, and nought after *death*;
If, when men died, at once they ceas'd to be,
Returning to the barren womb of nothing,
Whence first they sprung, then might the debauchee
Untrembling mouth the heavens:—Then might the
        drunkard
Reel over his full bowl, and, when 'tis drain'd,
Fill up another to the brim and laugh
At the poor bugbear *death*: Then might the wretch
That's weary of the world, and tir'd of life,
At once give each inquietude the slip,
By stealing out of being when he pleas'd,
And by what way, whether by hemp or steel,
Death's thousand doors stand open. Who could force
The ill-pleas'd guest to sit out his full time,
Or blame him if he goes. Sure he does well,
That helps himself as timely as he can,
When able. But if there is a *hereafter*,
And that there is, conscience, uninfluenc'd,
And suffered to speak out, tells every man;
Then must it be an awful thing to *die*:
More horrid yet to die by one's own hand.
Self-murder! name it not; our island's shame,
That makes her the reproach of neighb'ring states,
Shall nature, swerving from her earliest dictate,
Self-preservation, fall by her own act?

Forbid it, Heaven!—Let not, upon disgust,
The shameless hand be fully crimson'd o'er
With blood of its own lord.   Dreadful attempt!
Just reeking from self-slaughter, in a rage
To rush into the presence of our Judge;
As if we challeng'd him to do his worst,
And matter'd not his wrath.   Unheard-of tortures
Must be reserv'd for such: these herd together;
The common damn'd shun their society,
And look upon themselves as fiends less foul.
Our time is fix'd, and all our days are number'd;
How long, how short, we know not;—This we know,
Duty requires we calmly wait the summons;
Nor dare to stir till Heaven shall give permission:
Like sentries that must keep their destin'd stand,
And wait th' appointed hour, till they're reliev'd.
Those only are the brave that keep their ground,
And keep it to the last.   To run away
Is but a coward's trick: to run away
From this world's ills, that at the very worst
Will soon blow o'er, thinking to mend ourselves
By boldly vent'ring on a world unknown,
And plunging headlong in the dark;—'tis mad;
No frenzy half so desperate as this.

    " Tell us, ye dead; will none of you in pity
To those you left behind, disclose the secret ?
Oh ! that some courteous ghost would blab it out;
What 'tis *you* are, and *we* must shortly be.
I've heard that souls departed, have sometimes
Forewarn'd men of their death :—'Twas kindly done,
To knock and give the alarm.   But what means
This stinted charity ?—'Tis but lame kindness
That does its work by halves.   Why might you not
Tell us what 'tis to *die ?*—Do the strict laws
Of your society forbid your speaking
Upon a point so nice ?—I'll ask no more;
Sullen, like lamps in sepulchres, your shine
Enlightens but yourselves.   Well—'tis no matter,

A very little time will clear up all,
And make us learn'd as you are, and as close.
   " *Death's shafts* fly thick: Here falls the village
       swain,
And there his pamper'd lord. The cup goes round:
And who so artful as to put it by?
'Tis long since death had the majority:
Yet strange! *the living lay it not to heart.*
See yonder maker of the dead man's bed,
The *sexton*, hoary headed chronicle,
Of hard, unmeaning face, down which ne'er stole
A gentle tear; with mattock in his hand
Digs through whole rows of kindred and acquaintance,
By far his juniors. Scarce a scull's cast up,
But well he knew its owner, and can tell
Some passage of his life. Thus hand in hand,
The sot has walk'd with *death* twice twenty years:
And yet ne'er yonker on the green laughs louder,
Or clubs a smuttier tale: When drunkards meet,
None sings a merrier catch, or lends a hand
More willing to his cup. Poor wretch! he minds not,
That soon some trusty brother of the trade
Shall do for him what he has done for thousands.
   " On this side, and on that, men see their friends
Drop off, like leaves in autumn; yet launch out
Into fantastic schemes which the long livers
In the world's hale and undegen'rate days
Could scarce have leisure for. Fools that we are,
Never to think of *death* and of *ourselves*
At the same time: as if to learn to *die*
Were no concern of ours. Oh! more than sottish,
For creatures of a day, in gamesome mood,
To frolic on eternity's dread brink,
Unapprehensive; when for ought we know,
The very first swoln surge shall sweep us in.
Think we, or think we not, time hurries on
With a resistless unremitting stream;

Yet treads more soft than e'er did midnight thief,
That slides his hand under the miser's pillow,
And carries off his prize. What is *this world?*
What but a spacious *burial field* unwall'd,
Strew'd with death's spoils, the spoils of animals,
Savage and tame, and full of dead men's bones.
The very turf on which we tread once liv'd ;
And we that live must lend our carcasses
To cover our own offspring: In their turns
They too must cover their's. 'Tis here all meet :
The shiv'ring *Icelander*, and sunburnt *Moore ;*
Men of all crimes, that never met before ;
And of all creeds, the *Jew*, the *Turk*, the *Christian.*
Here the proud *prince*, and *favourite* yet prouder,
His sovereign's keeper, and the people's scourge,
Are huddled out of sight. *Here* lie acash'd,
The great *negociators* of the earth,
And celebrated *masters of the balance*,
Deep read in stratagems, and wiles of courts.
Now vain their *treaty skill.* Death scorns to treat.
Here the o'erloaded *slave* flings down his burden
From his gall'd shoulders ; and when the stern *tyrant,*
With all his guards and tools of power about him,
Is meditating new unheard-of hardships,
Mocks his short arm ;---and quick as thought escapes
Where tyrants vex not, and the weary rest.
Here the warm *lover*, leaving the cool shade,
The tell-tale echo and the babbling stream
(Time out of mind the fav'rite seats of love)
Fast by his gentle mistress lays him down,
Unblasted by foul tongue. *Here* friends and foes
Lie close ; unmindful of their former feuds.
The lawn-rob'd *prelate*, and plain *presbyter*,
Ere while that stood aloof, as shy to meet,
Familiar mingle *here*, like sister streams
That some rude interposing rock has split.
Here is the large limb'd *peasant ;---Here* the *child*
Of a span long, that never saw the sun,

Nor press'd the nipple, strangled in life's porch.
Here is the *mother*, with her sons and daughters:
The barren *wife* and long-demurring *maid*,
Whose lonely, unappropriated sweets
Smil'd like yon knot of cowslips on the cliff,
Not to be come at by the willing hand.
Here are the *prude* severe, and gay *coquette*,
The sober *widow*, and the young green *virgin*,
Cropp'd like a rose before 'tis fully blown,
Or half its worth disclos'd. Strange medley *here!*
Here garrulous *old* age winds up his tale;
And jovial *youth* of lightsome vacant heart,
Whose ev'ry day was made of melody,
Hears not the voice of mirth. The shrill-tongu'd *shrew*
Meek as the turtle-dove, forgets her chiding.
Here are the wise, the generous, and the brave;
The just, the good, the worthless, and profane,
The downright clown, and perfectly well bred;
The fool, the churl, the scoundrel, and the mean
The supple statesman and the patriot stern;
The wrecks of nations and the spoils of time,
With all the lumber of six thousand years.
Poor *man!* how happy once in thy *first state!*
When yet but warm from thy Great Maker's hand,
He stamp'd thee with his image, and, well pleas'd,
Smil'd on his last fair work. Then all was well.
Sound was the *body*, and the *soul* serene;
Like two sweet instruments, ne'er out of tune,
That play their sev'ral parts. Nor head, nor heart,
Offer'd to ache: nor was there cause they should;
For all was pure within: no fell remorse,
Nor anxious castings up of what might be,
Alarm'd his peaceful bosom. Summer seas
Shew not more smooth, when kiss'd by southern winds
Just ready to expire.—Scarce importun'd,
The generous soil, with a luxurious hand,
Offer'd the various produce of the year.

And ev'ry thing most perfect in its kind.
Blessed! thrice blessed days!—But, ah! how short!
Bless'd as the pleasing dreams of holy men!
But fugitive like those, and quickly gone.
Oh! slipp'ry state of things!—what sudden turns!
What strange vicissitudes in the first leaf
Of man's sad history!—To-day most happy,
And ere to morrow's sun has set, most abject.
How scant the space between these vast extremes!
Thus far'd it with *our sire :*—Not long enjoy'd
His paradise. Scarce had the happy tenant
Of the fair spot, due time to prove its sweets,
Or sum them up, when straight he must begone,
Ne'er to return again. And must he go ?
Can nought compound for the first dire offence
Of erring man ? Like one that is condemn'd,
Fain would he trifle time with idle talk,
And parley with his fate; but 'tis in vain.
Not all the lavish odours of the place,
Offer'd in incense, can procure his pardon,
Or mitigate his doom—a mighty angel,
With flaming sword, forbids his longer stay,
And drives the loiterer forth; nor must he take
One last farewell round. At once he lost
His glory and his GOD. If mortal now,
And sorely maim'd, no wonder—*man has sinn'd.*
Sick of his bliss, and bent on new adventures,
Evil he would needs try :—nor tried in vain,
(Dreadful experiment! destructive measure!
Where the worst thing could happen, is success,)
Alas! too well he sped :—the *good* he scorn'd
Stalk'd off reluctant like an ill us'd ghost,
Not to return ;—or if it did, its visits,
Like those of *angels*, short, and far between :
Whilst the black *demon* with his hell-scap'd train,
Admitted once into its better room,
Grew loud and mutinous, nor would begone ;
Lording it o'er the *man ;* who now too late

Saw the rash error which he could not mend.
An error, fatal not to him alone,
But to his future sons, his fortunes heirs.
Inglorious bondage !—Human nature groans
Beneath a vassalage so vile and cruel,
And its vast body bleeds through every vein.

   " What havoc hast thou made, foul monster, *sin*
Greatest and first of ills----the fruitful parent
Of woes of all dimensions !----But for *thee*
Sorrow had never been ! All noxious thing,
Of vilest nature, other sorts of evils
Are kindly circumscrib'd, and have their bounds,
The fierce *volcano*, from its burning entrails,
That belches molten stone, and globes of fire ;
Involv'd in pitchy clouds of smoke and stench,
Mars the adjacent fields for some leagues round,
And there it stops. The big swoln *inundation*,
Of mischief more diffusive, raving loud,
Buries whole tracts of country, threatening more ;
But that, too, has its shore it cannot pass.
More dreadful far than these ! *Sin* has laid waste,
Not here and there a country but a *world :*
Dispatching at a wide extended blow
Entire mankind ; and for their sakes defacing
A whole creation's beauty with rude hands ;
Blasting the foodful gain, and loaded branches,
And marking all along its way with ruin.
Accursed thing !----Oh ! where shall fancy find
A proper name to call thee by, expressive
Of all thy horrors ?----Pregnant womb of ills !
Of temper so transcendently malign,
That toads and serpents of most deadly kind,
Compar'd to thee, are harmless----sicknesses
Of every size and symptom, racking pains
And bluest plagues are thine. See how the fiend
Profusely scatters the contagion round !
Whilst deep mouth'd slaughter, bellowing at her heels,

Wades deep in blood new spilt ; yet for to-morrow
Shapes out new work of great uncommon daring,
And inly pines till the dread blow is struck.
    " But hold ;—I've gone too far : too much discover'd
My father's nakedness, and nature's shame.
Here let me pause and drop an honest tear,
One burst of filial duty and condolence,
O'er all those ample deserts *death* hath spread,
This *chaos* of mankind.   O, great *man-eater !*
Whose every day is *carnival*, not sated yet !
Unheard of *epicure !* without a fellow !
The veriest *gluttons* do not always cram ;
Some intervals of abstinence are sought
To edge the appetite ; *thou* seekest none.
Methinks the countless swarms thou hast devour'd,
And thousands that each hour thou gobblest up,
This, less than *this*, might gorge thee to the full,
But, ah ! rapacious still, thou gap'st for more ;
Like one, whole days defrauded of his meals,
On whom lank hunger lays her skinny hand,
And wets to keenest eagerness his cravings,
As if diseases, massacre, and poison,
Famine and war, were not thy caterers.
    " But, know that thou *must render up the dead*,
And with high int'rest too. They are not thine ;
But only in thy keeping for a season,
Till the great promis'd day of restitution ;
When loud diffusive sound from brazen trump,
Of strong lung'd cherub, shall alarm thy captives,
And rouse the long long sleepers into life,
Day-light and liberty.———
Then must thy doors fly open, and reveal
The minds that lay long forming under ground,
In their dark cells immur'd ; but now full ripe,
And pure as silver from the crucible,
That twice has stood the torture of the fire,
And inquisition of the forge. We know

Th' illustrious deliverer of mankind,
The son of God, thee foil'd. Him in thy pow'r
Thou couldst not hold :—Self-vigorous he rose,
And, shaking off thy fetters, soon retook
Those spoils his voluntary yielding lent ;
(Sure pledge of our releasement from thy thrall !)
Twice twenty days he sojourn'd here on earth,
And show'd himself alive to *chosen witnesses,*
By proofs so strong, that the most slow assenting
Had not a scruple left. This having done,
He mounted up to Heaven. Methinks I see him
Climb the aerial heights, and glide along
Athwart the severing clouds : but the faint eye,
Flung backwards in the chase, soon drops its hold ;
Disabled quite, and jaded with pursuing.
Heaven's portals wide expand to let him in ;
Nor are his friends shut out : as a great prince,
Not for himself alone procures admission,
But for his train. It was his royal will,
That where he is, there should his followers be,
Death only lies between. A gloomy path !
Made yet more gloomy by our coward fears :
But not untrod, nor tedious : the fugitive
Will soon go off. Besides there's no by-road
To bliss. Then why, like ill-condition'd children,
Start we at transient hardships in the way
That leads to purer air, and softer skies,
And a ne'er setting sun ?—Fools that we are !
We wish to be where sweets unwith'ring bloom ;
But straight our wish revoke, and will not go.
So have I seen, upon a summer's ev'n,
Fast by the riv'lets brink, a youngster play :
How wishfully he looks to stem the tide !
This moment resolute, next unresolv'd :
At last he dips his foot ; but as he dips,
His fears redouble, and he runs away
From th' inoffensive stream, unmindful now
Of all the flowers that paint the further bank,

And smil'd so sweet of late,   Thrice welcome *death*
That after many a painful, bleeding step
Conducts us to our home, and lands us safe
On the long wish'd for shore.   Prodigious change!
Our bane turn'd to a blessing! *death*, disarm'd,
Loses his fellness quite.   All thanks to him
Who scourg'd the venom out.   Sure *the last end*
Of the good man is *peace!* How calm his *exit!*
Night dews fall not more gently to the ground,
Nor weary worn out winds expire so soft.
Behold him in the evening tide of life,
A life well spent, whose early care it was
His riper years should not upbraid his green
By unperceiv'd degrees he wears away ;
Yet, like the sun, seems larger at his setting.
(High in his faith and hopes) look how he reaches
After the prize in view ? and, like a bird
That's hamper'd, struggles hard to get away ;
Whilst the glad gates of sight are wide expanded
To let new glories in, the first fair fruits
Of the fast coming harvest.   *Then!* oh *then!*
Each earth-born joy grows vile or disappears,
Shrunk to a thing of nought.   Oh ! how he longs
To have his passport sign'd, and be dismiss'd !
'Tis done, and now he's happy !—the glad *soul*
Has not a wish uncrown'd.   Ev'n the *lag flesh*
Rests too *in hope* of meeting once again
Its batter half, never to sunder more.
Nor shall it hope in vain :—The time draws on,
When not a single spot of burial earth,
Whether on land, or in the spacious sea,
But must give back its long committed dust
Inviolate.—And faithfully shall these
Make up the full account : not the least atom
Embezzl'd or mislaid, of the whole tale.
Each *soul* shall have a *body* ready furnish'd
And each shall have his own.   Hence, ye profane
Ask not how can this be ?—Sure the same pow'r

That rear'd the piece at first, and took it down,
Can re-assemble the loose scatter'd parts,
And put them as they were.   Almighty God
Has done much more, nor is his arm impair'd
Through length of days ; and what he can he will,
His faithfulness stands bound to see it done.
When the dread trumpet sounds, the slumb'ring dust,
(Not inattentive to the call) shall wake :
And ev'ry joint possess its proper place,
With a new elegance of form unknown
To its first state.   Nor shall the conscious *soul*
Mistake its partner, but amidst the crowd
Singling its other half, into its arms
Shall rush with all the impatience of a man
That's new come home, and having long been absent,
With haste runs over ev'ry different room,
In pain to see the whole.   Thrice happy meeting !
Nor *time* nor *death* shall ever part them more.
'Tis but a night, a long and moonless night ;
We make the *grave* our bed, and then are gone.
  " Thus at the shut of ev'n, the weary bird
Leaves the wide air, and in some lonely brake
Cow'rs down, and dozes till the dawn of day,
Then claps his well-fledg'd wings and bears away."

We have just witnessed the exit of the
vain and volatile votary of fashion ; we
will now take our eyes from this gloomy
picture of human depravity and wretchedness, and place them on the more refulgent delineation of the pursuits, the pleasures, and the end of the votary of religion
and virtue.

We have already said, that the appetites
of the body are soon cloyed, and the most

delicious and luxurious banquets soon become, if not disgustful, at least common and insipid. But the mind can never be cloyed with the plenitude of intellectual gratification, which the charming female proves to be the case, who turns a deaf ear to the syren's song, despises the harmonious hypocrite, and relinquishes all the illicit, the vile, the fashionable follies of the age; nay, all the vain things that charms her most, she sacrifices them for the ardent love she cherishes for her Almighty Parent. Her love augments with her years, and her divine enjoyments still increase, with all the luxuriancy of mental delight: yet she is so far from being surfeited with their accumulation, that she still pants for more of these holy, heavenly, happy pleasures :— Her listening to the commands of her gracious Parent, with her intellectual ear, or viewing the glories of his kingdom, or the superlative beauties of his person with her intellectual eye, does not preclude her from viewing, with admiration and veneration, the handy works of the Architect of nature ; the flowery gardens, the vernal groves, the scented meadows, the fragrant woods, the chrystal streams, the terraqueous globe itself-teeming with abundance for man and beast, the firmament sprinkled with gold-

en planets, all ether interspersed with numerous worlds, and irradiated with innumerable comets and constellations; the whole
universe pregnant with life : all these things
she views with the most reverential devotion and sentimental delight : but her views
are not confined to visible objects. She enters
the intellectual world majestically bold. She
views, with one comprehensive glance of her
mind's eye, dominions, thrones, principal-
ities, virtues, and powers, arranged in imperial order ; with starry hosts, and myriads of
smiling cherubs ; and hears the melodious lays
of the celestial world ; and though it is through
a glass darkly, yet she sees the eternal great
First Cause shrouded with refulgent and
inaccessible glory, from whose sacred presence, streams of light, life, and love, inces-
santly distil, and enrapture the heavenly
hosts, who continually see more of his munificence displayed, more of his magnificence developed, and more of his clemency
exercised over all his creatures, celestial
and terrestrial, at whose head he sits majestically glorious, holds the helm of affairs,
keeps in motion the machinery of the universe, and looks from heaven's high arch
with indignation upon that pitiful, that sordid, that voluptuous wretch, in his splendid
mansion, who, for the sake of indulging his

appetite, sacrifices the intellectual pleasures peculiar to the first born sons of heaven; while, with the same glance he descries, under the embowering shade of the lofty oak, and at the door of his rustic hovel, the unlettered savage, surveying with admiration the rude scenery and romantic beauties of the forest, the transparency of heaven's blue arch, the velocity of the vivid lightning, and listening to the distant bellowing of the rolling thunder : while with reverential awe he renders his Creator the grateful offering of untutored homage.

All these pleasures, and more than tongue can express, are the sure inheritance of this virtuous and pious female. Wherever she goes, she disseminates benefactions, and receives in return benedictions; she is the orphan's mother, the poor widow's comforter, and the social and sympathetic friend of the poor in general. If sudden danger threatens, her eyes are constantly fixed upon her Almighty Friend : if sudden blessings descend, her heart, her grateful heart, is instinctive in pouring out praises and thanksgivings in the ears of her Heavenly King.

Thus she continues, " for ever blessing and for ever blessed," till the period arrives in which death, with heavenly smiles, will

give her a passport to her Father's king
dom, where she ascends with glorious exultation, borne on the golden wings of arch-
angels, and is congratulated by the heavenly
host, and conducted to the presence of God
to enjoy his smiles and sublime approbation, for " *eye hath not seen, nor ear heard,
neither hath it entered into the heart of
man to conceive*," the glorious brilliancy of
that starry diadem, with which this virtuous
female is crowned in the celestial world.

There is another powerful motive I would
suggest, to stimulate my juvenile readers in
the pursuit of piety and virtue ; and that is,
the impossibility of avoiding the maledic-
tion and penalties of that august tribunal,
that omnipresent monitor, that inexorable
reprover, conscience ; though you may escape the laws and censures of men, you cannot escape this divinity (if I may call it so),
planted in your own breast, who is always
accusing or excusing, commending or re-
prehending you according to the merit or
demerit of your actions. If you take the
wings of an angel and fly into the heavens,
the pit of hell, or the uttermost parts of the
earth, you cannot possibly escape the scru-
tiny of this impartial judge, this good monitor, who will always watch you wherever
you go, as close as a tiger watches his prey,

and will seize you with the same impetuosity and fury, when you act counter to the mandates of the Eternal. Even if there were no future rewards and punishments, would it not be wisdom in you to live a virtuous life in order to avoid the lashes of a guilty conscience? I would ask, which of the faculties of the human mind are improved by following the fashions and fopperies of the present age? For my part I do not know of any. It rather poisons their energies, prevents their useful tendencies, and contaminates eventually the innocent pleasures of life ; nay, ruins the constitutions of its votaries. That young woman, who caught a cold, a consumption, and a premature death, by following the fashions, proves the force of my arguments ; as well as her companion, whose pallid countenance and emaciated body, declares to every candid mind that the shrine of fashion commonly called the temple of pleasure, is rather the receptacle of pollution, the repository of disorder, and the sepulchre of death. Survey it, therefore, with horror, and avoid it with avidity. Remember, that those who expose their bodies and prostitute their minds, counteract the laws of nature, and bid defiance to nature's God. If, therefore, your vain and volatile (I will not say vile and vulgar,)

companions or relatives, solicit you inces-
santly and importunately to participate the
unhallowed pleasure, the superficial delights,
the interdicted indulgencies, which depraved fashion legalizes, and depravation of
manners has rendered popular; do not,
my young readers, do not, I conjure you,
listen to the seductive, the enchanting, the
syren voice: it leads to the chambers of
death, and poor satisfaction will it be in
the event of your participating the chimerical and romantic pleasure with real and perpetual pain, to reflect that thousands of your
fellow creatures have acted in the same manner. But rush from the enchanting, the fascinating voice, as the innocent dove precipitates her flight from the infatuating presence
of the speckled serpent, which she beholds
charming, and destroying her cotemporary
warblers of the vernal groves! she seeks the
deep recesses of the embowering shade, and
though seated on the lofty bough of the
spreading foliage, and in perfect security, yet
still her heart beats against the branches.

Thus, shun the dreadful snare; and thus,
tremble for your subsequent safety. A flood
of interesting thoughts, intimately connected
with your future tranquillity, crowd profusely on my mind, the majority of which

I must reject, as I have almost exceeded my limits already; some of which, however, are of such magnitude and importance, that I must humbly beg the reader to exert her patience, and maintain her composure, while I merely hint them.

I would first, therefore, warn you from the commission of a certain diabolical crime of infernal origin, which, alas! too often is the companion of the convivial associations of your sex, as well as their tea-parties. I mean intellectual assassination. Oh! how often is the character of an unsuspecting neighbour, acquaintance, or even relative, in such parties, dissected, scrutinized, scandalized, and analyzed, with as mush insensibility as that of the butcher when he is cutting up the innocent lamb for market; and as void of the finer feelings which ennoble human nature, as the lion while devouring his mangled prey. Shun, I beseech you, this pestilential vapour, that breathes defamation; it springs spontaneously from the bottomless pit, and is the emmissary, the auxiliary, or, I might say, the prime minister of Satan, by which his malevolence is displayed in miniature, disseminated in superabundance, and retailed with avidity. The impetuosity and fury of the lion, and the subtilty and vileness of the

serpent, are united reciprocally in this offspring of hell. Yet, alas! notwithstanding
the blackness and deformity of this baneful
crime, it pervades every grade, and contaminates every party in society with its pestilential effluvia. It finds admission into the
rustic, and resplendent habitations of the poor
and rich, the noble and ignoble, the peasant
and potentate, the philosopher and the divine; it hovers over the courts of judica-
ture, visits periodically the pulpit and pre-
sidential chair, resides in the imperial
throne; is depictured on the lawyer's physiognomy, the poet's brain, and the itinerant
scribbler's closet is its perpetual and welcome habitation. It was this hell-born fury
that kindled the fires which consumed the
martyrs; that blows the clarion of war;
that drenches th earth with human blood;
that peoples and re-peoples the regions of
eternal death; that promotes anarchy and
intestine commotion in nations, discord and
inquietude in families, and all the boisterous
and turbulent passions in the breasts of individuals:—in one word, it renders this earth
an hospital, the land of sickness and sorrow;
which would otherwise be a terrestrial paradise, the land of concord and peace. Instead, therefore, of encouraging, theoretically or practically, by silence, or by lending

your name, hands, or tongue, to accelerate
this work of intellectual massacre, use your
utmost power to extirpate it from every circle you move in, and from every house you
enter; remember the proverb, " Silence
speaks consent." If you listen with composure or complacency to the voice of slan-
der, you are virtually its abettor. In this
respect sufferance is pusillanimity, silence
inhumanity, and forbearance treason ; for,
even by silence you reanimate, if you do not
retail, this execrable filth of hell.

There is another gigantic foe, which I
would warn you above all things to beware
of : I mean the proselyte and votary of seduction. He has already been held up to
popular animadversion and contempt in
this performance, which is principally intended to defend you from his innovations
and machinations. I need not say much to
you on this subject, only to advise you to
avoid vile and vulgar fashions ; and, in so
doing, you will avoid those innovators.
For the adept at seduction is encouraged by
the voluptuous appearance of the fashionable female, to commence his attack on her
virtue. Dress prudently and modestly, and
they will not dare to attempt it ; but will
view you with respect and admiration.
For, no man admires a prudent and modest

woman, and despises an unchaste and vicious woman, more than a libertine. Before I conclude this subject, I would wish to inculcate on the minds of my fair readers, one truly important lesson; which is, to view with horror, and repulse with magnanimity and scorn, the man who makes the smallest attack on your virtue. Let it shock you with the quickness of electricity, and let the repulse be instantaneous, and the battle is won. But, alas! how many thousands of unsuspecting, unconscious, and virtuous females, have been ruined by neglecting this precaution. The lover, or suitor, first appears with diffidence and conscious shame, to assault the delicacy of the silly fair one. She repulses him, indeed, with gentle reproof, but not with suitable indignation, and horror of heart; and her pusillanimity only tends to render still more invincible the guilty intentions of the amorous lover. Her coyness, in short, only tends to inflame his unhallowed passions to the highest pitch of voluptuous delirium. The sequel verifies th proverb, "give an inch and he will take an ell." And I will be bold to affirm, that such a man, though his intentions, affections, and resolutions, be ever so ardent, disinterested, and sincere, towards the girl he ruined, prior to that tragical event; yet posteriòr to it, his good intentions and resolutions will be eventually vanquished, and nothing, I am confident, not even the loss of fortune, friends, and health, or even life itself, will so effectually annihilate the love that man entertains, as imprudence and immodesty on the part of that woman ; and this is very natural. If I love a woman ardently and affectionately, and really intend to make her my wedded wife ; if that woman will allow me, previous to the matrimonial alliance, to take liberties incompatible with her chastity—this imprudence on her part destroys all confidence on mine ; and, consequently, vanquishes my love, though not my pity : for I must believe, indeed I cannot help believing, that she would give another person, under the same circumstances, and with the same opportunity and importunity, the same liberties she gave to me ; and she is not, of course, a fit person for an honourable man's wife : and, indeed, I could not marry her without sacrificing my future mental and domestic peace ; for I never could have real confidence in her ; and, consequently, jealousy would be always, on the most trivial occasions, lifting up its distracted head, and, with the keenest pangs, imbittering my future days.

A great deal might be said to elucidate this topic, and a long deduction of examples might be adduced to consolidate what has already been said; but, I very much fear that I am enlarging the subject too much; suffice it, therefore, to add, that the only sure and certain means you can successfully use to secure your lover's heart and hand, is by an exemplary modest demeanour, a prudent reservedness, an open cheerfulness, void of even the appearance of coquetry; and, to crown all, a modest ingenuousness, which, in the sight of an intelligent man, is a pearl of great price. Again, the most effectual means you can possibly use to cause your lover, though virtuous and honourable, "for strong temptations with the best prevail," to forsake you forever, is by allowing him to take liberties incompatible with your delicacy; and, if you let him go a step farther, and storm the ramparts that defends your chastity, the moment this is effected he is fled, however ardent and pure his passion may have been before; for ever fled, and leaves you in silent sadness to bewail your credulity, imbecility, duplicity, and premature prostitution.

"Ruin ensues, reproach, and endless shame,
And this false step for ever blasts her fame!

"In vain with tears the loss she may deplore,
In vain look back, to what she was before,
She sets like stars, that fall to rise no more."

You see the dreadfully formidable precipice extended beneath you; therefore beware and approach it not on your peril, as its environs are enchanted ground. Remember, also, the magnitude of the crime, and that according to the Mosaic dispensation, the female who suffered herself to be violated, when it was in her power to call for help, and receive assistance, was considered guilty of the crime of whoredom, and stoned to death for the same.

There is one sentiment I would particularly wish to inculcate upon your minds, where it should always hold a distinguished place; and that is, the great danger resulting to your sex, from precipitate and imprudent associations. You should compare your character to a clean sheet of white paper, which, if once stained, will be always visibly unclean and unfit for use, unless for the most common purposes. Remember your reputation may as easily be stained by associating with vain and vicious companions, as a clean sheet of paper, when deposited with unclean materials. Many unsuspecting innocent females have been ruined by keeping company with vicious persons of their own sex, whose credulity proved a prelude to their degradation and infamy. This is beautifully exemplified in the pathetic History of Charlotte Temple, a tale of truth, written by Mrs. Rowson; and perhaps, I might say, without stepping over the line of veracity, thousands of unhappy, unconscious females, for the want of this caution, are led to destruction in the same manner. A secret desire, which lurks in the breasts of most young women, often is the cause of innumerable evils to themselves in particular, and society in general: and that is, the love of being admired. They are stimulated by this propensity, to embrace every opportunity of attending places of public resort. Many a beauteous female appears in the temple of God, for the sake of seeing, and being seen and admired; as well as the theatre and ball room: but, alas! the incense, the adulation, the admiration they receive, is too often from the characters they should avoid and despise; namely, coxcombs and libertines, who flatter in order to ruin them. Too many of your sex, while they feel the most cogent ambition to be admired for their personal charms, pay no respect whatever to their mental qualifications; by this neglect they become the dupes of their own designs, the victims of

the artful rake, and the contempt of the discerning part of both sexes : and, while they
are admired by the licentious many, they
are disesteemed by the virtuous few.

Were young females convinced of the
dangers by which they will be surrounded,
the moment they shake off the manacles of
maternal restraint, they would tremble for
their safety ; but, alas ! this they seldom
think of, till environed by seductive foes,
like the beauteous lamb that wanders from
the fold into the woodlands, it seeks the vernal groves and embow,ring shades, it crops
the verdant green, and skips about every
bush ; when, lo ! the beasts of prey surround and devour it ; while its dam bleats
and laments its loss in vain. No tongue
can tell the danger resulting to young women from this fatal propensity ; too many
unhappy (I will not say infamous) women
are the most beautiful to be found, as it respects personal charms : their beauty proves
their destruction. Hence the more beautiful a woman is, the more fearful and guarded
(not vain and proud), she ought undoubtedly to be.

" The prudent nymph whose cheeks disclose,
The lily and the blushing rose,
From public view her charms will screen,
And rarely in the crowd be seen ;

"This simple truth shall keep her wise,
The fairest fruits attract the flies."

Is it not a fact, that females, when making choice of what are called lovers, do not
select prudent, discreet, and honourable persons of our sex, to place their affections
upon ; but rather the most volatile and dissipated ; so that the loquacious fop, versatile
rake, and artful villain, who can laugh, sing,
swear, dance, and dress fashionably, is preferred as a female favourite ; while the prudent unassuming young man is sent in silent sadness away. Is it not truly astonishing, that a young woman, with a particle of
common sense in her head, or generosity in
her heart, would prefer a libertine newly returned from a brothel, to the most discreet
of our sex. Yet it is a lamentable fact
that such connections are frequently the
cause of everlasting distress and misery to
the unhappy injudicious female, who has to
endure a life of woe for the imprudence and
indiscretion of a moment. The only way,
therefore, to avoid the misery resulting
from such imprudent connections, is, for
the unexperienced female not to give (I will
not say her heart or hand, but even) her
company for a moment in private, to a man
of a dissipated character ; for, if she gives

one indulgence, the rest will be taken of course.

In order to demonstrate the fatality of indulging injudicious attachments, and allowing men of loose morals too much familiarity, I need only point to the histories of many unhappy females, who became the victims of matrimonial infelicity through injudicious prepossessions ; and (I had almost said), the omnipotence of first impressions, and of premature attachments, with our sex. Some females, who profess to be discerning and discreet, will not hesitate to affirm, that " a reformed rake makes the best husband." I am truly astonished that a woman of common discretion and virtue, would harbour such a thought, much less express such a sentiment! Surely she cannot be acquainted with human nature, the depravity of the heart and the invincibility of bad habits, or she would not suppose that such a man can make a good virtuous husband, without the converting grace of God. I will be bold to say, that it is utterly impossible, without that all-conquering grace, for any man who may properly be denominated a libertine, to make (I will not say a good, but even) a just husband. No evil propensity is more unconquerable when consolidated by habit, and constitutional weakness, than incontinence ;

and though such men, when they place their affections on women, and find seduction impractible to accomplish their wishes, they of course marry them, previously making promises of eternal constancy; but, alas! the moment opportunity offers (for, by the by, they will not require importunity to solicit), they turn like the dog to his vomit, or the sow that was washed to her wallowing in the mire; and, indeed, I will say this much for them, they cannot conquer their inclinations, while under the influence of this dreadful depravity.

I refer to facts to prove my arguments: —witness how many wives are neglected and despised by their husbands, who are the uniform attendants of brothels and places of infamous resort, and the violent votaries of seduction. But, we will admit, for argument's sake, that the reformed rake proves always faithful to the bridal bed; yet then, even then, let the virtuous female make a comparative estimate of his character, and that of a uniformly modest man— the latter of whom has a pure heart and unadulterated affections, to present to the woman of his choice; who can never, in the moments appropriated to reflection, think or say of her husband, as follows:—he has by intemperance corrupted his principles, vitiated his taste for domestic, enjoyments, enslaved himself to the most detestable crimes, often laid the snares of seduction, ruined female innocence, and abandoned to infamy and shame the girls who adored him, and whom he seduced from the paths of virtue; he has haunted all the brothels within his reach, and, after all, presented me with the leavings of strumpets, a ruined constitution, a depraved heart, and a corrupt taste, which only requires an opportunity when it will be immediately gratified.——In short, the bitter lamentations and unutterable sorrow of thousands of slighted consorts, will give the lie in form to the absurd assertion, that a " reformed rake makes the best husband."

With respect to the necessary directions, which might be given you to facilitate your safe and happy passage through the changing scenes of life, many volumes would not contain them; suffice it to recommend to your constant perusal, our dear Redeemer's inimitable sermon on the mount; it is full of matter the most judicious, advice the most appropriate, and reproofs the most heavenly and divine; and I might recommend the most attentive imitation of his unblemished life; take him for your model, for he has commanded you so to do. " *Learn of me*," says he, *"for I am meek and lowly in heart, and ye shall find rest unto your souls."* Attend to all his precepts with religious punctuality ; but, above all, to that where duty to parents is enforced ; love them affectionately, obey them diligently, and serve them unweariedly. Let me tell you, that filial ingratitude is more enormous than the sin of witchcraft. What have they done ; or, rather what have they not done, to promote your happiness ! How great, therefore, is the debt of love you owe them. And you, whose parents unhappily lead you astray, far from the fold of Christ—Oh ! pity and pray for them ; being blinded by the god of this world, the prince of darkness, they lead you where they think you will find happiness and pleasurable sensations ; but which, alas ! prove to be the chambers of pain and pollution.

Though you are bound with great deference to obey your parents in every thing else, yet you must not on any account obey them, when their injunctions tend to cause you to disobey God, and murder your own souls. You should forego your parental home, and even sacrifice your life, before you should obey them in this instance ; yet, notwithstanding their degeneracy and depravity, you are to remember they are still your parents, and you should nurture, cherish, venerate, love, and serve them, to the utmost extent of your power, and to the last moment of their lives. Remember how they supplied your wants in helpless infancy, bore with the peevishness of your childhood, and protected and directed you while in the slippery paths of youth. They warded off the danger by which you were threatened ; and, perhaps, risked their own lives to save your's. They pitied and pardoned your wayward indiscretions, and youthful folly ; and, when they used the rod, it was with parental tears trickling down their cheeks ; and even now, when they lead you on the stage of fashionable life, though it is as slippery as glass, while fiery billows roll below it ; they do it, I am confident, with the most earnest desire, and anxious solicitude to promote your happiness. Do not detest, but pity them ; let the magnitude of your filial and sympathetic compassion run parallel with their blindness and degeneracy, their fashionable follies and splendid wretchedness. Remember what anxiety and labour they endured, while making provision for your comfortable and respectable accommodation. You are now in the morning of life ; but, remember, your sun may set at noon. View the churchyard, and it will teach you an useful lesson, relative to the shortness of time, and certainty of the approach of death :) yet, if you should live to see many years, and in the morning of your life unhappily prove disobedient to your parents, perhaps, in your own turn also, you will be cursed with disobedient children, and all the woes connected with filial ingratitude : you will then feel, as well as know, how incumbent it is upon children to honour their parents, to attend to their precepts, to reverence their grey hairs, support their declining natures, as well as to solace their minds in sickness, and close their eyes in death ; you will then abhor your unfilial conduct, and blush at the remembrance of your disobedience : and were not the dead regardless of the cries of the living, you would approach, with solemn sadness, the solitary tombs of your sainted parents, and lament, with tears of penitential sorrow, your filial ingratitude ; and with those tears would you bedew the graves which contain their ashes ! This you would do, I know, and judge from my own feelings, for I have myself proved (I speak it to my shame) an undutiful child.

Finally, remember you were created for the special purpose of being the temples of the Holy Ghost here on earth, and the celebraters of the glorious praises of the Holy Trinity hereafter in heaven ; therefore, let your conduct correspond with your high vocation.

I will now conclude, by illustrating the caution I have already given, respecting the prudence you must use in your intercourse with the other sex, with an appropriate poem. It is from the writings of a woman who was blessed with an ingenious head, but an erring heart : let this also be a lesson to teach you, that the most inimitable talents, incomparable personal charms, literary acquirements, with artificial brilliancy, riches and fame, will be like a feather, when put in competition with female delicacy ; therefore avoid not only the just censures of the world, but also be so scrupulously circumspect and religiously discreet, as to leave it out of the power of calumny itself to stain your good name, or depreciate your moral character, and take the apostle's advice by avoiding even the appearance of evil.

May the Almighty Parent of Good render these friendly admonitions a tenfold blessing to you, and a benediction to thousands of your sex, when I am wrapped in the cold embraces of the tomb.

The danger to which the female sex are exposed, from implicitly trusting to the professions and protestations of libertines, is beautifully exemplified in the following poem, written by the celebrated Mrs. Pilkington, a sketch of whose biography precedes it.

———

" Mrs. Pilkington was daughter to Dr. John Van Lewen, and was born in Dublin, in the year 1712. She had a lively genius, and a natural turn to poetry, which qualifications very early gained her the friendship of Dr. Swift, and several other persons of learning and distinction in Ireland. But as this lady has been her own biographer, we shall refer the curious reader, for further particulars concerning her, to her own memoirs : and shall only observe, that it is a pity this lady was not blessed with discretion, and, we may add, good fortune, in some proportion to her genius."

THE STATUES,

OR,

TRIAL OF CONSTANCY.

" In a fair Island in the southern main,
Blest with indulgent skies, and kindly rain,
A princess liv'd, of origin divine,
Of bloom celestial, and imperial line.

" In that sweet season, when the mountain sun
Prepares with joy his radiant course to run,
Led by the graces, and the dancing hours,
And wakes to life the various race of flowers;
The lovely queen forsook her shining court,
For rural scenes, and healthful sylvan sport.

" It so befel, that as, in cheerful talk,
Her nymphs and she pursu'd their evening walk;
On the green margin of the oozy deep,
They found a graceful youth dissolv'd in sleep,
Whose charms the queen survey'd with fond delight,
And hung enamour'd o'er the pleasing sight;
By her command the youth was straight convey'd,
And, sleeping, softly in her palace laid.

" Now ruddy morning purpled o'er the skies,
And beamy light unseal'd the stranger's eyes,
Who cried aloud, ye gods, unfold this scene!
Where am I! what can all these wonders mean?

" Scarce had he spoke, when with officious care,
Attendant nymphs a fragrant bath prepare;
He rose, he bath'd, and on his lovely head
Ambrosial sweets, and precious oil they shed.

To deck his polish'd limbs, a robe they brought,
In all the various dies of beauty wrought:
Then led him to the queen, who on a throne
Of burnish'd gold, and beamy diamonds shone;
But, Oh! what wonder seized her beauteous guest!
What love, what ecstasy his soul possess'd!
Entranc'd he stood, and on his falt'ring tongue
Imperfect words, and half-formed accents hung;
Nor less the queen the blooming youth admir'd,
Nor less delight and love her soul inspir'd.

  " O stranger! said the queen, if hither driven
By adverse winds, or sent a guest from heaven,
To me the wretched never sue in vain,
This fruitful isle acknowledges my reign;
Then speak thy wishes and thy wants declare,
And no denial shall attend your pray'r;
She paus'd and blush'd,—the youth his silence broke,
And kneeling, thus the charming queen bespoke:

  " O goddess! for a form so bright as thine
Speaks thee descended of celestial line:
Low at your feet a prostrate king behold,
Whose faithless subjects sold his life for gold;
I fly a cruel tyrant's lawless hand,
And shipwreck drove my vessel on your strand.
But why do I complain of fortune's frowns?
Or what are titles, honours, sceptres, crowns,
To this sweet moment? while in fond amaze
On such transporting excellence I gaze!
Such symmetry of shape! so fair a face!
Such finish'd excellence! such perfect grace!
Hear then my only wish, and oh! approve
The ardent prayer which supplicates thy love.

  " From *Neptune* know, O Prince, my birth I claim,
Replies the queen, and *Lucida's* my name;
This island, these attendant nymphs he gave,
The fair-hair'd daughters of the azure wave!
But he whose fortune gains me for a bride
Must have his constancy severely tried,

One day each moon am I compell'd to go
To my great father's wat'ry realms below,
Where coral groves, celestial red display,
And blazing di'monds emulate the day.
In this short absence, if your love endures,
My heart and empire are for ever your's ;
And hoary *Neptune* to reward your truth,
Shall crown you with immortal bloom and youth ;
But instant death will on your falsehood wait,
Nor can my tenderness prevent your fate.
Twice twenty times in wedlock's sacred band
My royal father joined my plighted hand ;
Twice twenty noble youths, alas ! are dead,
Who in my absence stain'd the nuptial bed ;
Your virtues, prince, may claim a nobler throne,
But mine is yielded on these terms alone.

 " Delightful terms ! replied the raptur'd youth,
Accept my constancy, my endless truth,
Perfidious, faithless men ! enrag'd, he cried,
They merited the fate by which they died ;
Accept a heart incapable of change,
Thy beauty shall forbid desire to range ;
No other form shall to mine eye seem fair,
No other voice attract my list'ning ear,
No charms but thine shall e'er my soul approve,
So aid thy vot'ry, potent god of love !

 " Now loud applauses through the palace ring,
The duteous subjects hail their godlike king :
To feastful mirth they dedicate the day,
While tuneful voices chant the nuptial lay,
Love ditied airs, hymn'd by the vocal choir,
Sweetly attemper'd to the warbling lyre ;
But when the sun descending sought the main,
And low brow'd night assum'd her silent reign ;
They to the marriage bed convey'd the bride,
And laid the raptur'd bridegroom by her side.

 " Now rose the sun, and with auspicious ray
Dispell'd the dewy mists, and gave the day ;

When *Lucida*, with anxious care opprest,
Thus wak'd her sleeping lord from downy rest:
" Soul of my soul and monarch of my heart,
This day she cried, this fatal day we part ;
Alas ! my boding soul is lost in woe,
And from mine eyes the tears unbidden flow.
" Joy of my life, dismiss those needless fears,
Replied the king, and stay those precious tears ;
Should lovely *Venus* leave her native sky,
And, at my feet, imploring fondness, lie,
E'en she, the radiant queen of soft desires,
Should, disappointed, burn with hopeless fires.
" The heart of man the queen's experience knew
Perjur'd and false, yet wish'd to find him true :
She sigh'd retiring, and in regal state,
The king conducts her to the palace gate ;
Where sacred *Neptune's* chrystal chariot stands,
The wondrous work of his celestial hands :
Six harness'd swans the bright machine convey
Swift through the air, or pathless wat'ry way ;
The birds with eagle speed the air divide,
And plunge the goddess in the sounding tide.
" Slow to the court the pensive king returns,
And sighs in secret, and in silence mourns ;
So in the grove sad *Philomel* complains
In mournful accents, and melodious strains :
Her plaintive woes fill the resounding lawn,
From starry vesper to the rosy dawn.
" The king, to mitigate his tender pain,
Seeks the apartment of the virgin train,
With sportive mirth sad absence to beguile,
And bid the melancholy moments smile ;
But there deserted lonely rooms he found,
And solitary silence reign'd around.
" He call'd aloud, when lo ! a hag appears,
Bending beneath deformity and years,
Who said, my liege, explain your sacred will,
With joy your sov'reign purpose I fulfil.

My will! detested wretch! avoid my sight,
And hide thy hideous shape in endless night.
What! does thy queen, o'er-run with rude distrust
Resolve by force to keep a husband just?

" You wrong, replied the hag, your royal wife,
Whose care is love, and love to guard your life.
The race of mortals are by nature frail,
And strong temptations with the best prevail.
Be that my care he said, be thine to send
The virgin train, let them my will attend.

" The beldam fled—The cheerful nymphs advance,
And tread to measur'd airs the mazy dance ;
The enraptur'd prince with greedy eye surveys
The blooming maids ; and covets still to gaze !

" At length a maid, superior to the rest,
Array'd in smiles, in virgin beauty drest,
Receiv'd his passion, and return'd his love,
And softly woo'd him to the silent grove.
Enclos'd in deepest shades of full grown wood,
Within the grove a spacious grotto stood,
Where forty youths in marble seem to mourn,
Each youth reclining on a fun'ral urn ;
Thither the nymph directs the monarch's way,
He treads her footsteps, joyful to obey.
There, fir'd with passion, clasp'd her to his breast
And thus the transport of his soul confest.

" Delightful beauty ! deck'd with every charm
High fancy paints ! or glowing love can form !
I sigh, I gaze, I tremble, I adore !
Such lovely looks ne'er blest my sight before !
Here, under covert of th' embowering shade,
For love's delights and tender transports made,
No busy eye our raptures to detect,
No envious tongue to censure or direct ;
Here yield to love, and tenderly employ
The silent season in ecstatic joy.

" With arms enclos'd, his treasure to retain,
He sigh'd and woo'd, but woo'd, and sigh'd in vain

She rush'd indignant from his fond embrace,
While rage with blushes paints her virgin face;
Yet still he sues with suppliant hands and eyes,
While she to magic charms for vengeance flies.

    " A limpid fountain murmur'd through the cave;
She fill'd her palm with the translucent wave,
And sprinkling cried, receive, false man, in time,
The just reward of thy detested crime.
Thy changeful sex in perfidy delight,
Despise perfection, and fair virtue slight;
False, fickle, base, tyrannic, and unkind,
Whose heart no vows can chain, nor honour bind:
Slaves to the bad, to the deserving worst,
Sick of your twentieth love, as of your first.
The statues, which this hallow'd grot adorn,
Like thee were lovers, and like thee forsworn;
Whose faithless hearts no kindness could secure,
Nor for a day preserve their passion pure;
Whom neither love nor beauty could restrain,
Nor fear of endless infamy and pain.
In me behold thy queen; for know, with ease,
We deities assume each form we please;
Nor can the feeble ken of mortal eyes
Perceive the goddess through the dark disguise.
Now feel the force of heaven's avenging hand,
And here inanimate for ever stand.

    " She spoke—Amaz'd the list'ning monarch stood
And icy horror froze his ebbing blood;
Thick shades of death upon his eyelids creep,
And clos'd them fast in everlasting sleep;
No sense of life, no motion he retains,
But fix'd, a dreadful monument remains:
A statue now, and if reviv'd once more,
Would prove, no doubt, as perjur'd as before."

APPENDIX.

———◆◆———

SINCE closing the prefixed desultory strictures, which has been some months ago, a variety of thoughts, connected with the subject, have periodically struck my mind. I neglected to attend to them, as I feared I had been too prolix already: however, the return of these reflections, which were sufficiently distinct from the antecedent, seemed to impress my mind with the idea, that something more should be said on the subject. Wishing, therefore, to obey the dictates of conscience, without attending to the formality of the literati; indeed were I to attend to them, I would lop off two-thirds of the most useful matter in the performance, in order to render the remainder systematic, and thus please the vitiated taste of pedants; I will, in this appendix, suggest some of the thoughts alluded to, assured that it will unburthen the writer's mind, if it fails in reforming the readers heart.

In the first place, I have not only anticipated the acrimony which the votaries of fashion will manifest towards my performance; but, I almost already hear, vociferated and reverberated, the hue and cry of legions of libertines, coquettes, and prudes, against my hypothesis. Say they—behold the bombastical rhapsody of that sentimental moralist which eventually tends to rob us of innocent pleasures, and darken the atmosphere of the juvenile, jovial, and volatile mind, with the gloom of solemn sadness, or monastic restraint! Nothing can be more false, nothing can be more uncandid, than such a conclusion. The very reverse of the above supposition is the true case.

D d

The primary object of the performance is to bring the versatile sons and daughters of folly, into the delectable path in which true pleasure abounds. Pleasure is the first gift of the Eternal, the most amiable and most beloved daughter of Heaven; but, alas! the fugitive sojourner on earth, the inmate of the social and sentimental philanthropist, which expands, humanizes, and exhilarates his heart: but, the exile and outcast of the unsocial, the selfish, the parsimonious and the penurious votaries of sensuality. The pleasure I allude to, is not what was taught in the school of Epicurus. The pleasure I preach is not the offspring of sordid or voluptuous gratification; but the child of God, the first born of the skies. The epicurean philosophy teaches the sons of folly to seek pleasure, exclusively, in the gratification of sense, and perpetration of crimes; the doctrine is, of course, selfish and devilish, without any reference to futurity or moral justice, and degrades its votaries to brutes. Is pleasure to be found at the table of riotous festivity, in the venial arms of illicit love, in the haunts of debauchery and disgust, meanness and madness? Surely not. Pleasure was made for man, and man was made for pleasure; for we cannot suppose that God, who is, was, and ever will be, great in goodness, and good in greatness, would make man for pain, and pain for man—it is impossible. The moment we form such an estimate of the Deity, we literally insinuate, that he is great in badness, and bad in greatness. The pleasure I advocate is of a delicate temperature. She is social, not sensual; she is god-like, and not satanic; she disclaims consanguinity with indelicacy and excess, and is always solicitous to maintain the honour of human nature; promotes at all times, in all places, and upon all occasions, the pleasurable feelings not only of humanity, but of the whole sensitive creation. She views, with a tender tear, the bleating lamb, and wooing turtle dove, consigned to death by the ruthless hand of power and pride. Her language is,

" No flocks that range the valley free,
To slaughter I condemn ;
Taught by that power that pities me,
I learn to pity them."

Love is her partner : wisdom, modesty, delicacy, cheerfulness, benignity, tenderness, and temperance, are her attendants. She enables her votaries to participate measurably the supreme delight, and taste the ineffable transports peculiar to the first born sons of glory, and even the Sovereign of the Universe.

Wisdom commands, and love her lectures teach,
With more than mortal eloquence they preach.
Ye connoisseurs and epicures come here,
'Tis pleasure calls, lend an attentive ear.

She delights to dwell in the sympathetic bosom of the fair philanthropist ; she nurtures luxuriancy of thought, benevolence of sentiment, and munificence, practically as well as theoretically ; she shrinks with horror from the rude alarms of war, from the clarion and clangour of anarchy, and rushes precipitate and disrobed from the panting, boisterous, and turbulent bosom of the ardent and impetuous warrior, and seeks in the sequestered abode of female modesty, the shelter she is bereaved of in the habitations of men . she makes the bed of death a bed of roses : she carpets the intermediate space between the grave and paradise, with ambrosial flowers, and her votary is transplanted from an earthly to a heavenly garden : as a gardener, when he sees the atmosphere big with showers, and hears the bellowing of the distant thunder, removes his tender flowers from the exposure of the descending deluge, the pattering hail, or the howling whirlwinds, to the safe temperature of the summer house. In short, the pleasure of the sensualist, when compared to those of the philanthropist, is like comparing the rattling of mighty thunder to the noise of a death watch.

" Who aids the cause of innocence oppress'd,
Is by the act alone supremely blest.
No greater rapture man on earth can know,
Than that of feeling and relieving woe."

An interesting thought strikes my mind, which I will put down at once, lest it slips my memory, which is very treacherous, and that is, that women in their sphere are more capacitated, and by the endowments of nature, are more qualified to obtain a proficiency in all the diversified luxuriancies of this sacred pleasure, than our sex, who are too often, and I was going to add, almost naturally estranged from the divine compassion, that tender sensibility, that sacred charity, which is necessarily productive of the pleasure under consideration. I would, therefore, encourage my amiable readers to nurture this sacred plant of heavenly growth; which, perhaps, lies dormant for want of cultivation in their tender breasts. Without hesitation, therefore, lay it under contribution, for you will find many intervening causes for so doing: you need not walk many steps to find objects to bestow your liberality and sympathy upon, and to receive in return the pleasure, as you enjoy the employment, which the highest and most exalted angels in heaven would be ambitious to participate; and which would reanimate the pleasurable feelings they now inherit, and which you will then enjoy. Believe me, you should think for yourselves, and think at large, how noble you are by nature, susceptible of transcendent improvements, fearfully and wonderfully made. Liberty of opinion is as much your privilege as ours, and is your natural inheritance, as much as your personal liberty.

Human nature has long groaned, and still groans under the tyranny of custom. By this means, the female mind is imprisoned in christian, as well as pagan countries. Vindicate, therefore, the transcendent prerogatives of your nature, and magnanimously receive no more to be the slaves of fashion, and the dupes of our sex. It is the interest of our's to encourage freedom of investigation among your sex. Some of us have had the effrontery to assert, that women should be confined to domestic avocations alone, and should leave the pursuits of arts, sciences, and politics, to men; and, of course, reprobated the freedom of investigation for which I contend. In order to demonstrate the cogency of this remark, and the fallacy, fatality, and absurdity of such subterfuges, I would ask, what kind of a partner, or, to use scriptural language, helpmate, will a woman, who has been educated as they generally are at present, make for an intelligent and benevolent man What harmony can exist between them in a social point of view ? Surely none at all. He can take no more pleasure in her conversation than if she was of another species; consequently, though their connubial tenderness may be reciprocal, their intellectual and social intercourse is far from being so. What pleasure can a man have in conversation with his consort, when all her thoughts, and talk, and gestures, are about fine clothes, fashionable appendages, and splendid equipage? I answer, as much as he would enjoy in conversation with his dog. Surely then social and sentimental intercourse cannot exist between such a couple. They are, of consequence, necessitated to seek in other circles, and in other company, the enjoyment they wish for, but cannot find at home. By this means, conjugal love is infringed, if not annihilated. Hence men consider such a woman merely as the apparatus of a seraglio. As a rational companion she cannot be esteemed; and such a woman, to such a man, is, in fact, nothing else but a domestic; not for want of capacity, but through neglect: for, surely, the one is by nature as susceptible of improvement as the other; if, therefore, you wish to be united to a man of parts, first qualify yourself for his company.

I hope my fair readers will excuse my candid and pointed phraseology, in the present momentous discussion. What subject can be more interesting to them? It is intended to teach them, in the most compendious way, how to be respectable, happy, and glorious in this life, and that which is come. Ignorance is the characteristic of the savage in the wilderness; and the civilian in his palace, if ignorant, is no better. The mind that is uninformed, though in body propped on a staff, and shaking as it goes, is in a puerile and pitiable state. Attend to the economy of Providence, and the curiosity of the human mind: the thoughts of futurity, the contemplation of the great First Cause. All these will demonstrate, that for something more noble and exalted were you formed, than to offer incense at the shrine of fashion, and to adorn the perishing body, while the immortal soul lies in ruins.

These inquiries are worthy of a rational creature, worthy of the genius with which the liberal hand of nature has endowed you. Use her prolific gifts as it becomes intelligent beings; despise the sneer of the supercilious pedant, who will flatter to deceive you; they are jealous of superior attainments in, and dread the knowledge of a woman. Let the pedantic libertine once believe a female is intelligent, and he can not, he dare not, intellectually, much less actually, meditate an attack on her virtue: and, you will generally find, that those silly fair ones, who become the victims of their artifice, were previously the foolish and illiterate votaries of fashion.

I would ask, for what was every faculty adapted to scientific improvement given you, in the same quota as to us? Were they given by another god, or by a discriminating hand? Surely not. God is not, and why shall man be, a respecter of persons. These qualifications and capacities were given to you for improvement; and, by neglecting to improve them, you sin against the law of nature, and nature's God. And, believe me to be your friend, when I tell you, that he is a fallacious foe to your sex, who attempts to establish the worst kind of tyranny over them—I mean the tyranny of the mind. What illiberal monopolizers of dignity are to be found amongst the sons of men, in every part of the world. How can they be such implacable enemies to your charming sex? But it is your business to counteract their malevolent machinations, by using unwearied assiduity, in attaining a liberal education : and, if you should already have arrived at the years of maturity, and cannot attend to scholastic resources and researches, you may attain, notwithstanding, by indefatigable perseverance, a sufficiency of polite information, to put you on an equality, in point of intellectual improvement, with a great majority of our sex. For my part, I have attained more information in nine months, by my individual endeavours, than I did from the most ingenious tutors, in one of the principal cities of Europe, in the same number of years. I, therefore, can speak with certainty on this head. The study of astronomy is my greatest delight; on this subject have I written, and on it do I still contemplate, not only with ineffable delight, but with great benefit; nothing can give us more glorious ideas of the creation, more humiliating thoughts of ourselves, or more confidence in the goodness of our Heavenly Father, than astronomical contemplations.

I would, therefore, encourage my fair readers, to appropriate less time to the decoration of their persons, and more to the improvement of their minds. The study of astronomy will be to them a most useful as well as entertaining source of luxurious investigation. The perusal of sacred and civil history will greatly enrich the mind; while the lighter study of belles lettres will embellish and ornament it. I would caution them to avoid the voluptuous rhapsody of the novelist, the romancer, and the new philosophy, as they would the face of a fiery serpent. These deleterious vehicles have ruined their millions of the human race ; yet works of philanthropy morality, and christian philosophy, which develope what is harmonious and amiable in moral life, may be read with avidity, and be productive of utility. From them we derive a degree of mechanical virtue, and learn to abhor systematical vice. The humanizing influence of virtuous poetry, and its pathetic powers, may likewise be productive of charming sensibility, enthusiastic tenderness, and luxuriancy of sentiment. But in all your literary researches, you should never forget, that the ingenuity of the head, without ingenuousness of heart, will never render you amiable in the estimation of your own or our sex. If local circumstances should leave it out of your power to attain any degree of proficiency from the treasures of antiquity, remember that the august book of creation is open to all for investigation. In it study the philosophy of nature. By this you may not only embellish your natural genius, but replenish your heart with unperishable beauties, from the inexhaustible magazine of benefactions. And you should ever bear in mind, in your laborious and scientific pursuits, that you are not toiling for the acquisitions, fashions, and fopperies which perish in the using : but rather for *the bread which endureth unto eternal life.*

I think it should prove a formidable stimulus to recollect, that while your corporeal charms languish and fade, your mental accomplishments will be improving to all eternity.

Here we see and know more, and consequently improve more, from day to day ; yet still we cannot ascertain the thousandth part of the un nvestigable wonders of creation, and the unfathomable benefits, astonishing munificence, super-eminent privileges, and intrinsic excellencies of the covenant of grace and wonders of redeeming love. And it will be the same, no doubt, with us hereafter. We shall see as much more of the immutable architecture and unutterable benevolence of our heavenly Father, as this earth exceeds in magnitude the circumference of a particle of dust. And yet what we shall then see (though endowed with the same visual rays as the most exalted cherubims and seraphims), when compared to what is to be seen of his inaccessible glory, brilliancy, magnificence, and munificence, will be like comparing the thousandth part of a moment to boundless eternity. If, then, we are susceptible of such amazing and divine improvement, both here and hereafter, how reprehensible must we be to neglect the improvement of our minds, not only almost but altogether? Instead of promoting, by our conduct, conversation, or writings, the cause of piety, and facilitating the intellectual improvement of our fellow travellers to the grave; we contaminate their minds and poison the whole moral system. Surely, we cannot meet the approbation of a just and holy God, if the sacred rememberance of the former conduct is pregnant with prolific pleasures, whether in a world of sycophants or a world of spirits! Surely, the reflection of the latter must be big with the triple thunders of Jehovah's indignation and the vengeance of eternity.

May I humbly and earnestly beg the patience of my fair reader, while I drop a few hints on a subject that I have scarcely suggested in the antecedent strictures, from a tenacious wish to accommodate my matter to the taste of the volatile and gay, who, I am confident, do not wish to hear or read much about vital religion, having reserved that subject for the consideration of old age. Millions of prolix and puerile discourses have been delivered from the pulpit and the press, doctrinal and practical, on this subject, which have tended to lead the mind into a labyrinth of uncertainties, both premises and conclusions having often been equally ambiguous. By such performances, religion is made to appear the greatest mystery and phenomenon in nature; whereas it is, in reality, the most simple thing under the broad can-opy of heaven, which I will endeavour to make appear in a few words.

It is, in short, nothing more than pure love to God and man. This love will stimulate the soul to the performance of actions, which will be well pleasing to God and beneficial to man. The omission of duties, or the commission of sins, will grieve such a one more than any pain or punishment ; and the performance of duties will be productive of the sacred pleasures which I have pointed out in the prefixed pages. Such a soul loves God for his own intrinsic excellence, and not for what he can give or take away. It is neither sinister nor selfish. The religion of such a man is seated in his heart, not his head.

Few can say this much ; and I will assign an authentic reason, namely, a mistaken notion of the severity of Providence, whose despotism is magnified at the expence of his munificence. It is ungenerous and unjust to impute to God the evils we bring upon ourselves, by our imprudence and disobedience. That freedom of will, which is the quintessence of our natural and moral powers, is perverted and corrupted by our perverseness, and misery is the necessary result. God is not, nor indeed can he be, the author of evil. Could I believe this of him, the supposition would not only shake my confidence, but annihilate my love, though not my fear.

Alas ! how has religion been dishonoured by blind and bloody zealots, and fanatics, by whom the source of benevolence has been metamorphosed to a blood thirsty monster. O, conscience, thou vicegerent of Heaven ! assume thy legal prerogatives, vindicate the honour of the Eternal, and let loose thy tenfold vengeance upon such enthusiastic and impious calumniators. To be blinded by such fanaticism, I might say heresy ; and, of course, to be ignorant of the simple religion of Christ ; *i. e.* repentance towards God, and faith in our dear Redeemer, is the greatest curse that can befal a human being. Reader, may the good God open your eyes to see the truth, as it is in Jesus, before you sleep the sleep of death. The most refined pleasure results from the candid investigation of sacred truths. For instance, when I find that God not only loves the whole human family collectively, but myself as an individual, surely this sentiment will create love in mine or any generous breast. Gratitude will revive, and tears of penitential sorrow will begin to flow ; that is, when we readily see, feel, and believe this truth. One expression of gratitude from such a person, will be more acceptable than a thousand volumes of formal declamatory and systematical prayers. One sincere penitential sigh is more efficacious than all the wicked prayers carried by proud, perverse, and petulent devotees to the church militant for a thousand years.

How many make a pompous profession of religion, and implicitly depend on forms and ceremonies for salvation, while they are utterly destitute of that christian philanthropy which is the nerve of religion, and without which it is an empty name. Woe be to such professors, if God shows them no more compassion than they show to their brethren.

Before I conclude, I must inform the reader, that I have for many months past been occasionally preparing a manuscript work on christian perfection, for the press. What induced me to compose this work, was a happy deliverance I experienced from the manacles of the guilt and power of in-dwelling sin some years ago ; and I may add, the false notions I entertained of the severity of God, which kept me unutterably wretched ; though I had been seeking sincerely and striving to serve affectionately my Maker from my minor state. Alas ! by looking too much to the ceremonies of men, I neglected to descry the sympathy of God. While listening to the controversial lectures of men, I forgot to listen to his small still voice, who often cried in reason's ear, *" this is the way, walk ye in it.*" In short, I rushed upon the immediate performance of the whole moral law, without previously taking Christ and his righteousness for my guide and help therein, and of consequence found both wind and tide were against me. I never considered the due place of holiness in the mystery of salvation : nor the impossibility of bringing forth the fruit of the spirit without its aid. I knew that holiness was absolutely necessary to salvation, as the means to the end ; but never recollected that it was part of the end itself. Such was the madness of my folly, that I believed I was saved by good works, as the procuring cause of my salvation ; and forgot that we are saved from bad to good works, as the fruits and effects of grace, to which alone praise should redound, and not to the miserable creature.

Now, blessed be God, I see that holiness is not only a distinguished, but a central part of our salvation, where all the means of grace, and ordinances, of religion terminate. To be saved from the bondage of sin and misery here, is synonimous with being saved from the punishment of sin hereafter.

Attend with scrupulosity to these important truths, my amiable readers, and your persons or minds, will not be subject to the usurpation of temporal or spiritual invaders. Pardon me for enlarging these strictures, such is the solicitude I feel for your present and eternal welfare, that when I begin to write, I know not when to conclude.

FINIS.

CONTENTS.

E e

CHAPTER V.

CHAPTER VI.

American Women: Images and Realities
An Arno Press Collection

[Adams, Charles F., editor]. **Correspondence between John Adams and Mercy Warren Relating to Her "History of the American Revolution," July-August, 1807.** With a new appendix of specimen pages from the "History." 1878.

[Arling], Emanie Sachs. **"The Terrible Siren": Victoria Woodhull, (1838-1927).** 1928.

Beard, Mary Ritter. **Woman's Work in Municipalities.** 1915.

Blanc, Madame [Marie Therese de Solms]. **The Condition of Woman in the United States.** 1895.

Bradford, Gamaliel. **Wives.** 1925.

Branagan, Thomas. **The Excellency of the Female Character Vindicated.** 1808.

Breckinridge, Sophonisba P. **Women in the Twentieth Century.** 1933.

Campbell, Helen. **Women Wage-Earners.** 1893.

Coolidge, Mary Roberts. **Why Women Are So.** 1912.

Dall, Caroline H. **The College, the Market, and the Court.** 1867.

[D'Arusmont], Frances Wright. **Life, Letters and Lectures: 1834, 1844.** 1972.

Davis, Almond H. **The Female Preacher, or Memoir of Salome Lincoln.** 1843.

Ellington, George. **The Women of New York.** 1869.

Farnham, Eliza W[oodson]. **Life in Prairie Land.** 1846.

Gage, Matilda Joslyn. **Woman, Church and State.** [1900].

Gilman, Charlotte Perkins. **The Living of Charlotte Perkins Gilman.** 1935.

Groves, Ernest R. **The American Woman.** 1944.

Hale, [Sarah J.] **Manners; or, Happy Homes and Good Society All the Year Round.** 1868.

Higginson, Thomas Wentworth. **Women and the Alphabet.** 1900.

Howe, Julia Ward, editor. **Sex and Education.** 1874.

La Follette, Suzanne. **Concerning Women.** 1926.

Leslie, Eliza . **Miss Leslie's Behaviour Book: A Guide and Manual for Ladies.** 1859.

Livermore, Mary A. **My Story of the War.** 1889.

Logan, Mrs. John A. (Mary S.) **The Part Taken By Women in American History.** 1912.

McGuire, Judith W. (A Lady of Virginia). **Diary of a Southern Refugee, During the War.** 1867.

Mann, Herman . **The Female Review: Life of Deborah Sampson.** 1866.

Meyer, Annie Nathan, editor.**Woman's Work in America.** 1891.

Myerson, Abraham. **The Nervous Housewife.** 1927.

Parsons, Elsie Clews. **The Old-Fashioned Woman.** 1913.

Porter, Sarah Harvey. **The Life and Times of Anne Royall.** 1909.

Pruette, Lorine. **Women and Leisure: A Study of Social Waste.** 1924.

Salmon, Lucy Maynard. **Domestic Service.** 1897.

Sanger, William W. **The History of Prostitution.** 1859.

Smith, Julia E. **Abby Smith and Her Cows.** 1877.

Spencer, Anna Garlin. **Woman's Share in Social Culture.** 1913.

Sprague, William Forrest. **Women and the West.** 1940.

Stanton, Elizabeth Cady. **The Woman's Bible** Parts I and II. 1895/1898.

Stewart, Mrs. Eliza Daniel . **Memories of the Crusade.** 1889.

Todd, John. **Woman's Rights.** 1867. [Dodge, Mary A.] (Gail Hamilton, pseud.) **Woman's Wrongs.** 1868.

Van Rensselaer, Mrs. John King. **The Goede Vrouw of Mana-ha-ta.** 1898.

Velazquez, Loreta Janeta. **The Woman in Battle.** 1876.

Vietor, Agnes C., editor. **A Woman's Quest: The Life of Marie E. Zakrzewska, M.D.** 1924.

Woodbury , Helen L. Sumner. **Equal Suffrage.** 1909.

Young, Ann Eliza. **Wife No. 19.** 1875.

Hale, [Sarah J.] Manners: or, Happy Homes and Good Society All the Year Round, 1868.

Higginson, Thomas Wentworth. Women and the Alphabet, 1900.

Howe, Julia Ward, editor. Sex and Education, 1874.

... Folly of Silence: Concerning Women, 1926.